# Law, Drugs and the Making of Addiction

This book considers how largely accepted 'legal truths' about drugs and addiction are made and sustained through practices of lawyering.

Lawyers play a vital and largely underappreciated role in constituting legal certainties about substances and 'addiction', including links between alcohol and other drugs, and phenomena such as family violence. Such practices exacerbate, sustain and stabilise 'addicted' realities, with a range of implications – many of them seemingly unjust – for people who use alcohol and other drugs. This book explores these issues, drawing upon data collected for a major international study on alcohol and other drugs in the law, including interviews with lawyers, magistrates and judges; analyses of case law; and legislation. Focussing on an array of legal practices, including processes of law-making, human rights deliberations, advocacy and negotiation strategies, and the sentencing of offenders, and buttressed by overarching analyses of the ethics and politics of such practices, the book looks at how alcohol and other drug 'addiction' emerges and is concretised through the everyday work lawyers and decision makers do. Foregrounding 'practices', the book also shows that law is more fragile than we might assume. It concludes by presenting a blueprint for how lawyers can rethink their advocacy practices in light of this fragility and the opportunities it presents for remaking law and the subjects and objects shaped by it.

This ground-breaking book will be of interest not only to those studying and working within the field of alcohol and drug addiction but also to lawyers and judges practising in this area and to scholars in a range of disciplines, including law, science and technology studies, sociology, gender studies and cultural studies.

**Kate Seear** is an Associate Professor in Law at Monash University, Australia. She is an Australian Research Council Discovery Early Career Researcher Award (DECRA) Fellow (2016–2019), the Academic Director of the Springvale Monash Legal Service, an Adjunct Research Fellow in the Social Studies of Addiction Concepts research programme at the National Drug Research Institute in the Faculty of Health Sciences at Curtin University and a practising lawyer. She is the author of *Making Disease, Making Citizens: The Politics of Hepatitis C* (with Suzanne Fraser) and *The Makings of a Modern Epidemic: Endometriosis, Gender and Politics,* and co-editor of the collection *Critical Perspectives on Coercive Interventions: Law, Medicine and Society* (with Claire Spivakovsky and Adrian Carter).

# Law, Drugs and the Making of Addiction

## Just Habits

Kate Seear

R Routledge
Taylor & Francis Group

LONDON AND NEW YORK

First published 2020
by Routledge
2 Park Square, Milton Park, Abingdon, Oxon OX14 4RN

and by Routledge
605 Third Avenue, New York, NY 10017

First issued in paperback 2020

*Routledge is an imprint of the Taylor & Francis Group, an informa business*

A GlassHouse book

*British Library Cataloguing-in-Publication Data*
A catalogue record for this book is available from the British Library

*Library of Congress Cataloging-in-Publication Data*
Names: Seear, Kate, author.
Title: Law, drugs and the making of addiction : just habits / Kate Seear.
Description: New York, NY : Routledge, 2019.
Identifiers: LCCN 2019013332 (print) | LCCN 2019013676 (ebook) |
ISBN 9780429450792 (ebk) | ISBN 9781138324633 (hbk)
Subjects: LCSH: Drugs of abuse—Law and legislation. | Drug addiction. |
Narcotic laws. | Drug addiction—Australia. | Drug addiction—Canada.
Classification: LCC K3641 (ebook) | LCC K3641 .S44 2019 (print) |
DDC 344.04/46—dc23
LC record available at https://lccn.loc.gov/2019013332

ISBN 13: 978-0-367-72714-7 (pbk)
ISBN 13: 978-1-138-32463-3 (hbk)

Typeset in Galliard
by codeMantra

For Kara. And for her – and my – homegirls.

# Contents

*Acknowledgements*                                                    ix

Introduction: Slowing down. Peering in.                               1

1  *Legislative practices*: On human rights, jurimorphs and
   the fragile ontology of law                                       33

2  *Advocacy practices*: On legal strategies, habits and the
   action of anticipation                                            61

3  *Negotiation practices*: On addiction veridiction and
   the gendering of agency in family violence and child
   protection cases                                                  88

4  *Sentencing practices*: On assembling 'alcohol effects' and
   the 'Aboriginal community' in criminal law                       113

5  *Ethical practices*: On rules, values and ethics as a 'matter
   of concern'                                                      143

   Conclusion: Making just habits. A blueprint for
   onto-advocacy                                                    168

*Index*                                                            177

# Acknowledgements

This book is the product of several years of work, supported by many people. It is based on research funded by an Australian Research Council DECRA fellowship (DE160100134). I acknowledge and thank the Council, and all those involved in the assessment and selection process, for supporting my project. I undertook my DECRA fellowship in the Faculty of Law at Monash University. I wish to acknowledge all of my colleagues at Monash University who provided assistance or advice in the preparation of my DECRA fellowship application and to the faculty and university more broadly for their support.

My DECRA research in fact began as a pilot study in 2013, when I was a post-doctoral research fellow in the Social Studies of Addiction Concepts research programme in the National Drug Research Institute, which is part of the Faculty of Health Sciences at Curtin University. The National Drug Research Institute receives core funding from the Australian Government under the Substance Misuse Prevention and Service Improvements Grants Fund, and my postdoctoral fellowship in the Social Studies of Addiction Concepts research programme was supported by the Office of Research and Development at Curtin University.

Throughout the project I was supported by an expert advisory board, whose guidance, contacts and input were invaluable to the project. Thanks go to all of them: Professor Suzanne Fraser, Dr Alex Wodak, Professor The Honourable Judge Nahum Mushin, Ms Jenny Kelsall (who sadly passed away over the course of this research), Ms Annie Madden, Mr Greg Denham, Professor Susan Boyd, Ms Kristen Wallwork and Mr Dave Taylor.

This book would not have been possible without the generosity of my anonymous interview participants from Australia and Canada. They included lawyers, judges, magistrates and other statutory decision makers. I am indebted to all of them for their time and expertise. I also thank the many individuals and organisations who assisted with recruitment, not all of whom I can name here for reasons of confidentiality. I am especially indebted to Susan Boyd and Ryan McNeil, who assisted with recruitment for the Canadian limb of my pilot study and whose invaluable knowledge and insights on Canadian alcohol and other drug policy was enormously helpful in the early stages of my research.

Many people have listened to me talk about this research and provided helpful suggestions over many years. They include Adrian Evans; Abbe Smith; Christine

Parker; Kenneth Tupper; Kari Lancaster; Barry Judd; David Moore; Helen Keane; kylie valentine; Cameron Duff; Ross Hyams; Becky Batagol; and many other friends and colleagues at workshops, roundtables and conferences. I have also benefitted immensely from the opportunity to present early drafts of this work or elements of my findings at conferences and events, including the Social Studies of Addiction Concepts Thinking Addiction symposium; the research seminar series of the LaTrobe Centre for Health Law and Society; the Yarra Drug Health Forum event; Harm Reduction Victoria's Law Reform Forum; the Castan Centre for Human Rights Law's annual conference; the International Legal Ethics Conference (first in New York and later in Melbourne); the Law and Society Association conference; events of the Students for Sensible Drug Policy, including its inaugural conference; the Society for Social Studies of Science (4S) conference; the Australasian Viral hepatitis Conference; the Somatechnics international conference; the Centre for Social Research in Health conference at the University of New South Wales; and the bi-annual Contemporary Drug Problems Conference.

Some of my colleagues went above and beyond, reading drafts of my work and offering feedback and advice. I am deeply indebted to Steven Angelides, Patrick Emerton and Jamie Walvisch for their careful reading, support and suggestions as well as their friendship. Thank you to Claire Spivakovsky for also reading drafts and providing advice; for her friendship and reassurance; and for listening to me, quite literally for weeks on end, especially during our travels through Canada and the United States, when I was grappling with the book's core ideas.

I am particularly grateful to Suzanne Fraser. Suzanne has been an amazing friend and colleague all the way through this project. As well as offering me the initial postdoctoral fellowship that sparked this work, she has read drafts and provided feedback throughout, listened to my worries, offered insightful suggestions and kept me motivated. She has been extraordinarily generous, enthusiastic and encouraging, including towards the end of the work, when I needed it most.

Thanks also to my colleagues at Springvale Monash Legal Service. Many of the ideas that later formed part of this book were formed while teaching Monash Law students at Springvale Monash Legal Service as part of the Monash programme of clinical legal education. I am grateful to the clients, staff, students and volunteers of that service.

The book was commissioned by Colin Perrin at Routledge. I am grateful to Colin for commissioning and supporting this project, and to all those at Routledge.

The book was only possible due to the generous research assistance provided by many people over the course of the project. Huge thanks to Kara Ward, Liam Elphick, Julia Walker, Liza Miller, Jarryd Bartle, Emily Domingo and Nikkie Geschke.

Portions of Chapter 3 were previously published, as: Seear, K., & Fraser, S. (2016). Addiction veridiction: Gendering agency in legal mobilisations of addiction discourse. *Griffith Law Review*, 25(1), 13–29.

I want to acknowledge my sisters at the Outer Sanctum, and our producer, Tess Armstrong, who make me laugh and cry on a weekly (if not daily) basis. I have learned so much from all of you.

Thanks to all my friends and family, especially my sister Claire and my mum, Wendy, for their support.

And finally, to my partner in everything, Stewart Dugmore. Thank you for keeping me going through the slow and arduous process of writing this book, including during the challenges we endured in 2017. I owe everything to you, as my biggest champion and closest confidant. I share this book with you and our truest love, our dog, Cyril, who brings joy to our lives every day and who sat by my feet (as only the best dogs do) through the long days and nights I toiled over this book.

# Introduction
## Slowing down. Peering in.

## Introduction

Addiction is a relatively recent historical concept (Room, 2003; Levine, 1978). It first emerged in relation to the consumption of alcohol and was later extended to include illicit drugs (Room, 2006). The nomenclature of addiction has since been deployed even further and is now applied to a range of different activities, such as sex, Internet use, gambling, gaming, eating, exercise and shopping. Consumables such as coffee, sugar, cheese and ice cream are increasingly characterised as dangerous substances with 'addictive' properties. Famously, Eve Sedgwick (1993) described this process – of recasting certain behaviours and substances as addictions – as a growing 'epidemic of addiction-attribution'. The epidemic of addiction-attribution raises urgent questions, especially within legal settings. Do addicts have limited capacity to control their behaviour, or is habitual drug use a choice? Is addiction a 'disease' for which addicts bear little or no responsibility? What causes addiction? And what are the consequences? How should we deal with addiction when it surfaces in the criminal law, family law and civil law? Should addicts be punished and jailed or offered treatment? To what extent should governments be able to coerce addicts into treatment? Is it a disability? If so, do those characterised as 'addicts' deserve special accommodations or rights? In Australia and other parts of the world, courts are regularly being asked to consider questions such as these in relation to many different kinds of addictions. They are also being asked to weigh such considerations against conceptions of moral culpability and legal responsibility, legal symbolism, risk, protection and deterrence. These issues are playing out across a broad range of cases, including personal injury lawsuits pertaining to tobacco, pharmaceuticals, food and video games; lawsuits involving the liability of casinos to cover heavy losses sustained by gambling 'addicts'; family law disputes about parents who use drugs; and public health lawsuits regarding access to particular treatments for people labelled as 'addicts'. I suggest that these cases are part of a growing global trend of what might be termed, following Eve Sedgwick, 'legal addiction-attribution'. The issues at stake in these cases are of substantial personal, public and commercial interest.

The nature and meaning of addiction is still very much 'under construction' (Fraser & Seear, 2011). In many fields, there is a lack of consensus regarding what the term 'addiction' actually means as well as the key concepts that underpin it (e.g. Carter et al., 2014; Karasaki et al., 2013). For instance, in 2014, 94 experts were signatories to an open letter to the prestigious journal *Nature*, in which they challenged claims by other experts about addiction, thus highlighting the complexity and contestation in the field (Heim et al., 2014). Similarly, there has been significant contestation and debate about appropriate terminology in the alcohol and other drugs field. A particularly notable example involved the attempt to revise and update the *Diagnostic and Statistical Manual of Mental Disorders* – a key text of the American Psychiatric Association (subsequently published as the *DSM-5*) (American Psychiatric Association, 2013). The DSM-5 contained major revisions related to substance use, and these were the subject of significant controversy, criticism and debate. Importantly, debates about terminology and associated 'changes are not just a matter of terminology but represent a redefining of addiction and a redrawing of its boundaries' (Fraser, Moore, & Keane, 2014: 45). Addiction has been described, variously, as 'contentious and complex' (Hammer et al., 2013: 28), and as an 'ambiguous concept', with a diverse range of approaches found across medicine, science, psychology, criminology, law and other social sciences (Karasaki et al., 2013: 195). Articulations of addiction and the key concepts that underpin it have a long and complex history, and tend to differ depending on the substance in question (Fraser, 2015). Debates about the meaning and regulatory function of addiction concepts have given rise to a growing body of scholarship on concepts of addiction in policy, science and service provision (e.g. Fomiatti, Moore, & Fraser [In press]; Fraser, valentine, & Ekendahl, 2018; Fraser & Ekendahl, 2018; Dwyer & Fraser, 2016a; Moore et al., 2015; Fraser, Moore, & Keane, 2014; Karasaki et al., 2013; Moore & Fraser, 2006; Room, 2006; Keane, 2002). In this work, scholars have drawn attention to the implications that different addiction concepts have, especially for those characterised as experiencing addiction. Research on addiction and addiction concepts in legal settings is far less common, however. Although a number of studies focus on how specialist drug courts operate, as well as how they approach drug use (Lyons, 2014; Murphy, 2011; Tiger, 2011; Vrecko, 2009; Fitzgerald, 2008; Moore, 2007), addiction is rarely the central object of analysis in such research. Indeed, beyond a few examples, including my own work (Seear, 2017, 2015; Seear & Fraser, 2016, 2014a, 2014b), few critical analyses have been conducted on the models of addiction operating in the law and the many implications of these approaches for people caught up in legal processes, whether as plaintiffs, defendants or victims. How addiction is conceptualised and stabilised in law matters for several reasons. For example, where addiction is underpinned by an assumption that addicts lack volition or the capacity for self-control, the use of coercive practices and paternalistic policies – including involuntary treatment, detention and sterilisation – might follow (Spivakovsky, Seear, & Carter, 2018; Lucke & Hall, 2014). These practices raise vital questions about 'justice' and fairness. If an addict is 'sick', should they be punished more or less harshly than another offender? What would be just, in such a case? What are the implications for victims of crime? Will they view approaches to offenders as just or unjust?

This book engages with these questions. Its focus is broadly threefold. First, I explore how addiction features in various legal contexts and how the law and key stakeholders (lawyers and decision makers, such as judges) constitute addiction through their work. Second, encouraged by Fraser, Moore and Keane (2014), I consider what is at stake in these processes. Finally, I consider whether what the law does with respect to addiction is desirable and whether things might be done otherwise. My analysis draws inspiration from a range of theoretical traditions, including feminist and queer theory, poststructural policy analysis, legal ethics and – most prominently – science and technology studies (STS). Taking my cue from the work of STS scholars such as Annemarie Mol and John Law, I argue that addiction is not a stable, pre-existing 'object' but an object that is made in practice (Law, 2011; Mol & Law, 2002; Mol, 2002, 1999). The central premise of this book is that legal practices are central to realities. The law constitutes addiction 'facts' and 'truths', rather than simply 'unearthing' or 'describing' them. I argue that these practices raise vital political and ethical questions, and have implications for race, sex/gender and more. In the next sections I provide an overview of the history of addiction and addiction concepts, outline some of the key literature on addiction and addiction concepts, and introduce the theoretical framework for the book. I also provide an introduction to some basic legal concepts and practices for readers unfamiliar with the law.

## Concepts of addiction

The word 'addiction' comes from the Latin term *addicere*, which refers to the relationship between masters and slaves in Roman law (Alexander, 2008; Seddon, 2007). The notion of 'enslavement' is thus arguably foundational to addiction, with the will of the addict seen to be compromised or attenuated in some way (West, 2001). Writing about metaphors of drug addiction and enslavement, Kenneth Tupper notes that drugs are often constituted as malevolent agents that overwhelm one's resolve. A drug is a:

> diabolical force with talismanic or magical power to subjugate the will: even being in its proximity is dangerous, simple possession is reprehensible, distribution or sale is nefarious, and any indication of such transgressions merits swift and forceful preventive or punitive intervention.
>
> (Tupper, 2012: 477)

Common addiction concepts include that addicts are irrational, duplicitous, weak, emotional and chaotic. Such tropes have been widely criticised (Fraser & Seear, 2011; Seear & Fraser, 2010a, 2010b; Fraser & valentine, 2008; Moore & Fraser, 2006; Fraser, 2004; Keane, 2002). Importantly, such addiction concepts are not necessarily *intrinsically* problematic. Instead, their meaning emerges via a 'binary logic', an idea most closely associated with the French philosopher Jacques Derrida (2002, 1976). Derrida argued that Western thought is steeped in binary logic. Examples of common binary pairings include: mind/body, reason/emotion, objective/subjective, voluntarity/compulsivity, object/subject, nature/culture, authentic/inauthentic, passive/active and order/chaos. According to binary logic, the meaning of each term of the pair is forged through its relation to the other. Crucially, terms in a binary are constituted as mutually exclusive, where one term enjoys a dominant status, and the other enjoys a subordinate one. So, as Elizabeth Grosz (1989: 27) explains:

> Within this structure the opposed terms are not equally valued: one term occupies the structurally dominant position and takes on the power of defining its opposite or other. The dominant and subordinated terms are simply positive and negative versions of each other, the dominant term defining its other by negation.

To take an example: 'Body is ... what is not mind, what is distinct from and other than the privileged term' (Grosz, 1994: 3). To return to the example of 'addiction', then, the meaning of drug use, addiction and other forms of 'compulsive' conduct are often secured through reference to what they are not or, perhaps more accurately, by what they are *claimed* not to be (their binary 'other').

In a now famous formulation on the process by which the meaning of addiction as devalued compulsivity is secured, Eve Sedgwick argued that:

> So long as 'free will' has been hypostatized and charged with ethical value, for just so long has an equally hypostatized 'compulsion' had to be available as a counterstructure always internal to it, always requiring to be ejected from it.
>
> (Sedgwick, 1993: 133–134)

She goes on to argue that:

> The scouring work of addiction attribution is propelled by the same imperative; its exacerbated perceptual acuteness in detecting the compulsion behind everyday voluntarity is driven, ever more blindly, by its own compulsion to isolate some new, receding but absolutized space of pure voluntarity.
>
> (Sedgwick, 1993: 134)

The effects of these conceptualisations can be 'wide-ranging' for people who use drugs (Simmonds & Coomber, 2009: 122). In conceptualising the addict as weak of will, untrustworthy, deluded, inauthentic and lacking volition, addiction discourse can justify 'the suspension of [the individual's] personal autonomy, installing an imperative that they be governed by others' (Brook & Stringer, 2005: 319). Similarly, Davies (1992: 163) argues that dominant conceptualisations of addicts as non-volitional result in a framing of them as 'helpless victims' or 'helpless junkies driven by forces beyond their capacity to control'. In other words,

> when the rescuing abstainer directs the user's will, imposing 'cruel to be kind' punishments, it is justified as being in the user's best interests. In short, *marking drug users with the stigma of debility and delusion simultaneously creates an arena of domination*, situating heroin users as appropriate targets for shows of strength, therapeutic or otherwise.
>
> (Brook & Stringer, 2005: 319; emphasis added)

As noted already, the use of coercive practices and paternalistic policies – including involuntary treatment, detention and sterilisation – is a genuine possibility for many people labelled as 'addicts' (Spivakovsky, Seear, & Carter, 2018; Lucke & Hall, 2012). Indeed, and as I argue later in this book, coercive interventions are sometimes justified on the basis that they are in the best interests of addicts.

Depictions of people who use alcohol and other drugs as inherently chaotic, irrational, duplicitous and weak may also be stigmatising. The relationship between alcohol and other drugs and stigma is well known and has been widely documented (e.g. Lancaster, Seear, & Ritter, 2018; Fraser et al., 2017; Seear, Lancaster, & Ritter, 2017; Lloyd, 2013, 2010). It was even acknowledged by Erving Goffman (1963) in his hugely influential work on stigma. Addiction-related stigma can lead to the view that people who use drugs are either less worthy or less deserving of support and services than others (Simmonds & Coomber, 2009). It may result in people who use drugs being reluctant to admit to such use or to seek help from health services where they want help. It may even result in outright discrimination, including through denial of access to vital rights and services (Lancaster, Seear, & Ritter, 2018). As Fitzgerald, McDonald and Klugman (2004) argue, stigma can also disproportionately affect some groups, including those who live in rural, regional and remote areas, where it is difficult to hide such use, and where people who use are often excluded from social networks and opportunities. The effects of stigma can last a lifetime (Lloyd, 2013). Crucially, as I argue in this book, approaches to addiction are thus symbolically and materially important. As I explain in the next section, however, concepts of addiction are changeable across cultures and time.

## Addiction concepts across cultures and time

An important body of scholarship notes that the nature and meaning of addiction changes across cultures and throughout history. In his classic article titled 'The discovery of addiction', Harry Levine (1978: 147) argues that in the American colonial period:

> 'addicted' meant habituated, and one was habituated to drunkenness, not to liquor. Almost everyone 'habitually' drank moderate amounts of alcoholic beverages; only some people habitually drank them to the point of drunkenness.

In the eighteenth century, American drunkenness was fairly unremarkable, and alcohol was considered as both a food and a medicine as well as a social lubricant (Levine, 1978). These ideas changed over time, however. Levine notes that Americans first began to report being 'addicted' to alcohol in the late eighteenth and early nineteenth centuries. For them, being 'addicted' to alcohol meant being overwhelmed with a desire to consume it. Influenced by the temperance movement, drunkenness was eventually reworked as 'alcoholism'/'addiction', and abstinence was prescribed as the solution. As noted earlier, the language of addiction was later extended to other substances and behaviours, including illicit drug use. According to Mariana Valverde, contemporary Western approaches to 'addiction' were shaped by a combination of two sets of concerns. The first appeared in the early 1900s and involved 'an international panic about the opium traffic, [… alongside] a more generalized panic about the figure of the drug fiend' (1998: 5). Valverde notes that opium derivatives, morphine and cocaine came to be viewed 'as highly dangerous substances that would immediately cause addiction in virtually anyone' (1998: 5). The panic about particular substances was inextricably linked to racism and sexism, including fears about the use of opium by the Chinese; about African-American men; and about the sexual vulnerability of white women, especially if they consumed intoxicating substances in the presence of non-white men (see, for example, Ziegler, 2008). The second factor involved in the contemporary emergence of addiction, according to Valverde, was the growing concern with 'problem' drinkers and the push by some experts and institutions, including the World Health Organisation, to reclassify alcohol as a 'drug'. The emergence of the concept of 'alcohol and other drugs' (AOD) brought illicit substances and alcohol together, mixing the concepts of the 'drug addict' with the 'alcoholic'.

The work of scholars such as Levine (1978), Valverde (1998), Ziegler (2008), Reinarman (2005) and Room (1985) suggests that particular concepts of addiction, including the notion that addicts 'lose control', are historically and culturally specific (for a more detailed discussion with additional literature, see Weinberg, 2011, and on the 'invention of quitting', see White, Oliffe & Bottorff, 2013). They have also identified links between the emergence of addiction and addiction concepts, and phenomena such as industrialisation, globalisation (Room, 1985) and the rise of empire (Sedgwick, 1993). Mariana Valverde argues that:

> Alcohol has been a problematic substance for modern European societies because questions of addiction have been and continue to be important sites upon which the complex dialectic of personal freedom and control/self-control has worked itself out historically.
>
> (1998: 5)

The point here is that addiction has come to be conceptualised as a 'problem' – at least in Western, liberal, discursive contexts – in part because of what it ostensibly reveals about free will. Mariana Valverde (1998: 3), referencing Eve Sedgwick's work, describes an 'intense valuation of personal freedom' and free will underpinning cultural anxieties about addiction in the West. Importantly, implicit in the work of many of the addiction scholars cited above is a sense of addiction as constructed, unstable and variable, themes I will return to later in this chapter and which will be of central concern in this book.

Several authors have also critiqued formulations of addicted subjecthood for their relation to citizenship in late, Western, liberal, discursive contexts. As I have previously argued (with Suzanne Fraser), for example, 'the "proper" subject of late modernity [is constituted as] responsible, autonomous, rational, enterprising and choosing' (Seear & Fraser, 2010b: 450). As such, claims that 'addicts' are irresponsible, dependent, irrational and non-volitional 'operate to produce people who use drugs as less-than-full citizens' (Seear & Fraser, 2010b: 450) or the antithesis of the ideal Western subject. In other words, key addiction concepts reflect and reproduce notions of 'addicts' as illegitimate members of society. Taking these ideas further, and inspired by Steve Woolgar's work on 'gerunding', Fraser, Moore and Keane (2014) have coined the term '*addicting*' to acknowledge addiction's co-constitutive action and to emphasise the ways that society is increasingly being subjected to (and by) the logic of addiction. There are other reasons why conceptualisations of addicted agency (or non-agency) may be cause for concern. According to William Garriott (2013: 215), for example, the link between drugs, addiction and crime is now a 'social fact' in America. When drugs are viewed as 'inherently criminogenic', addicts are 'viewed as perpetually inclined toward criminality, making her or him a constant threat' (Garriott, 2013: 217). In this sense, addiction is very often inscribed – at least in American criminal justice settings – with a highly value-laden and stereotyped set of meanings in which crime is a defining feature (Bourgois, 1995). In recent years, there has been a growing debate about whether different theories about addiction – what it is and how it works – have the potential to disrupt the highly stereotyped set of meanings attached to it. I now turn to outline some of those theories and the relevant debates.

## Theories of addiction

There are a number of different theories about what addiction is and what causes it, as well as its consequences. The two most common frameworks deployed to try and 'explain' addiction are the moral and medical models (Hall & Carter, 2015). The moral model sees drug use as a choice and addiction as a form of personal or moral failing, evil or wickedness. In contrast, the disease model sees addiction as an 'illness' or 'sickness' (West, 2006a, 2006b). Versions of these two models appear frequently in multiple fields, including law, media, public health and popular culture. Scientific versions of the disease model generally 'share the common view that control over drug use is somehow impaired', although they differ as to the precise mechanisms involved (Carter et al., 2014: 206). According to disease models of addiction, although some people may choose to use drugs in the first instance, a minority of them will go on to develop an addiction characterised by a pattern of repetitive or 'compulsive' drug use (Leshner, 1997). In that they are thought to relieve those who use drugs from responsibility and blame for their behaviour (see Fox, 1999), disease models of addiction are often thought to be more generous and progressive than moral ones. As Brook and Stringer explained:

> When harm reductionists assert that heroin use should be conceptualised, first and foremost, as a health problem, it is generally in the hope that drug users might be treated with more dignity, better resources and less judgmental attitudes [...] The aim of describing users as ill is to destigmatise them while contrasting harm reduction with punitive approaches.
>
> (2005: 318)

In recent years, a particular disease model of addiction known as the 'brain disease model' has become increasingly popular and influential. This is largely a result of the work of the US National Institute on Drug Abuse (NIDA), which first articulated this view under the leadership of Alan Leshner (1997), and has since invested heavily in it under the direction of Nora Volkow. For leading proponents of this model, addiction is a chronic, relapsing disease which represents 'the neurobiology of behavior gone awry' (Volkow & Li, 2004). It holds that drugs 'hijack' the brain's reward system by binding to the receptors in the brain that produce sensations of pleasure (Nestler & Malenka, 2004; Robinson & Berridge, 2004). Nancy Campbell argues that this definition 'provided scaffolding for a new optics that reorganized the federal research apparatus, reorienting it toward neuroscience with the goal of pinpointing molecular "targets" for medications development' (2010: 90).

As noted earlier, there has been enthusiasm in some circles about the potential of the brain disease model to revolutionise understandings of drug use and those characterised as experiencing addiction. This includes people most directly affected by these models: those characterised as suffering from the disease itself (e.g. Hammer et al., 2013). There have been important criticisms, however, of both disease models in general and the brain disease model in particular. For example, Nancy Campbell has questioned the claim that disease models are wholly distinct from moral ones, noting that the latter is an historical antecedent to the former:

> Presented as novel outcomes of neuroscience, social constructs of compulsion, disruption and disinhibition owe a debt to a historical past when addiction was considered a moral weakness or disease of the will. Such notions were the very moral and cultural constructs that early architects of the neurophysiology of addiction devoted their scientific careers to avoiding. These pioneers advanced new cultural constructs of addiction and relapse as neural and physiological phenomena in order to make each tractable in science.
>
> (2010: 93)

Other scholars have similarly highlighted the conceptual links between neuroscientific accounts of the 'hijacked brain' and earlier accounts of overborne will. Disease models share 'certain similarities in logical structure with seventeenth-century theological narratives in which demonic possession was thought to be causal' (Reinarman, 2005; see also Tupper, 2012; Room, 2003). Importantly, even when people who use drugs are characterised as 'addicts' experiencing an illness, value judgements about their conduct and character persist (Fraser & Seear, 2011; Reinarman, 2011; Courtwright, 2010; Fraser & valentine, 2008; Brook & Stringer, 2005; Keane, 2002). This might occur where the addicted individual is conceptualised as perpetually sick, in 'thrall' to their addiction, unable to make sensible decisions and/or diminished in capacity. For example, some folk and self-help traditions (such as Alcoholics Anonymous) utilise disease concepts, holding that 'an alcoholic who has not had a drink for twenty years nevertheless still suffers from the incurable disease of alcoholism' (Keane, 2002: 2). Some have thus highlighted the failure of both disease models in general, and the neuroscience of addiction in particular, to live up to its potential, including in the reduction of stigma (Hall, Carter, & Forlini, 2015).

So where does all of this leave us? As these analyses reveal, there is a lack of consensus in the literature about what different theories of addiction do for key addiction concepts, such as those pertaining to rationality and volition. The literature is marked by a set of claims, on the one hand, that ideas about addiction have changed or evolved over time, opening up new and more generous possibilities. On the other is the claim that key concepts of addiction are remarkably persistent, stigmatising and marginalising. Notions of stasis and change are thus a preoccupation in much of the literature. Questions about the ontology of addiction have become even more central in recent years, with the emergence of a body of critical literature that takes inspiration from numerous traditions, including poststructuralism, feminist theory, queer theory and STS. These theories inform the approach that I take in this book. Before I get to these, however, I provide a general introduction to how addiction figures in the law.

## Addiction in the law

As I outlined at the start of this chapter, alcohol and other drug 'addiction' appear in a wide range of legal settings, including settings beyond the familiar criminal law (Seear, 2015; Seear & Fraser, 2014a, 2014b). This includes civil law, family law, child protection, social security and administration law, disability and discrimination law, international human rights law and public health law, to name just a few. In the course of undertaking this research there was an almost constant array of commissions of inquiry, law reform references, legislative reviews and proposed bills that in some way engaged with or referenced 'addiction'. When addiction features in legal settings, its status varies, as does the terminology used to describe it. In Australia, and in Australian law, the terms 'addiction' and 'dependence' are both used interchangeably and often undefined. Addiction or dependence may be a central object in legislation. For example, the *Drug and Alcohol Treatment Act* (2010) (New South Wales) allows for the temporary detention and treatment of people experiencing 'severe substance dependence', where it is deemed necessary to protect them from serious harm, or where others are likely to be in need of protection from serious physical harm, and where the person is likely to benefit from treatment. Addiction or dependence can be found centrally in several other pieces of legislation, such as the criminal statutes pertaining to sentencing of offenders and public health laws pertaining to how specific drugs can be described. There are other examples too. In Victoria, the *Infringements Act* (2006) is the main law that deals with the administration of fines for various activities, such as driving on roads without a toll, and other minor traffic offences. The Act allows people with a 'serious addiction' to drugs, alcohol or other volatile substances to be excused from paying their fines, if it can be shown that addiction resulted in them being unable to understand that they had committed an offence, or if it meant that they could not control conduct that constituted an offence. In another example, this time from the state of New South Wales, the *Anti-Discrimination Act* (1977) precludes discrimination against people on the basis of race, sex and other grounds, but makes an exception for 'persons addicted to prohibited drugs'. Even a cursory introduction to legislative examples like these gives us a sense of what kind of object addiction is thought to be: something that is dangerous and a potential threat to the health and safety of the 'addict' or others, something that may impact upon a person's capacity to understand or control their own behaviour and something – at least in one jurisdiction – that should not afford a person protection under discrimination law. Some possible tensions between these approaches are also apparent. Indeed, as Suzanne Fraser and I have previously argued, legal approaches to addiction are multiple:

> it is not possible to speak of a single or consistent legal response to alcohol and other drug issues, including addiction, whether within a single jurisdiction involving pieces of legislation enacted at the same point in time, or within a broader area where more than one legislative instrument may apply.
>
> (Seear & Fraser, 2014a: 447)

When we move away from legislation and towards legal practices, we see that 'addiction' surfaces for a variety of reasons. In legal practice, lawyers may need to advise their clients about their legal rights or responsibilities under one of the laws I have already mentioned. Addiction may otherwise be *proactively asserted* by a party to a legal proceeding in circumstances where it is considered useful or necessary to make such assertions as a means of pursuing a legal argument, or seeking a legal remedy. It may also be *reactively asserted:* where, for example, drug use becomes known in a legal proceeding (via expert evidence, for instance), and a strategic decision is made to respond to that revelation by developing an argument designed to manage or mitigate one's drug use by constituting it as an 'addiction'. (These issues will be examined in more detail in Chapter 2.) In recent years, addiction has been a central feature in a number of cases across the world. Some notable examples include:

- *McCabe v British American Tobacco Australia Services Limited* (2002) VSC 73. This was a landmark, high-profile Australian civil case in which a woman (Rolah McCabe) dying of lung cancer sued a major tobacco company, arguing that the manufacturer knew cigarettes were addictive, had targeted children in its advertising and had taken no reasonable steps to reduce the addictive nature of smoking. McCabe originally won the case, after it was revealed that the tobacco company had disposed of documents that might be relevant to the case under its so-called 'document retention policy'. The verdict was eventually overturned on appeal (*British American Tobacco Australia Services Limited v Cowell (as representing the estate of Rolah Ann McCabe, deceased)* (2002) VSCA 1) by which time Ms McCabe had passed away.

- *Canada (Attorney General) v PHS Community Services Society* (2011) 3 SCR 134 (known as the 'Insite' case). *Insite* was concerned with the legality of Vancouver's supervised drug consumption facility (which is called 'Insite'): a clinic designed to allow on-site consumption of illicit drugs such as heroin and crystal methamphetamine so as to support illicit drug consumers in avoiding forms of harm that can be associated with drugs including overdose. The facility was established as a pilot facility in 2003 via special government exemptions but the Federal Minister for Health later decided not to grant further exemptions, meaning that the facility would have to close. Proponents and consumers of the service facilitated legal action and the case was eventually heard in the Supreme Court of Canada. A crucial issue in the case was how drug use was to be conceptualised. The Supreme Court concluded that drug addiction was an 'illness'. The case is revisited later in this book.

- *Commonwealth v Julie A. Eldred* (2018) SJC 12279. Julie Eldred was convicted of theft and granted probation. She was ordered to remain drug-free as a condition of her probation, and to undergo regular drug screening tests. On her first drug screen she tested positive for fentanyl, and was sent to jail. On appeal Ms Eldred asked the court to consider whether it was appropriate for a person to be sent to jail if they were in fact suffering from a 'disease' in the form of 'addiction'. The court was thus asked to address quite directly the question of what addiction is, whether it was a disease, how positive drug tests might be understood (i.e. whether this was a form of uncontrollable 'relapse' or a choice) and whether punitive approaches to 'addiction' were thus unconstitutional. Notably, many high-profile experts and organisations submitted petitions to the court on these issues. There was no clear consensus among experts on these questions. Ms Eldred ultimately lost her appeal on quite specific grounds. Although the outcome of the decision was widely anticipated, the court did not decide these questions for technical legal reasons. The issues examined in *Eldred* are likely to be considered again in future cases.

These and other cases have all attracted considerable academic attention (e.g. Bunn, 2019; Morse, 2017; Flacks, 2012; Murphy, 2012; Oliphant, 2012; Calder, 2011; Lessard, 2011; Gibson, 2009; Joh, 2009; Brown, 2008; Cameron, 2002; Liberman, 2002; Taylor, 2002; Morse, 2000). Importantly, however, addiction is rarely a central object of analysis in this work, and the use of critical theory is rare. One exception is Rebecca Bunn's work (2019) on the constitution of addiction in discrimination law. Bunn explores some of the implications of conceptualising addiction as a disability for the purposes of discrimination law, using intersectionality theory. She argues that systems of power such as ableism and neoliberalism work through disability discrimination law to co-constitute both addiction and disability in ways that are stigmatising and counterproductive, even as they aim to improve the lives of those labelled as experiencing addiction. Some critical insights appear in other literature, too. For instance, Elizabeth Joh makes the point that understandings of substances and subjects can be remade as a result of legal outcomes. She notes that evidence about the extent of corporate knowledge regarding tobacco helped to reshape conceptualisations of smoking and addiction, such that:

> The prevailing portrait of the smoker evolved from that of a voluntary decision-maker to that of a victim harmed by an industry bent on deception.
>
> (2009: 188)

A separate but related body of critical literature examines drug courts. This literature examines issues such as best practice approaches to treatment and offending, the 'effectiveness' of courts in reducing recidivism and alcohol and other drug use, the history and logics of drug courts, their processes for establishing eligibility including alcohol and other drug dependence, the consequences of merging therapy with punishment and logics of expertise and power in hybrid medico-legal systems (e.g. Gowan & Whetstone, 2012; Tiger, 2012, 2011; Jones, 2011; Murphy, 2011; Vrecko, 2009; Fitzgerald, 2008; Cappa, 2006; Roberts & Indermaur, 2006; Bull, 2005, 2003; Indermaur & Roberts, 2005, 2003; Freiberg, 2001, 2000). Importantly, again, addiction is rarely a central object of analysis in this work (although see Sarmiento, 2018). This can be contrasted to the field of alcohol and other drug studies more broadly, which has seen a surge in critical literature in recent years. The literature examined here also has limited engagement with critical theory of the kind that has become increasingly influential in alcohol and other drug studies. I now turn to this work.

## Addiction and ontological politics

Approaches to addiction are typically underpinned by one of two theoretical frames: realism or constructionism. John Law (2011: 156) describes realism (or what he calls 'Euro-American common-sense realism') as having six features: (1) it assumes that reality exists 'out there', (2) it claims that reality exists independently of our actions, (3) it asserts that reality precedes our actions and our attempts to know it, (4) it assumes that reality takes a definite form, (5) it takes for granted the notion that reality is singular and (6) it assumes such reality to be coherent. In contrast, social constructionists challenge taken-for-granted assumptions about the world, as well as 'claims to the existence of essential truths' (Lupton, 2003: 12) and focus instead on the discursive-material processes by which reality is enacted, or made. As Annemarie Mol (2002: 42) explains:

> The term 'construction' was used to get across the view that objects have no fixed and given identities, but gradually come into being. During their unstable childhoods, their identities tend to be highly contested, volatile, open to transformation. But once they have grown up objects are taken to be stabilized.

Mol goes on to critique this idea in her now classic book *The Body Multiple* (2002). According to Mol, a central flaw in constructionism is its implication that objects are constructed as a once-off, never-to-be-repeated process. Instead, she argues, the ontology of objects is 'fragile'; they have not simply a complex past but a 'complex present', with identities that 'may differ between sites' (2002: 43). Mol goes on to suggest that 'maintaining the identity of objects requires a continuing effort' and notes that 'over time [those identities] may change' (2002: 43). A classic early articulation of these ideas appeared in Mol's work on anaemia (1999). There, she argued against pluralism, perspectivism and constructionism, instead emphasising an approach that has come to be known as ontological multiplicity:

> The reality of anaemia takes various forms. These are not perspectives seen by different people [...] neither are they alternative, bygone constructions of which only one has emerged from the past [...] they are different versions, different performances, different realties that co-exist in the present.
>
> (1999: 79)

There are several implications of this work. The first is that a new nomenclature is needed: 'reality' must give way to 'realities'. The second is that realities are unstable, changeable and multiple, rather than stable, fixed and singular. The third is that realities are made and remade through processes of constant iteration or repetition (see also Butler, 1990). Fourth, in order to understand how objects and subjects come to be, one must attend to the specific practices and processes by which realities are enacted, formulated and maintained. Crucially, Mol's work also disrupts taken-for-granted assumptions about the inherent nature of things. This concern is encapsulated in Mol's work, as well as that of John Law – one of her most frequent collaborators. As Law puts it:

> In this scheme of things, entities have no inherent qualities: essentialist divisions are thrown out on the bonfire of the dualisms ... there *are* no divisions. It is rather that such divisions or distinctions are understood as *effects or outcomes*. They are not given in the order of things.
>
> (1999: 3)

As I have noted elsewhere, one implication of these ideas is that 'any number of actions, gestures, movements, practices and articulations are suddenly materially, politically and ethically significant' (Seear, 2014: 14). Importantly, both human and non-human actors are considered essential objects for analysis in such approaches (see, for example, Law, 1999; Callon & Law, 1997; Casper, 1994; Latour, 1988a, 1988b). Practices are also a central focus, given that 'reality does not precede the mundane practices in which we interact with it, but is rather shaped within these practices' (Mol, 1999: 75). Such practices can be found everywhere: 'wherever you look, whether this is a meeting hall, a talk, a laboratory or a survey, there is no escape from practice. It is *practices all the way down*, contested or otherwise' (Law, 2011: 171; emphasis added). Law offers some insights into how this approach might be mobilised in different fields of research, and suggests paying attention to five issues. First, attend to how practices produce realities. This involves looking, empirically, at how it is relations are assembled and ordered to 'produce objects, subjects and appropriate locations'. Second, attend to how realities become and remain stable. Third, consider how such processes obscure their role in the production of realities, instead creating an appearance of realities as existing prior to the processes that produce and stabilise them. Fourth, as noted earlier, practices are everywhere and always behind realities. And finally, 'look for the gaps, the aporias and the tensions between the practices and their realities' as this is where realities become vulnerable and might be made otherwise (Law, 2011: 171). Crucially, then, an important implication of Law's approach is that 'by attending to specific practices, articulations, gestures, and more, we might simultaneously intervene in the making and maintenance of ontologies, so that new versions [of an object] may materialise' (Seear, 2014: 14). These ideas are sometimes encapsulated in the overarching phrase, coined by John Law, of 'ontological politics' (or 'ontics'). As Mol explains:

> *Ontological politics* is a composite term. It talks of *ontology* – which in standard philosophical parlance defines what belongs to the real, the conditions of possibility we live with. If the term 'ontology' is combined with that of 'politics' then this suggests that the conditions of possibility are not given.

That reality does not precede the mundane practices in which we interact with it, but is rather shaped within these practices. So the term *politics* works to underline this active mode, this process of shaping, and the fact that its character is both open and contested.

(1999: 74–75; original emphasis)

These ideas have become increasingly influential in alcohol and other drug studies. Researchers have been inspired to explore new and different questions. For instance, in *Habits: Remaking addiction*, Fraser, Moore and Keane make the point that STS-inspired studies of addiction are not concerned with what addiction '*is*' (if indeed such a conclusion could ever be drawn) but what addiction '*does*'. They ask:

What is 'addiction'? What does it say about us, our social arrangements and our political preoccupations? Where is it going as an idea, and what is at stake in its ongoing production?

(2014: 1)

Applying and adapting the work of Mol, Law and others, scholars have also problematised foundational concepts in alcohol and other drug research. Areas that have attracted attention include alcohol and other drug policy (Fraser, 2016; Moore et al., 2015); service provision (Moore & Fraser, 2013), including online counselling (Savic et al., 2018); health promotion (Fraser & Seear, 2011); drug education (Farrugia, 2017); addiction screening tools (Dwyer & Fraser, 2016a); social media practices, such as tweeting (Dwyer & Fraser, 2016b); autobiographical accounts of addiction (Fraser, 2015); personal accounts of addiction (Moore et al., 2017; Pienaar et al., 2017); medical interventions (Rhodes et al., 2016); reports on 'recovery' (Lancaster, Duke & Ritter, 2015); and drug consumption events and practices (Dilkes-Frayne & Duff, 2017; Dilkes-Frayne, 2016; Demant, 2013). Collectively this work questions claims about the biological properties and 'effects' of drugs as ontologically singular, stable or fixed (see Seear & Moore, 2014; Dwyer & Moore, 2013; Duff, 2013; Fraser & Moore, 2011). To use the words of Woolgar and Lezaun (2013: 333), they often 'interrogate the whatness of things' and how they come to exist. Importantly, this work also reveals the ways that policies and practices might be revised for more effective interventions into alcohol and other drug-related harms, through the recognition that such harms are products of neither 'nature' nor 'discourse' alone. These ideas have had a profound impact on alcohol and other drug research. This is reflected in the establishment of a bi-annual international conference dedicated to STS and drugs, run by the journal *Contemporary Drug Problems* (see Lancaster, 2017; Seear & Moore, 2014).

Researchers have also combined STS ideas with the work of feminist, poststructuralist and performativity scholars. Although there are important differences between such approaches they often overlap or complement each other in important ways. A performativity approach asserts that objects and subject positions such as 'nature', 'gender', 'femininity', 'drugs', 'addiction' and 'addicts' are themselves *made*, rather than natural, fixed or biologically given (e.g. Butler, 2010, 1997, 1993, 1990). A key component of performativity theory is the notion that 'descriptive, calculative, and gestural practices' (Race, 2012: 328) are formative, so that discourses and practices systematically shape subjects and objects, with ontological effects. Put another way: 'If we think performatively, then reality is not assumed to be independent, priori, definite, singular or coherent' (Law, 2011: 156). Performativity theory has been influential in several disciplines, including feminism, queer theory and economics (Race, 2012). An important aspect of performativity theory is the notion that realities are made through processes of repetition (Butler, 1993, 1990). Feminists have deployed these approaches to challenge essentialising claims about the 'nature' or 'naturalness' of women's oppression, highlighting instead the ways that oppression is made and maintained via discourse and practice (Fraser & Moore, 2011). Extending these ideas to the study of addiction, Moore and Fraser (2013: 916) have argued that systems and practices can function 'to produce "addicts" as an effect of policy' and as this work happens, 'the scale of the problem appears to be growing rather than shrinking'. In later work building upon and expanding these ideas, Fraser, Moore and Keane (2014: 5–6) argued that 'the kind of problem that addiction is depends on institutional location and the ontological politics of the substance involved'. Implicit in this suggestion is the need to study how addiction is understood, represented, dealt with, managed and thus *enacted* across different institutional settings. Surprisingly, there has been very little work that responds to this call and seeks to study the enactment of addiction in one of the most important and influential of all institutional contexts: the law. This is despite the fact that there is a growing interest in the application of STS and related theoretical approaches to law, and an existing conceptual and methodological toolbox that can be readily applied to legal practices.

## Science and technology studies and the law

One of the best-known proponents of STS is Bruno Latour. His early work dealt with scientific practices and institutions, but in recent years, Latour has turned his attention to other institutions, including the law. An early example of this was Latour's ethnography of a French administrative court (Latour, 2009). On and off, over a period of four years, Latour had privileged access to the inner workings of the court – not only sitting in the public gallery, but behind closed doors, where cases were discussed by those tasked with reviewing them. His interest was in what it means to 'speak legally', but also, more broadly, in how one of the 'central institutions' of our culture produces 'truth' (Latour, 2009: ix). Latour was concerned to capture something about what he called '*the essence of law*' (2009: x; original emphasis). His conclusion is that the essence of law 'does not lie in a definition *but in a practice*' (2009: x; emphasis added). Law's essence is forged via overlapping and situated material practices and networks. To make this point, Latour draws an analogy between law and other entities and modes of inquiry, including science, noting that:

> Law is not made 'of law' any more than a gas pipe is made *of* gas or science *of* science. On the contrary, it is by means of steel, pipes, regulators, meters, inspectors and control rooms that gas ends up flowing uninterruptedly across Europe; and yet it is well and truly gas that circulates, and not the land, nor steel.
>
> (2009: 264)

As such, Latour's legal analyses have sought to track the various processes by which the content of law is made, and stabilised. This has been described as a form of 'tracing' (Matthews & Veitch, 2016: 355). Kyle McGee (2014: 159) has elsewhere argued that legal scholarship often obscures these processes, however, instead being dominated by 'a ceaseless tendency to obliterate the demos, the entire population of mediators through which the normativity of law is constructed'. The Latourian approach to law thus seeks to identify these mediators and lay bare their role in the production of law. A foundational idea in Latourian legal scholarship is thus that:

> Such mediators – human and non-human – are what carry the force of law and in so doing generate the legal form, rather than the legal form being the presupposition of valid law that will somehow 'diffuse' into the world.
>
> (Matthews & Veitch, 2016: 359)

Later, in *An Inquiry into Modes of Existence*, Latour made the point that the law was a 'highly distinctive world' (2013: 54), with its own processes of 'veridiction' – or truth making. He argues that *'law is its own metalanguage'* (2015: 334; original emphasis). Latour was of the opinion that studying the peculiarities and specificities of law was important. In other words:

> For Latour, and his followers, we must come to law as an ethnographer. In doing so we must try to ascertain of what exactly law's specificity consists. Here, witnessing what happens in the process of making the law, the *content* of the law is not of major significance. Rather, the ethnographer finds in law a way of linking, of establishing a whole series of *vindicula juris*, which alone establishes its unique character as a form of veridiction and mode of existence.
>
> (Matthews & Veitch, 2016: 352; original emphasis)

Notably, Latour's approach emphasises not 'transcendence' and 'externality' as the core of law, but its 'modes of connecting' (Matthews & Veitch, 2016: 355). In a lengthy passage on law's connective modes in *The Making of law* (2009: 264), Latour argues that:

> there is no domain, no territory that belongs to law. Notwithstanding the claims of jurists served by the sociologists of systems, it does not form a sphere; without the rest holding it, law would be nothing. Yet it holds

everything, in its own way. If we have so much difficulty focusing precisely on the form of autonomy peculiar to Law, if it requires so much care to deploy its fabric without damaging it, this may be due to another feature which can but strike the observer: its superficiality. If it holds everything, if it makes it possible to link all people and all acts, if by way of a continuous route it authorizes the Constitution to be linked to a tiny case, it is also because it extracts only a tiny part of their essence from all situations. Its fabric resembles that of a delicately knitted lace.

As this passage reveals, Latour's critical interest is in more than just the fundamental precepts of law (such as legal precedents). Of equal interest, according to Latour, is the study of law's mechanisms, of how law comes to be constituted and stabilised, and from where it draws its 'force'. This distinction requires a little explanation.

## What does an STS approach to law involve?

The doctrine of *stare decisis* is at the heart of Australia's common law system (and other common law systems around the world). Latin for 'to stand by things decided', the doctrine dictates that a principle or rule decided in a previous legal case is to be binding, or persuasive, on subsequent cases with similar issues or facts. (For an overview of these issues, see Hyams, 2017.) Under this doctrine of precedent, rules pronounced by higher courts are binding on lower courts. Importantly, the ratio of a case is not always clear. Written judgements can run for several pages, and in some instances, in excess of 100 pages. Judges rarely pause at any point in the judgement to say, 'and now we come to the ratio'. Lawyers are thus taught how to 'read' cases with a view to extracting the relevant principle, a process that generally involves drawing distinctions between two kinds of utterances. These are known as the *ratio decidendi* (Latin for the 'rationale of the decision') and the *obiter dicta* (Latin for comments 'by the way'). The *ratio* is considered to be the core legal principle of the case (and thus of, legal and material import), while the *obiter* are considered as mere remarks made in passing, with little or no legal significance. It is the ratio that has precedent value and can be 'carried' from case to case. In some instances, obiter can itself be persuasive, such as where a higher court provides a detailed commentary on issues that might not be central to the case it is deciding, but which it still feels are worth making. In such a case, the obiter might be taken up in a later case, or lay the foundations for the evolution of a legal principle in subsequent cases. Both the ratio and obiter are important to the meaning and content of the law (the former more so). But it would be wrong to assume that the complexity of law can be reduced to these utterances alone. A focus on legal principles ignores the important work that is done in articulating, developing, construing and applying the law, among other things. For instance, the process of extracting the ratio from a case, or distinguishing between the ratio and obiter, requires work, and might itself be the subject of disagreement or debate. The process of applying the ratio to subsequent cases with similar facts or issues raises further questions, including what 'similarity' might look like, how much similarity is needed, how much dissimilarity can be tolerated and with regard to what. It also overlooks the work done in deciding what a relevant 'issue' involves, as well as how 'facts' are determined or constituted. Importantly, as I have argued elsewhere (see Seear, 2015, discussed below), a focus on the ratio of a case neglects the way in which cases can stabilise other realities – subjects and objects – as 'collateral realities' (following Law, 2011), along the way. It also misses an important opportunity to leverage critical insights from queer and feminist theory, in particular, on the constitutive work of repetition. More plainly, that is, the doctrine of *stare decisis* is a practice explicitly invested in and characterised by repetitive practices, suggesting an immediate compatibility between such theoretical concerns and law. Moreover, such repetition may be vulnerable to rupture, thus opening up interesting questions about legal futures. Finally, underpinning all of these practices are vital questions about the proper role and function of lawyers, including the ethics and politics of different approaches to lawyering (see, for example, Parker & Evans, 2014; Evans, 2014). Although I will return to a more detailed discussion of these issues in Chapter 5, it is important to note that there is no single, universal approach to lawyering. There is ongoing debate about how lawyers should approach their work, including the extent to which lawyers should be concerned with the wider implications of what they do. A focus on the doctrine of precedent elides the importance and centrality of these processes and considerations to the making of law, and thus to the implications of legal practices.

Latour has encouraged a wider look at legal practices of the kind described above, including a focus on what they materialise, make possible and foreclose. This work has been interpreted as meaning that critiques of legal content are now to some extent 'redundant', and that we should now 'forget ideology' (Matthews & Veitch, 2016: 354–355). For some, the Latourian 'emphasis on law's *superficiality*, with its apparent lack of attention to the content of the law, might well be troubling. Does it make no difference to our understanding of law's practice whether the law condones or condemns slavery, exploitation, genocide?' (2016: 354). In my reading of Latour, the point is not that legal content is now wholly redundant but that it is simply one of several subjects that should be of interest to critical legal scholars. One scholar to take up Latour's ideas and interpret, revise and expand them is Kyle McGee. Latour has explicitly endorsed McGee's approach to law (Latour, 2015). McGee argues that Latour's work responds to a greater crisis in legal scholarship, including a preoccupation with narrow fields of inquiry. On this, McGee (2015c: 62) writes:

> This failure of legal studies is basic and spread widely beyond the field, in virtually every domain for which rules, standards, principles and other normative artifacts are endowed with quasi-spiritual powers to regulate, restrict, govern, dominate or rule quite effortlessly. It is a metaphysical failure. Thought and speech, things and practices alike are delocalised so that their normative effects become untraceable and emanate, somewhat mysteriously,

from no particular site or act of enunciation. Unbound from such terrestrial constraints, disembedded legal articles move swiftly through the normative void. There is, therefore, tremendous value in modes of thought that slow down to peer into these sorts of artifacts and the material, conceptual and semantic constructs that enable law.

'Slowing down' and 'peering in' necessitate moving beyond precedent and towards legal practices as implicated in the making of worlds. As McGee (2015c: 64) explains, 'the content of law is not only irremediably bound up with its conditions of enunciation, but is fully identical with those conditions. And some of those conditions are packaged in *legal devices* that we can unwrap and explore'. In explaining this process of unwrapping and exploring, Latour and McGee both draw upon the metaphor – closely associated with Latour's earlier work on science – of the 'black box'. In that work, the metaphor of the black box refers to the notion that 'scientific and technical work is made invisible by its own success. When a machine runs efficiently, when a matter of fact is settled, one need focus only on its inputs and outputs and not on its internal complexity' (Latour, 1999: 304). Latour has long been concerned with how to open black boxes. He suggests that this might be done by exploring the 'conditions of production' (Latour, 1987: 23). Put another way, the aim is: 'to open a black box and reveal its constitutive assemblage, to lead it back to the process that gave rise to it' (McGee, 2014: 19; see also Valverde & Weaver, 2015).

These calls to action – to slow down, peer in, unwrap, explore and open legal black boxes – require scholars to move beyond traditional areas and methods of inquiry. For example, although litigation is a 'key site for the production of the sense or truths of law' (McGee, 2015c: 67), it is also true that 'the public focus on litigation obscures the sources of power and hegemony of law' (Silbey, 2005: 331). Thus, STS-inspired approaches to law gesture towards understanding how law is made, and the processes and practices that sustain it. Kyle McGee (2018) has also developed a 'materiological' account of law, which focusses on non-textual modalities (such as fences, signs and speed bumps) and their function in the production of law. It also means looking at the work of various actors in the legal process, including lawyers. Lawyers, like judges, can play a vital and oft-overlooked role in the production of legal 'facts' (Lynch, 2007) and the stabilisation of taken-for-granted notions and 'realities'. By way of example, McGee's chapter for his own edited collection on Latour and the passage of law (McGee, 2015a) examines a single motion in a single case in the United States. He describes this work as narrowing 'the scope of inquiry to an almost unbearable degree [through a focus on…] a single, most ordinary American legal case in a most ordinary procedural posture at the trial court level. Yes, one decision on one motion' (2015c: 62). The value in so doing is:

> To track the slow composition of a unique trajectory of legal truth; to register the specific processes and techniques deployed to fuse a continuous pathway out of scattered elements of uncertain relevance and to thus achieve an order that is witnessably legal; to map the decisive yet easily overlooked

transformations of volatile value-objects into disciplined obligations or the multiple transfers of agency implicated in the fabrication of a legal statement; none of these 'earthbound' jurisprudential phenomena are accessible without a dogged insistence on a kind of casuistry that places a premium on the actions occurring in courts of first instance. The conceptual point of this casuistic method is that, when we bypass the radically uncertain, tenuous, hesitant production of judgments, we carelessly afford a set of pricey values – neutrality, objectivity, certainty, integrity, *sécurité juridique* even the rule of law – to wonky artifacts that perhaps do not deserve them or, more interestingly, that have in fact acquired alternative versions of some of these values in ways quite different than we had imagined.

(McGee, 2015c: 62–63; original emphasis)

In other words, an STS approach to law has the effect of demystifying and deconstructing it. I have previously applied similar ideas to the study of addiction in legal contexts. In a detailed study of one Australian High Court case dealing with gambling addiction, for instance, I argued that legal judgements ostensibly dealing with one object (in that case, 'pathological gambling') can simultaneously materialise and stabilise other realities, including the 'realities' of addiction more broadly and other 'types' of addiction such as drug addiction (Seear, 2015). I argued that it was important to attend to legal specificities in different areas of law, including the procedural and technical minutiae of different legal realms (Seear, 2015), since these were likely to be important in shaping addiction realities. Crucially, I also made the point that legal minutiae and procedural rules play a vital role in the production of addiction, and that in 'a different legal realm, where slightly different questions and remedies were at issue, another version of addiction might have been produced' (2015: 82). I have also explored how lawyers talk about addiction in the work that they do (a theme that I will return to in this book). Following on from Michael Lynch's observation, noted earlier, that lawyers play an important role in the production of legal 'facts', I examined how lawyers stabilise addiction facts in their work. I argued (2017: 185) that lawyers make 'quasi-expert determinations', because:

1   Legal practice is of a special nature, with its own unique approach to the constitution of facts/truths. This approach differs from veridiction processes that operate in science, and is shaped by a range of factors, including the peculiarities of legal rules and processes (e.g. rules that prevent lawyers from misleading the court but allow them to otherwise make arguments they deem to be strategically advantageous to their clients).
2   Just as the law has its own processes for the constitution of 'facts', it has its own methods for determining who may co-constitute facts, what constitutes expert knowledge in the production of facts, and how and when expert (or expert-like) determinations can be made. Multiple actors, including conventional expert witnesses, lawyers and judges, play a role in these processes of veridiction.

3   Important expert and 'expert-like' decisions are made at multiple points in the legal process (including many outside of the courtroom). Similarly, legal veridiction is not confined to the courtroom.
4   Expert-like deliberations and pronouncements (some that draw explicitly on science, others more implicitly) allow for idiosyncratic and ontologically unique 'facts' that may well differ from those that are constituted in other (non-legal) contexts (see also Seear, 2015). These 'expert' and 'quasi-expert' pronouncements will be shaped by a range of factors (following Jasanoff, 2004a, 2004b, 1995) including values, politics and emotions, and legal strategy.

Beyond these limited examples, there have been no attempts to utilise STS ideas and apply them to the study of addiction in the law. This book is an attempt to engage with these issues. Inspired by Mol and Law's *ontological multiplicity*, Fraser, Moore and Keane's work on *'addicting'*, STS analyses of law by Bruno Latour (2013, 2009) and Kyle McGee (2015a, 2015b, 2015c, 2014), and critical scholarship on the ethics of lawyering, among other things, this book examines how the law and legal practices constitute addiction. It also considers what these enactments *do*, why these doings matter and whether things might be done otherwise.

## The structure of this book

In keeping with John Law's (2011: 171) focus on 'practices all the way down', and the five issues he suggests paying attention to, each chapter of this book examines one aspect of legal practice. The practices dealt with are *legislative practices* (Chapter 1), *advocacy practices* (Chapter 2), *negotiation practices* (Chapter 3), *sentencing practices* (Chapter 4) and *ethical practices* (Chapter 5). Most chapters have the same structure, comprising an introduction (summarising key ideas in the chapter), a background section (outlining relevant legal and other contextual information) and a section in which the theoretical approach is introduced, before moving on to data analysis and the chapter conclusion. Each chapter contains an overview of the relevant legal issues and assumes no previous knowledge of Australian law or law more generally. It also assumes no knowledge of STS theory. The chapters draw upon a range of data sets collected for this research. These are: Australian legislation which refers to 'addiction' and/or 'dependence' and associated materials, such as statements of compatibility with human rights; cases from the Australian High Court that dealt with 'addiction' and/or 'dependence'; qualitative, in-depth interviews with Australia and Canadian lawyers and Australian decision makers (judges, magistrates and other statutory decision makers such as tribunal members and members of parole boards) (total number = 48). Interviews were confidential, digitally recorded and transcribed verbatim. In order to protect anonymity, all participants who are mentioned in this book have been given a pseudonym. Interviews were conducted according to an interview schedule covering themes including:

* definitions of addiction;
* the range of concepts or models of addiction participants draw on in their work;

- the relevance of statutes and/or case law from within and outside the participants' own fields of expertise;
- participants' experiences of and needs regarding education in understandings of alcohol and other drugs and addiction;
- participants' views on the strengths and weaknesses of existing approaches; and
- public policy implications of various legal approaches to addiction.

All data were analysed using the Miles and Huberman (1994) approach of data display, coding and analysis. The project was approved by the Monash University Human Ethics Research Committee. Not all of these data appear in each chapter.

Chapter 1 focusses on the legislative process, and examines two pieces of proposed legislation ('bills') that dealt with alcohol and other drug issues. In that chapter, I concentrate on one aspect of the process through which bills are developed in some Australian jurisdictions, in particular the requirement that bills take account of and incorporate human rights considerations. In that chapter I consider how this requirement plays out in practice, and what the process of bringing human rights into conversation with alcohol and other drugs does with both 'human rights' and 'dependence'. The analysis I undertake in the first chapter sets the scene for the rest of the book in three main ways. First, it sheds light on how law and legal content is produced. Second, and in a related sense, it highlights the central role that practices of articulation and connection play in the development of legal content, and thusly in the ontology of law. Third, it suggests that the content of law can be made anew if different connections are articulated, or if connections are expressed differently. In this sense, the law is more malleable and fragile than we might assume. This presents opportunities for remaking law, and the subjects and objects shaped by it. Chapter 2 continues this focus on the making of addiction through practices, drawing on interview data with lawyers and decision makers. I examine lawyers' accounts of how addiction features in their work, and why it features. Lawyers often make strategic decisions about how to manage alcohol and other drug use when it comes up in their work, the utility of framing alcohol or other drug use as 'addiction' and key concepts that underpin it. A central theme of this chapter is that lawyers anticipate how decision makers will think about alcohol and other drugs and 'addiction', and that this anticipation shapes lawyers' strategy and practice. In this sense, anticipation works to materialise and stabilise addiction as a (certain kind of) legal object. I also introduce interview data from decision makers, contrasting their opinions on alcohol and other drugs with those of lawyers. Somewhat surprisingly, decision makers afford themselves less agency in the enactment of legal realities than we might assume them to have. Whereas lawyers' enact addiction in ways they anticipate will accord with decision makers' conceptualisations, decision makers claim to be constrained in their enactments, with their judgements contingent upon the ideas that lawyers' put to them. This raises questions about the habituated nature of the strategies lawyers use, and whether those habits are 'just'.

Chapter 3 continues the focus on lawyers' practices, with a specific focus on the practice of negotiation. The chapter again draws upon interview data with lawyers, focussing in particular on their accounts of negotiation strategies outside court. This subtle shift in setting and focus are important for various reasons. I argue that lawyers play a central role in stabilising addiction 'facts' and establishing legal 'truths' about addiction. I explore how that plays out within the context of two areas, being family violence and child protection cases. The chapter explores the gender implications of these processes, and examines how legal practices of truth-making risk securing, reinforcing and perpetuating gendered inequalities for women. In Chapter 4, I turn to an examination of the case law, and provide a detailed reading of one case decided by the Australian High Court in 2013. Drawing upon Deleuzian 'assemblage thinking' on alcohol and other drug events, including those involving violence, I consider how legal approaches to sentencing Indigenous offenders constitute alcohol and other drug 'addiction'/'alcoholism', violence, race, gender and place in Australia. I argue that the process of sentencing offenders in the criminal law necessarily entails an attempt, on the part of courts, to assemble the relative agency of various human and non-human actors in the commission of a crime, and that processes of affording agency have political, ethical and material effects. In Chapter 5, I return to the interview data and explore lawyers' and decision makers' reflections on the ethics of existing legal approaches to alcohol and other drugs. Lawyers suggest that existing approaches to the practice of lawyering for people who use drugs are simultaneously beneficial and harmful, and can be implicated in the production of drug-related stigma, primarily through the enactment of the 'addict' as irrational and non-agentive. Lawyers raise concerns about the central emphasis placed on addiction in their work, and question whether different approaches might be possible. I also examine the views of decision makers on the utility of existing enactments of 'addiction'. The concluding chapter draws together the findings from each of the previous chapters. In this final chapter, I ask whether existing approaches can be said to be just and whether they might be otherwise. I introduce the concept of 'onto-advocacy' – an approach that combines ideas from the 'ontological turn' in alcohol and other drug studies with critical approaches to legal ethics. I argue that lawyers might consider working with their clients to deliberately leverage law's ontological fragility, and to rethink their advocacy practices in light of the power that they hold to constitute objects, subjects and outcomes. I ask whether alcohol and other drugs might one day be decentred, seen as just habits, and whether a more just approach to habits (both those in and of law, and those in and of consumption) is possible.

# References

Alexander, B. (2008). *The Globalisation of Addiction: A Study in the Poverty of Spirit.* Oxford: Oxford University Press.

American Psychiatric Association. (2013). *Diagnostic and Statistical Manual of Mental Disorders DSM-5.* Washington: American Psychiatric Press.

Bourgois, P. (1995). Disciplining addictions: The bio-politics of methadone and heroin in the United States. *Culture, Medicine and Psychiatry, 24*(2), 165–195.

Brook, H., & Stringer, R. (2005). Users, using, used: A beginner's guide to deconstructing drugs discourse. *International Journal of Drug Policy, 16*(5), 316–325.

Brown, S. (2008). Application of addiction neuroscience to moral and legal responsibility: Explanations not exculpations. *Criminal Law Journal, 32,* 239–247.

Bull, M. (2005). A comparative review of best practice guidelines for the diversion of drug related offenders. *International Journal of Drug Policy, 16*(4), 223–234.

Bull, M. (2003). *Just Treatment: A Review of International Programs for the Diversion of Drug Related Offenders from the Criminal Justice System.* Brisbane: Queensland University of Technology.

Bunn, R. (2019). Conceptualising addiction as disability in discrimination law: A situated comparison. *Contemporary Drug Problems, 46*(1), 58–77.

Butler, J. (2010). Performative agency. *Journal of Cultural Economy, 3*(2), 147–161.

Butler, J. (1997). *Excitable Speech: A Politics of the Performative.* New York: Routledge.

Butler, J. (1993). *Bodies that Matter: On the Discursive Limits of 'Sex'.* New York: Routledge.

Butler, J. (1990). *Gender Trouble: Feminism and the Subversion of Identity.* New York: Routledge.

Calder, G. (2011). Insite: Right answer, wrong question. *Constitutional Forum, 19*(3), 113–117.

Callon, M., & Law, J. (1997). After the individual in society: Lessons on collectivity from science, technology and society. *Canadian Journal of Sociology, 22*(2), 165–182.

Cameron, C. (2002). Hired guns and smoking guns: McCabe v British American Tobacco Australia Ltd. *UNSW Law Journal, 25*(3), 768–797.

Campbell, N. (2010). Toward a critical neuroscience of 'addiction'. *BioSocieties, 5*(1), 89–104.

Cappa, C. (2006). The social political and theoretical context of drug courts. *Monash University Law Review, 32*(1), 145–176.

Carter, A., Mathews, R., Bell, S., Lucke, J., & Hall, W. (2014). Control and responsibility in addicted individuals: What do addiction neuroscientists and clinicians think? *Neuroethics, 7*(2), 205–214.

Casper, M. (1994). Reframing and grounding nonhuman agency: What makes a fetus an agent? *American Behavioral Scientist, 37*(6), 839–56.

Courtwright, D. (2010). The NIDA brain disease paradigm: History, resistance and spinoffs. *BioSocieties, 5,* 137–147.

Davies, J. B. (1992). *The Myth of Addiction: An Application of the Psychological Theory of Attribution to Illicit Drug Use.* Reading: Harwood Academic Publishers.

Demant, J. (2013). Affected in the nightclub. A case study of regular clubbers' conflictual practices in nightclubs. *International Journal of Drug Policy, 24*(3), 196–202.

Derrida, J. (2002). *Writing and Difference* (A. Bass, Trans). London: Routledge.

Derrida, J. (1976). *Of Grammatology* (G. C. Spivak, Trans). Baltimore: Johns Hopkins University Press.

Dilkes-Frayne, E. (2016). Drugs at the campsite: Socio-spatial relations and drug use at music festivals. *International Journal of Drug Policy, 33,* 27–35.

Dilkes-Frayne, E., & Duff, C. (2017). Tendencies and trajectories: The production of subjectivity in an event of drug consumption. *Environment and Planning D: Society and Space, 35*(5), 951–967.

Duff, C. (2013). The social life of drugs. *International Journal of Drug Policy*, *24*(3), 167–172.

Dwyer, R., & Fraser, S. (2016a). Making addictions in standardised screening and diagnostic tools. *Health Sociology Review*, *25*(3), 223–239.

Dwyer, R., & Fraser, S. (2016b). Addicting via hashtags: How is Twitter making addiction? *Contemporary Drug Problems*, *43*(1), 79–97.

Dwyer, R., & Moore, D. (2013). Enacting multiple methamphetamines: The ontological politics of public discourse and consumer accounts of a drug and its effects. *International Journal of Drug Policy*, *24*(3), 203–211.

Evans, A. (2014). *The Good Lawyer*. Port Melbourne: Cambridge University Press.

Farrugia, A. (2017). Gender, reputation and regret: The ontological politics of Australian drug education. *Gender and Education*, *29*(3), 281–298.

Fitzgerald, J. (2008). Drug diversion: An intersection between law enforcement and the public health approaches to the control of illicit drug use. In P. Dietze & D. Moore (eds.), *Drugs and Public Health: Australian Perspectives on Policy and Practice* (pp. 103–113). Melbourne: Oxford University Press.

Fitzgerald, J., McDonald, K., & Klugman M. (2004). *Unspoken but Everpresent: Hepatitis C in a Regional Setting*. Melbourne: The University of Melbourne.

Flacks, S. (2012). Deviant disabilities: The exclusion of drug and alcohol addiction from the Equality Act 2010. *Social and Legal Studies*, *21*, 395–412.

Fomiatti, R., Moore, D., & Fraser, S. [In Press]. The improvable self: Enacting model citizenship and sociality in research on 'new recovery'. *Addiction Research and Theory*.

Fox, K. (1999). Ideological implications of addiction: Theories and treatment. *Deviant Behavior: An Interdisciplinary Journal*, *20*, 209–232.

Fraser, S. (2016). Articulating addiction in alcohol and other drug policy: A multiverse of habits. *International Journal of Drug Policy*, *31*, 6–14.

Fraser, S. (2015). A thousand contradictory ways: Addiction, neuroscience and expert autobiography. *Contemporary Drug Problems*, *42*(1), 38–59.

Fraser, S. (2004). 'It's your life!': Injecting drug users, individual responsibility and hepatitis C prevention. *Health: An Interdisciplinary Journal for the Social Study of Health, Illness and Medicine*, *8*(2), 199–221.

Fraser, S., & Ekendahl, M. (2018). 'Getting better': The politics of comparison in addiction treatment and research. *Contemporary Drug Problems*, *45*(2), 87–106.

Fraser, S., & Moore, D. (eds.). (2011). *The Drug Effect: Health Crime and Society*. Melbourne: Cambridge University Press.

Fraser, S., Moore, D., & Keane, H. (2014). *Habits: Remaking Addiction*. London: Palgrave Macmillan.

Fraser, S., Pienaar, K., Dilkes-Frayne, E., Moore, D., Kokanovic, R., Treloar, C., & Dunlop, A. (2017). Addiction stigma and the biopolitics of liberal modernity: A qualitative analysis. *International Journal of Drug Policy*, *44*, 192–201.

Fraser, S., & Seear, K. (2011). *Making Disease, Making Citizens: The Politics of Hepatitis C*. Aldershot: Ashgate.

Fraser, S., & valentine, k. (2008). *Substance and Substitution: Methadone Subjects in Liberal Societies*. Basingstoke: Palgrave.

Fraser, S., valentine, k., & Ekendahl, M. (2018). Drugs, brains and other subalterns: Public debate and the new materialist politics of addiction. *Body & Society*, *24*(4), 58–86.

Freiberg, A. (2001). Problem-oriented courts: Innovative solutions to intractable problems? *Journal of Judicial Administration*, *11*(1), 8–27.

Freiberg, A. (2000). Australian drug courts. *Criminal Law Journal*, 24(4), 213–235.

Garriott, W. (2013). 'You can always tell who's using meth': Methamphetamine addiction and the semiotics of criminal difference. In E. Raikhel & W. Garriott (eds.), *Addiction Trajectories* (pp. 213–237). Durham: Duke University Press.

Gibson, (2009). Drugs, discrimination and disability. *Journal of Law and Medicine, 17*, 400–411.

Goffman, E. (1963). *Stigma: Notes on the Management of Spoiled Identity.* New York: Simon & Schuster, Inc.

Gowan, T., & Whetstone, S. (2012). Making the criminal addict: Subjectivity and social control in a strong-arm rehab. *Punishment & Society, 14*(1), 69–93.

Grosz, E. (1994). *Volatile Bodies: Towards a Corporeal Feminism.* Indiana: Indiana University Press.

Grosz, E. (1989). *Sexual Subversions: Three French Feminists.* Sydney: Allen and Unwin.

Hall, W., & Carter, A. (2015). Are addicted individuals responsible for their behaviour? In W. Glannon (ed.), *Free Will and the Brain* (pp. 146–167). Oxford: Cambridge University Press.

Hall, W., Carter, A., & Forlini, C. (2015). The brain disease model of addiction: Is it supported by the evidence and has it delivered on its promises? *The Lancet Psychiatry, 2*(1), 105–110.

Hammer, R., Dingel, M., Ostegren, J., Partridge, B., McCormick, J., & Koenig, B. A. (2013). Addiction: Current criticism of the brain disease paradigm. *AJOB Neuroscience, 4*(3), 27–32.

Heim, D., Agrawal, R., Allamani, A., Arvers, P., Beccaria, F., & Berridge, V., et al. (2014). Addiction: not just brain malfunction. *Nature, 507,* 40. Available at: www.nature.com/nature/journal/v507/n7490/full/507040e.html (accessed 16 October 2017).

Hyams, R. (ed.). (2017) *Foundations of Law: A Custom Publication for Monash University* (2nd edn). Clayton: LexisNexis Butterworths.

Indermaur, D., & Roberts, L. (2005). Finding alternatives to imprisonment: Drug courts in Australia. *Reform, 86,* 28–32.

Indermaur, D., & Roberts, L. (2003). Drug courts in Australia: The first generation. *Current Issues in Criminal Justice, 15*(2), 136–153.

Jasanoff, S. (2004a). The idiom of co-production. In S. Jasanoff (ed.), *States of Knowledge: The Co-production of Science and Social Order* (pp. 1–12). London: Routledge.

Jasanoff, S. (2004b). Afterword. In S. Jasanoff (ed.), *States of Knowledge: The Co-production of Science and Social Order* (pp. 274–282). London: Routledge.

Jasanoff, S. (1995). *Science at the Bar: Law, Science and Technology in America.* Cambridge: Harvard University Press.

Joh, E. (2009). Imagining the addict: Evaluating social and legal responses to addiction. *Utah Law Review, 175,* 175–194.

Jones, C. (2011). Intensive judicial supervision and drug court outcomes: Interim findings from a randomised controlled trial. *Contemporary Issues in Crime and Justice, 152,* 1–16.

Karasaki, M., Fraser, S., Moore D., & Dietze P. (2013). The place of volition in addiction: Differing approaches and their implications for policy and service provision. *Drug and Alcohol Review, 32*(2), 195–204.

Keane, H. (2002). *What's Wrong with Addiction?* Melbourne: Melbourne University Press.

Lancaster, K., Duke, K., & Ritter, A. (2015). Producing the 'problem of drugs': A cross national-comparison of 'recovery' discourse in two Australian and British reports. *International Journal of Drug Policy, 26,* 617–625.

Lancaster, K., Seear, K., & Ritter, A. (2018). *Reducing Stigma and Discrimination for People Experiencing Problematic Alcohol and Other Drug Use. Drug Policy Modelling Program Monograph Series* (vol. 26, p. 119). Sydney: National Drug and Alcohol Research Centre.

Latour, B. (2015). The strange entanglement of jurimorphs. In K. McGee (ed.), *Latour and the Passage of Law* (pp. 331–353). Edinburgh: Edinburgh University Press.

Latour, B. (2013). *An Inquiry into Modes of Existence: An Anthropology of the Moderns.* Cambridge: Harvard University Press.

Latour, B. (2009). *The Making of Law: An Ethnography of the Conseil D'Etat.* Cambridge: Polity Press.

Latour, B. (1999). *Pandora's Hope: Essays on the Reality of Science Studies.* Cambridge: Harvard University Press.

Latour, B. (as Jim Johnson). (1988a). Mixing humans and nonhumans together: The sociology of a door-closer. *Social Problems, Special Issue: The Sociology of Science and Technology, 35*(3), 298–310.

Latour, B. (1988b). How to write *The Prince* for machines as well as machinations. In B. Elliot (ed.), *Technology and Social Change* (pp. 20–63). Edinburgh: Edinburgh University Press.

Latour, B. (1987). *Science in Action: How to Follow Scientists and Engineers through Society.* Cambridge: Harvard University Press.

Law, J. (2011). *Collateral realities.* In F. Rubio & P. Baert (eds.), *The politics of knowledge* (pp. 156–178). London: Routledge.

Law, J. (1999). After ANT: Complexity, naming and topology. In J. Law & J. Hassard (eds.), *Actor Network Theory and After* (pp. 1–14). Oxford: Blackwell.

Leshner, A. (1997). Addiction is a brain disease, and it matters. *Science, 278*, 45–47.

Lessard, H. (2011). Jurisdictional justice, democracy and the story of Insite. *Constitutional Forum, 19*(3), 93–112.

Levine, H. (1978). The discovery of addiction: Changing conceptions of habitual drunkenness in America. *Journal of Studies on Alcohol, 39*, 143–174.

Liberman, J. (2002). The shredding of BAT's defence: McCabe v British American Tobacco Australia. *British Medical Journal, 11*(3), 271–274.

Lloyd, C. (2013). The stigmatization of problem drug users: A narrative literature review. *Drugs: Education, Prevention, and Policy, 20*(2), 85–95.

Lloyd, C. (2010). *Sinning and Sinned Against: The Stigmatisation of Problem Drug Users.* London: UK Drug Policy Commission (UKDPC).

Lucke, J., & Hall, W. (2012). Under what conditions is it ethical to offer incentives to encourage drug-using women to use long-acting forms of contraception? *Addiction, 107*, 1036–1041.

Lupton, D. (2003). *Medicine as Culture* (2nd edn). London: Sage.

Lynch, M. (2007). Expertise, skepticism and cynicism. *Spontaneous generations, 1*(1), 17–23.

Lyons, T. (2014). Simultaneously treatable and punishable: Implications of the production of addicted subjects in a drug treatment court. *Addiction Research and Theory, 22*(4), 286–293.

Matthews, D., & Veitch, S. (2016). The limits of critique and the forces of law. *Law Critique, 27*, 349–361.

McGee, K. (2018). Hybrid legalities: On obligation and law's immanent materiology. In D. Matthews & S. Veitch (eds.), *Law, Obligation, Community* (pp. 163–182). Abingdon: Routledge.

McGee, K. (2015a). *Latour and the Passage of Law*. Edinburgh: Edinburgh University Press.

McGee, K. (2015b). Introduction. In K. McGee (ed.), *Latour and the Passage of Law* (pp. 1–16). Edinburgh: Edinburgh University Press.

McGee, K. (2015c). On devices and logics of legal sense: Toward socio-technical legal analysis. In K. McGee (ed.), *Latour and the Passage of Law* (pp. 61–92). Edinburgh: Edinburgh University Press.

McGee, K. (2014). *Bruno Latour: The Normativity of Networks*. Oxfordshire: Routledge.

Miles, M., & Huberman A. M. (1994). *Qualitative Data Analysis* (2nd edn). Thousand Oaks: Sage.

Mol, A. (2002). *The Body Multiple: Ontology in Medical Practice*. Durham: Duke University Press.

Mol, A. (1999). Ontological politics. A word and some questions. In J. Law & J. Hassard (eds.), *Actor Network Theory and After* (pp. 74–89). Oxford: Blackwell Publishers.

Mol, A., & Law, J. (2002). Complexities: An introduction. In J. Law & A. Mol (eds.), *Complexities: Social Studies of Knowledge Practices* (pp. 1–22). Durham: Duke University Press.

Moore, D. (2007). *Criminal Artefacts: Governing Drugs and Users*. Vancouver: University of British Columbia Press.

Moore, D., & Fraser, S. (2013). Producing the 'problem' of addiction in drug treatment. *Qualitative Health Research, 23*(7), 916–923.

Moore, D., & Fraser, S. (2006). Putting at risk what we know: Reflecting on the drug-using subject in harm reduction and its political implications. *Social Science and Medicine, 62*(12), 3035–3047.

Moore, D., Fraser, S., Törrönen, J., & Eriksson Tinghög, M. (2015). Sameness and difference: Metaphor and politics in the constitution of addiction, social exclusion and gender in Australian and Swedish drug policy. *International Journal of Drug Policy, 26*(4), 420–428.

Moore, D., Pienaar, K., Dilkes-Frayne, E., & Fraser, S. (2017). Challenging the addiction/health binary with assemblage thinking: An analysis of consumer accounts. *International Journal of Drug Policy, 44*, 155–163.

Morse, S. (2017). The science of addiction and the criminal law. *Harvard Review of Psychiatry, 25*(6), 261–269.

Morse, S. (2000). Hooked on hype: Addiction and responsibility. *Law and Philosophy, 19*(3), 3–49.

Murphy, E. (2012). Paved with good intentions: Sentencing alternatives from neuroscience and the policy of problem-solving courts. *Law and Psychology Review, 37*, 83–118.

Murphy, J. (2011). Drug court as both a legal and medical authority. *Deviant Behavior, 32*(3), 257–291.

Nestler, E., & Malenka, R. (2004). The addicted brain. *Scientific American, 290*(3), 78–85.

Oliphant, B. (2012). Prima facie discrimination: Is Tranchemontagne consistent with the Supreme Court of Canada's Human Rights Code Jurisprudence? *Journal of Law and Equality, 9*, 33–65.

Parker, C., & Evans, A. (2014). *Inside Lawyers' Ethics* (2nd edn). Port Melbourne: Cambridge University Press.

Pienaar, K., Moore, D., Fraser, S., Kokanovic, R., Treloar, C., & Dilkes-Frayne, E. (2017). Diffracting addicting binaries: An analysis of personal accounts of alcohol and other drug 'addiction'. *Health: An Interdisciplinary Journal for the Social Study of Health, Illness and Medicine*, 21(5), 519–537.

Race, K. (2012). Framing responsibility: HIV, biomedical prevention, and the performativity of the law. *Bioethical Inquiry*, 9, 327–338.

Reinarman, C. (2011). Cannabis in culture and legal limbo: Criminalisation, legalization and the mixed blessing of medicalization in the USA. In S. Fraser & D. Moore (eds.), *The Drug Effect: Health, Crime and Society* (pp. 171–188). Melbourne: Cambridge University Press.

Reinarman, C. (2005). Addiction as accomplishment: The discursive construction of disease. *Addiction Research and Theory*, 13(4), 307–320.

Rhodes, T., Closson, E., Paparini, S., Guise, A., & Strathdee, S. (2016). Towards 'evidence-making intervention' approaches in the social science of implementation science: The making of methadone in East Africa. *International Journal of Drug Policy*, 30, 17–26.

Roberts, L., & Indermaur, D. (2006). Timely intervention or trapping minnows? The potential for a range of net-widening effects in Australian drug diversion initiatives. *Psychiatry, Psychology and Law*, 13(2), 220–231.

Robinson, T., & Berridge, K. (2004). Addiction. *Annual Reviews in Psychology*, 54, 25–53.

Room, R. (2006). Addiction concepts and international control. *The Social History of Alcohol and Drugs*, 20, 276–289.

Room, R. (2003). The cultural framing of addiction. *Janus Head*, 6(2), 221–234.

Room, R. (1985). Dependence and society. *British Journal of Addiction*, 80, 133–139.

Sarmiento, E. (2018). *Producing alcohol or other drug 'dependence' in an Australian Drug Court: A Victorian case study*. Unpublished PhD thesis. National Drug Research Institute, Faculty of Health Sciences, Curtin University.

Savic, M., Dilkes-Frayne, E., Carter, A., Kokanovic, R., Manning, V., Rodda, S. N., & Lubman, D. I. (2018). Making multiple 'online counsellings' through policy practice: An evidence-making intervention approach. *International Journal of Drug Policy*, 53, 73–82.

Seddon, T. (2007). Drugs and freedom. *Addiction Research and Theory*, 15(4), 333–342.

Sedgwick, E (1993). Epidemics of the will. In E. Sedgwick (ed.), *Tendencies* (pp. 130–142). Durham: Duke University Press.

Seear, K. (2017). The emerging role of lawyers as addiction 'quasi-experts'. *International Journal of Drug Policy*, 44, 183–191.

Seear, K. (2015). Making addiction, making gender: A feminist performativity analysis of Kakavas v Crown Melbourne Limited. *The Australian Feminist Law Journal*, 41(1), 65–85.

Seear, K. (2014). *The Makings of a Modern Epidemic: Endometriosis, Gender and Politics*. Farnham: Ashgate.

Seear, K., & Fraser, S. (2016). Addiction veridiction: Gendering agency in legal mobilisations of addiction discourse. *Griffith Law Review*, 25(1), 13–29.

Seear, K., & Fraser, S. (2014a). Beyond criminal law: The multiple constitution of addiction in Australian legislation. *Addiction Research and Theory*, 22(5), 438–450.

Seear, K., & Fraser, S. (2014b). The addict as victim: Producing the 'problem' of addiction in Australian victims of crime compensation laws. *International Journal of Drug Policy*, 25(5), 826–835.

Seear, K., & Fraser, S. (2010a). The "sorry addict": Ben Cousins and the construction of drug use and addiction in elite sport. *Health Sociology Review*, 19(2), 176–191.

Seear, K., & Fraser, S. (2010b). Ben Cousins and the "double life": Exploring citizenship and the voluntarity/compulsivity binary through the experiences of a "drug addicted" elite athlete. *Critical Public Health, 20*(4), 439–452.

Seear, K., Lancaster, K., & Ritter, A. (2017). A new framework for evaluating the potential for drug law to produce stigma: Insights from an Australian study. *Journal of Law, Medicine and Ethics, 45*, 596–606.

Seear, K., & Moore, D. (eds.). (2014). Complexity: Researching alcohol and other drugs in a multiple world (Conference Special Issue). *Contemporary Drug Problems, 41*(3), 293–484.

Silbey, S. (2005). After legal consciousness. *Annual Review of Law and Social Science, 1*, 323–68.

Simmonds, L., & Coomber, R. (2009). Injecting drug users: A stigmatised and stigmatising population. *International Journal of Drug Policy, 20*, 121–130.

Spivakovsky, C., Seear, K., & Carter, A. (eds.). (2018). *Critical Perspectives on Coercive Interventions: Law, Medicine and Society*. London: Routledge.

Taylor, G. (2002). Should addiction to drugs be a mitigating factor in sentencing?' *Criminal Law Journal, 26*, 324–343.

Tiger, R. (2012). *Judging Addicts: Drug Courts and Coercion in the Justice System*. New York: New York University Press.

Tiger, R. (2011). Drug courts and the logic of coerced treatment. *Sociological Forum, 26*(1), 169–182.

Tupper, K. (2012). Psychoactive substances and the English language: 'Drugs', discourses, and public policy. *Contemporary Drug Problems, 39*, 461–492.

Valverde, M. (1998). *Diseases of the Will: Alcohol and the Dilemmas of Freedom*. Cambridge: Cambridge University Press.

Valverde, M., & Weaver, A. (2015). 'The crown wears many hats': Canadian aboriginal law and the black-boxing of empire. In K. McGee (ed.), *Latour and the Passage of Law* (pp. 93–121). Edinburgh: Edinburgh University Press.

Volkow, N., & Li, T. (2004). Drug addiction: The neurobiology of behaviour gone awry. *Nature Reviews, 5*, 963–970.

Vrecko, S. (2009). Therapeutic justice in drug courts: Crime, punishment and societies of control. *Science as Culture, 18*(2), 217–232.

Weinberg, D. (2011). Sociological perspectives on addiction. *Sociology Compass, 5*(4), 298–310.

West, R. (2006a). *Theory of Addiction*. Oxford: Blackwell.

West, R. (2006b). Towards a comprehensive theory of addiction. *Drugs and Alcohol Today, 6*(1), 28–32.

West, R. (2001). Theories of addiction. *Addiction, 96*, 3–13.

White, C., OLiffe, J. L., & Bottorff, J. L. (2013). Tobacco and the invention of quitting: A history of gender, excess and will-power. *Sociology of Health and Illness, 35*(5), 778–792.

Woolgar, S., & Lezaun, J. (2013). The wrong bin bag: A turn to ontology in science and technology studies. *Social Studies of Science, 43*(3), 321–340.

Ziegler, S. (2008). *Inventing the Addict: Drugs, Race, and Sexuality in Nineteenth-century British and American Literature*. Amherst: University of Massachusetts Press.

## *Cases*

*British American Tobacco Australia Services Limited v Cowell (as representing the estate of Rolah Ann McCabe, deceased)* (2002) VSCA 1.

*Canada (Attorney General) v PHS Community Services Society* (2011) 3 SCR 134.
*Commonwealth v Julie A. Eldred* (2018) SJC 12279.
*McCabe v British American Tobacco Australia Services Limited* (2002) VSC 73.

## Legislation

*Anti-Discrimination Act* (1977) (New South Wales).
*Drug and Alcohol Treatment Act* (2010) (New South Wales).
*Infringements Act* (2006) (Victoria).

# 1   *Legislative practices*
## On human rights, jurimorphs and the fragile ontology of law

## Introduction

What is law, and how is it made? What is it made *of* (following Latour, 2009)? And how stable is it? Conventional wisdom tells us that among other things law is comprised of 'formal sources' (see Gutwirth, 2015), in the form of legislation, regulations and rules. When law takes this form, the answer to the question of *how* law is made seems obvious: legislation is drafted by parliamentarians, and becomes law when parliaments pass it. What it is made *of* might seem similarly obvious: law is made of whatever is contained within an Act itself. Looking at law in this way implies there is not much to be learned from the practices that underpin the legislative process. In this chapter, I argue against such a reading. I argue that legislative practices are and should be of interest. For context, it's important to note as an initial point that laws are never proposed nor developed in a vacuum. Rather, they are developed under particular conditions and must take account of various things. These include principles of statutory interpretation and other established conventions regarding legal terminology. For example, the Latin term *noscitur a sociis* signals that a word is known by its associations, such that if its meaning in a statute is ambiguous, it can be determined by the rest of the Act. They may also have to take into account previous case law so as to ensure laws will withstand legal challenge. As well, there may be local, jurisdictional considerations. In several jurisdictions around the world, for instance, it is necessary to give consideration to human rights when developing laws. In some parts of the world, the practice of developing law with a view to human rights principles is referred to as a 'dialogue model' (Mathew, 2017: 53). The dialogue model 'aims at promoting thought and discussion about human rights, as legislation and policy are made, ensuring that the executive complies with human rights, and establishing a dialogue between the legislative and judicial arms of government' (Mathew, 2017: 53). In those jurisdictions that utilise a dialogue model, human rights considerations form part of the conditions under which legal content is developed. As I noted in the introductory chapter, Kyle McGee (2015a, 2015b) argues that legal content is fully identical with its conditions of enunciation. This chapter takes its cue from McGee's observation and explores the making of legislation where the dialogue model is a condition of enunciation. In so doing, I consider what happens when human rights are brought into conversation with alcohol and other drug 'problems' in the form of substance 'dependence', 'misuse' and 'addiction'. I examine how these conditions of enunciation shape legal content and how, in turn, legal processes operate to shape particular alcohol and other drug 'problems'. In this sense, the chapter addresses the double meaning of a keyword in law: *enact*. It examines how law is enacted (passed) and what the passage of law enacts along the way. My particular focus in this chapter is on two prominent and controversial laws that were proposed in Australian parliaments over the last decade. Both proposed laws ('bills') identified 'problems' pertaining to alcohol and other drugs and sought to solve them. One bill was introduced into the Victorian parliament in 2009, and was called the *Severe Substance Dependence Treatment Bill*. It sought to establish a scheme for the detention, assessment and treatment of people adjudged to be experiencing 'severe substance dependence'. The other was a bill introduced into the Commonwealth parliament in 2018, known as the *Social Services Legislation Amendment (Drug Testing Trial) Bill*. It sought to establish a pilot scheme for drug testing welfare recipients, for managing their income (and more) if they tested positive, and for directing them into alcohol or other drug treatment. As I will explain, the human rights compatibility of each bill had to be considered by each parliament. In what follows, I consider how these processes of compatibility assessment work and how they help to shape legal content. The analysis I undertake in this chapter sets the scene for the rest of the book in three main ways. First, it sheds light on how law and legal content is produced. Second, and in a related sense, it highlights the fundamental importance of practices of articulation and connection in the development of law. Third, it suggests that the content of law can be made anew if different connections are articulated, or if those links are enunciated differently. In this sense, the law is more fragile than we might assume. This presents opportunities for remaking law, and the subjects and objects shaped by it. I also make a series of observations about human rights. I argue that rights are not simply 'applied' to the bills, but constituted via the process of their application, and that these processes draw upon assumptions about what addiction is and how it works, along with how addiction impinges upon 'the human'. Similarly, the process of rights interpretation and application helps to make addiction as a certain kind of (legal) object. In making these arguments I draw upon Kyle McGee's (2015a, 2015b, 2014) concept of the 'jurimorph', along with insights from critical human rights scholars such as Hannah Arendt (1958), Costas Douzinas (2007) and John Erni (2019, 2012) on the ontology of the 'human' in human rights.

## Background

Aboriginal and Torres Strait Islander peoples have occupied Australia for an estimated 65,000 years (Clarkson et al., 2017). The British arrived in 1788, claimed the land and established a convict colony. They did not seek permission to take the land, nor pay compensation for it. Instead, they claimed the land using an international legal doctrine known as 'terra nullius' – the principle that 'land belonging to no-one' can be claimed. The assumption here was that Aboriginal people were 'uncivilised' and had no system for ownership of land, such that it *practically* belonged to no one. In 1992, the landmark Australian High Court case of *Mabo and Others v Queensland (No. 2)* [1992] HCA 23 turned that logic on its head, finding that terra nullius was irrelevant to pre-colonial Australia, as it was never land 'belonging to no-one'. The case allowed for a limited recognition of native title rights established via Indigenous customary law. Beyond this, Megan Davis (2006: 136) argues that Australia's public institutions have 'failed to accommodate difference and in some cases [...] have distorted and limited the practice of Indigenous culture and religion'. Australia's overarching legal infrastructure thus continues to primarily be a legacy of British invasion and colonisation. The current architecture of the Australian legal system was established on the occasion of federation, on 1 January 1901 (Williams, 2017). On that date, a Commonwealth Constitution was established, through which the parameters of Australian parliamentary power were set out (*Commonwealth of Australia Constitution Act* (1900) (Commonwealth)). A separation of powers between the parliament, executive and judiciary was also established. Australia has a three-tiered system of government, with governments at the Commonwealth (also known as 'federal'), state/territory and local levels. The Commonwealth, states and territories each have their own parliaments and court systems. Laws are principally made by the parliament, or they derive from judicial precedent under a system of common law imported from Britain. Several years after federation, the *Universal Declaration of Human Rights* (UDHR, 1948) was developed, establishing the United Nations' goal for a 'common standard' of basic freedoms and rights. The UDHR included a preamble and 30 rights. Australia voted in favour of the UDHR. Importantly, the Australian Constitution, which predated the UDHR by several decades, actually contained few explicit references to rights. Some rights were later read into the Constitution during a period of judicial activism by Australia's High Court, and take the form of 'implied rights' (Groves, 2017). Beyond this, rights protection in Australia has proceeded differently than in other Western nations. Unlike the United States, which has the *Bill of Rights* (1789); the United Kingdom, which has the *Human Rights Act* (1998); or Canada, which has the *Charter of Rights and Freedoms* (1982), Australian parliaments have long resisted calls for more formal and explicit rights protections (e.g. Groves, 2017; Williams, 2007). In recent years, however, two legislatures passed their own rights-based laws, in a bid to encourage a culture of human rights, and to offer some form of overarching rights protection for their citizens. (A third parliament, Queensland, passed the *Human Rights Bill 2018* in the final days of this research.) These laws were both inspired by and depart in important ways from the UK's *Human Rights Act* (1998) (Williams, 2017). The first parliament to pass such a law was the Australian Capital Territory (ACT), with its 2004 *Human Rights Act*. This was followed by the state of Victoria, which introduced the *Charter of Human Rights and Responsibilities Act* in 2006. These laws are often referred to as the 'charters'. The charters protect numerous rights, including the right to privacy, freedom of movement and a fair hearing. The two charters were later joined by a law passed at the federal level, called the *Human Rights (Parliamentary Scrutiny) Act* (2011) (Commonwealth), which offers some human rights protections. Section 3 of that Act defines 'human rights' as those rights and freedoms afforded under several specific international instruments to which Australia is a signatory.

Both the charters and the federal Act enshrine some rights, but in ways that fall short of the rights protections afforded by other countries, including Canada. The power of Australian courts does not extend to being able to strike down laws that are considered to be inconsistent with human rights, for example (Mathew, 2017). One way that both of the charters and the federal Act pertain to rights is through a process of parliamentary rights 'scrutiny'. Section 28 of the Victorian charter requires a member of parliament who introduces a bill to produce a 'statement of compatibility' alongside the bill, outlining how it is compatible with those rights recognised by the charter, and to flag any incompatibilities. A separate committee, known as SARC (the Scrutiny of Acts and Regulations Committee), also considers the compatibility of the bill and prepares a report to parliament on those issues. Under the Victorian charter, human rights can be 'limited' only if those limitations accord with Section 7(2) of the Act. That Section states:

> A human right may be subject under law only to such reasonable limits as can be demonstrably justified in a free and democratic society based on human dignity, equality and freedom, and taking into account all relevant factors including –
>
> a    the nature of the right; and
> b    the importance of the purpose of the limitation; and
> c    the nature and extent of the limitation; and
> d    the relationship between the limitation and its purpose; and
> e    any less restrictive means reasonably available to achieve the purpose that the limitation seeks to achieve.

The Victorian parliament is also empowered (under Section 31 of the charter) to make an override declaration, by which a law still 'has effect despite being incompatible with one or more of the human rights' in the charter. A similar process of scrutiny exists at the federal level, although the exact nature and mechanisms for scrutinising rights differs from those used in the charters. Under Section 5 of the federal Act, a Parliamentary Joint Committee on Human Rights is established. It is comprised of ten members: five from each of the two houses of parliament (the House of Representatives and the Senate). Among other things, the Joint Committee's role is to examine bills proposed in the parliament for their compatibility with human rights, and to report on these issues to the parliament (Section 7 of the Act). In order to aid in this process, the Act also requires any member of parliament who proposes a bill to prepare an accompanying 'statement of compatibility', which includes details on whether or not the bill is compatible with human rights. Where, for example, the bill would breach human rights, an explanation is required. The question of whether a right can be justifiably limited depends on the right in question, and from where it stems. If the right is one articulated under the *International Covenant on Economic, Social and Cultural Rights* (the ISECR) (1966), for example, rights limitations are only permissible if they are determined by law, compatible with the nature of the rights in the treaty in question, seek to achieve a legitimate objective and are a reasonable and proportionate means of achieving that objective.

These processes of parliamentary rights scrutiny ostensibly serve two broad functions – first, they are a means by which potential human rights infringements are identified, and second, they are a means by which to assess whether any proposed limitations are 'justifiable'. Boughey (2017: 37) argues that the key purpose of statements of compatibility is to ensure 'that members of the respective parliaments have access to relevant information and arguments to enable them to turn their minds to balancing rights and public interests' in the process of creating new laws. There are differing views on how effective these processes are, however. Australian models have been described as a 'weak form' (Gans, 2009) of human rights protection, because they do not cede power to courts to overturn laws that are not compliant with human rights. Instead, they grant power to 'various wings of government to *consider* human rights, without necessarily having to *comply* with them, hence preserving parliamentary sovereignty' (Gans, 2009; emphasis added). Speaking of the Victorian charter, Michael Brett Young (2015: 174) has pointed out that:

> the requirement for a statement of compatibility to accompany all Bills is a safeguard to ensure that any legislative departure from the human rights in the Charter is reasoned and explained. The role of parliamentary human rights scrutiny is essential in the Victorian context, because the Charter does not permit courts to strike down legislation for being incompatible with human rights. The mechanism for the Supreme Court to make a declaration of inconsistent interpretation refers incompatible legislation back to Parliament as the ultimate decision maker.

Still within the Victorian context, and speaking of the SARC process, Jeremy Gans (2009) notes that the Victorian charter 'doesn't specify what should go in an incompatibility report and, indeed, there is a view that the actual contents of SARC reports aren't the point'. He points to a statement by the Victorian Equal Opportunity and Human Rights Commission by way of example, in which it was said that:

> When reflecting on the Charter's overall impact on the legislative process during 2007, the Commission believes it is informative to ask one very simple question: if it was not for the Charter, would the human rights dimensions of these 93 Bills have been identified, analysed and debated? In all but a very few cases, the answer is clearly 'no'. For this reason alone, the initial impact of the Charter is significant: it has already comprehensively expanded

the parameters of public policy analysis to include the transparent assessment of new laws against a human rights framework. This is a substantial achievement.

(Victorian Equal Opportunity and Human Rights Commission, 2008)

Processes of rights scrutiny are variously understood as simple technicalities on the way to the implementation of law, check and balance mechanisms against excessive government power or mere 'check box' exercises designed to convey an appearance of human rights sensibility. As we will see, I am less concerned about the relative 'effectiveness' of human rights mechanisms in this chapter than with what happens when human rights are brought into conversation with alcohol and other drug 'problems'. I want to make a different argument in this chapter, which is about how human rights practices operate to 'morph' alcohol and other drugs and 'addicts' into particular kinds of legal objects and subjects. Before I come to these issues in more detail, I will introduce the two bills.

## The proposed bills

The *Severe Substance Dependence Treatment Bill* was introduced into the Victorian parliament in December 2009. The bill would repeal and replace an earlier Act known as the *Alcoholics and Drug-Dependent Persons Act* (1968) (Victoria), and establish an entirely new, statewide system of civil detention, assessment and treatment for individuals adjudged to be suffering from a 'severe substance dependence'. Similar laws exist in other Australian states and territories, and other parts of the world (Spivakovsky, Seear, & Carter, 2018), although the precise criteria and mechanism for assessment, detention and treatment differ between jurisdictions. In essence, the bill prescribed a process by which adults with a severe substance dependence would be assessed, detained for a maximum of 14 days and administered treatment in the form of medically assisted withdrawal. Detention would be strictly limited to those adults 'who require immediate treatment as a matter of urgency to save their life or prevent serious damage to the person's health' (Victorian Legislative Assembly, 2009: 4579), and where there are 'no less restrictive means reasonably available to ensure the treatment' (Victorian Legislative Assembly, 2009: 4579). A 'severe substance dependence' was defined in the bill as being characterised by a person having a tolerance to a substance and that person showing withdrawal symptoms when the person stops using, or reduces the level of use of, the substance, and where the person is incapable of making decisions about his or her substance use and personal health, welfare and safety, due primarily to their dependence on the substance (Clause 5). The bill had two objectives (Clause 3), which were to:

- Provide for the detention and treatment of persons with a severe substance dependence where this is necessary as a matter of urgency to save the person's life or prevent serious damage to the person's health; and
- Enhance the capacity of those persons to make decisions about their substance use and personal health, welfare and safety.

The Magistrates' Court would be tasked with making a decision about whether a detention and treatment order was warranted. Any application for such an order would need to be accompanied by a recommendation from a registered medical practitioner. In order to provide such a recommendation, the medical practitioner would need to be able to personally examine the person suspected of suffering from a severe substance dependence. To this end, the bill included a proposal for a process by which this could be done if the person would not submit to an examination voluntarily. Any person over the age of 18 years could apply to a magistrate seeking a 'special warrant' for a person to be examined. The applicant would need to show that they had 'reasonable grounds' for suspecting that the criteria in the bill would be met. If a special warrant were to be granted, a member of the police force would be permitted to enter a premises and 'to use such force as may be reasonably necessary to enable the prescribed registered medical practitioner to examine the person named in the warrant' (Clause 13). A statement of compatibility with human rights was prepared and delivered to the parliament, as required by the Victorian Charter, in December 2009 (Victorian Legislative Assembly, 2010: 836–841). The then Minister for Health, Daniel Andrews MP, tabled the statement into the parliamentary record, known as the Hansard. The statement indicated which of the charter's 20 articulated rights were thought to have been engaged by the bill, and explained the basis upon which any limitations on rights were thought to be justifiable. The statement suggested that the engaged rights were the right to be protected from any discrimination on the basis of an impairment (Sections 8(3) and 8(4) of the Charter); the right to life (Section 9 of the Charter); the protection of families and children (Section 17 of the Charter); cultural rights (Section 19 of the Charter); the right not to be subjected to medical treatment without the person's full, free and informed consent (Section 10(c) of the Charter); freedom of movement (Section 12 of the Charter); privacy (Section 13 of the Charter); liberty and security of the person (Section 21 of the Charter); and the right to a fair hearing (Section 24 of the Charter). This is the first bill that I will consider in this chapter.

The second bill began its journey through the federal system in 2017, when a number of changes to Australia's welfare system were being proposed. Schedule 12 of the *Social Services Legislation Amendment (Welfare Reform) Bill* (2017) (Commonwealth) ('the initial bill') contained a proposal to drug test welfare recipients. In June 2017, the Commonwealth Senate referred the provisions of the original bill to the Senate Community Affairs Legislation Committee for inquiry and report. Public submissions were sought and obtained, two public hearings were held and a report was finalised in September 2017. The first committee's report noted that a number of concerns were raised by research, legal, policy and welfare experts, in both submissions and oral evidence, regarding the proposal to establish drug-testing trials. These included:

a lack of evidence to support the use of drug testing; the cost, availability and reliability of drug testing; availability of treatment services to meet potential increased demand; and reliance on delegated legislation to set out significant detail about the operation of the trial; and income management.

(Commonwealth of Australia, 2017: 14)

The proposal to drug test welfare recipients did not gain support in the Senate, and was dropped from the initial bill. A proposal to drug test welfare recipients was later reintroduced to parliament, this time via the *Social Services Legislation Amendment (Drug Testing Trial) Bill* (2018) (Commonwealth) ('the second bill'). This second bill proposed the establishment of a drug testing pilot programme for recipients of welfare across three Australian locations: Canterbury-Bankstown, in the state of New South Wales; Logan, in the state of Queensland; and Mandurah, in the state of Western Australia. The drugs to be tested for were methamphetamine, methylenedioxy-methamphetamine, tetrahydrocannabinol, opioids or another substance prescribed by the drug test rules for the purposes of this definition. The proposed trial would have two objectives (Commonwealth of Australia House of Representatives, 2018a: 3):

- maintain the integrity of, and public confidence in, the social security system by ensuring that taxpayer-funded welfare payments are not being used to purchase drugs or support substance abuse; and
- provide new pathways for identifying recipients with drug abuse issues and facilitating their referral to appropriate treatment where required.

The bill envisaged a complex system of testing and sanctions. In essence, welfare recipients located in one of the three pilot locations would be notified of the need to present for a drug test, be tested, and then, if returning a positive result, be sanctioned. On the first occasion that a person tested positive to a drug, they would be subject to income management. According to the statement of compatibility with human rights accompanying the bill (Commonwealth of Australia House of Representatives, 2018a: 4), income management:

> does not reduce the total amount of income support available to a person, just the way in which they receive it. Under Income Management, a majority portion of a job seeker's normal payment is quarantined and the remaining amount is paid into their regular bank account and is accessible as cash. Job seekers placed on Income Management under this trial will still be able to purchase items at approved merchants and pay rent and bills with their quarantined funds. However, the recipient will not be able to use their quarantined funds to withdraw cash, gamble, buy alcohol, tobacco products, pornography or cash-equivalent products (such as gift cards).

No rationale was offered for restricting access to legal products such as alcohol, tobacco or pornography, and no rationale was offered for restricting one's capacity to engage in the lawful activity of gambling. The proposal contained no information outlining why these measures were thought to be valuable or necessary, or how they relate to the 'problems' the bill purported to address. The bill stated that people who return an initial (first) positive test would be subject to income management for a period of 24 months. This might even be extended if the secretary of the department considered it 'beneficial to a person's drug rehabilitation outcome to remain on income management for a longer period of time' (Commonwealth of Australia House of Representatives, 2018b: 20). The bill and accompanying documents contained no explanation as to why this length of time was deemed necessary. The proposal also stated that those who refused a drug test without a reasonable excuse would have their welfare payments cancelled. If they then made a new claim for a welfare allowance, they would need to wait a period of four weeks. In accordance with the requirements of the *Human Rights (Parliamentary Scrutiny) Act* (2011) (Commonwealth), the statement of compatibility examined whether the bill was compatible with the rights and freedoms recognised in various international instruments. The rights thought to be engaged were the right to social security, the right to an adequate standard of living and the rights of the family and child to special protection and assistance (Articles 9, 10 and 11 of the *International Covenant on Economic, Social and Cultural Rights*); the right to equality and non-discrimination (Article 2(2) of the *International Covenant on Economic, Social and Cultural Rights*); the right to equality before the law, the right to privacy and the rights of the child to special protection and assistance (Articles 10(3), 17 and 26 of the *International Covenant on Civil and Political Rights* (1966)); obligations under the *Convention on the Rights of Persons with Disabilities* (2006); obligations under the *Convention on the Elimination of all forms of Racial Discrimination* (1965); and obligations under the *Convention on the Rights of the Child*. At the time of writing this book, the bill was still undergoing passage through the Australian parliamentary system, and still the subject of debate. As I noted earlier, both the state and federal systems allow for rights limitations in certain circumstances. In both cases, those presenting the bill agreed that although particular rights had been engaged, the limitations proposed on those rights were justifiable.

## Human rights, jurimorphs and the making of legal content

Costas Douzinas (1996: 123) notes that in modernity, to have human rights has come to be seen as 'synonymous with being human'. A typical definition of human rights is that they are 'literally the rights one has because one is a human being', and that they are those rights that are essential not simply for life, but 'for a life of dignity' (Donnelly, 1989: 9, 17). Importantly, not everyone agrees with the notion that individuals possess rights simply by virtue of being human. Rights are not only or consistently given to people on the basis of their 'participation in the human race', a point Hannah Arendt (1958) famously made in her critique of the relationship between rights and citizenship. Reflecting on statelessness, refugees and citizenship in the aftermath of the Second World War, Arendt (1958: 297) argued that:

> the conception of human rights, based upon the assumed existence of a human being as such, broke down at the very moment when those who professed to believe it were for the first time confronted with people who had indeed lost all other qualities and specific relationships – except that they were still human.

For Arendt, the predicament of the stateless lays bare a fundamental paradox regarding human rights, which is that rights are not always bestowed upon or enjoyed by humans, equally. The conferral of rights is instead contingent: a process, connected to states, citizenship, nationalism, power and politics. If one must 'be human' to have rights, and not all subjects have rights, then surely not all subjects can be said to be human. Other scholars have raised related concerns about human rights, including that they are not particularly robust (see Erni, 2019), that they are often unenforceable – especially where nation-states breach the rights of their own citizens, that they are prone to 'confusion and rhetorical exaggeration' (Douzinas, 2007: 10) and that they lack 'shape and strength' (Zucca, 2016: 491).

There is also a critical literature examining which rights have been recognised and why, and what such recognition reveals about conceptions of 'the human'. John Erni (2012: 181) notes, for example, that 'the history of human rights leading up to the current moment continues to annex a history of encounter between industrial and post-industrial modernity of the West and alternative visions of modernity embodied chiefly by the colonized others'. The 'subject' of human rights is often understood to be a product of Western thinking, and to reflect particularly Western/late colonial concerns and preoccupations. Douzinas (2007: 7) notes in this respect that perhaps 'the greatest achievement of rights is ontological: rights contribute to the creation of human identity'. In other words:

> The legal recognition of a particular category of rights, say women's rights, is at the same time the partial recognition of a particular type of identity linked with these rights. Conversely, an individual recognized as a legal subject in relation to women's rights is accepted as the bearer of certain attributes and the beneficiary of certain activities and, at the same time, as a person of a particular identity which partakes amongst others of the dignity of human nature. The identity of a particular woman is not exhausted, of course, in her identification as a subject of women's rights or in her recognition as the beneficiary of the equality and freedom of human nature [...] What is crucial, however, is that [...] the legal subject and legal rights act as unified consequences of 'human nature' through which the law assigns categories and fixes identities and tries to stabilize the proliferation of social meaning.
>
> (Douzinas, 1996: 127)

For Douzinas, this is part of the appeal of human rights, in that they 'have acquired ideological and legal pre-eminence precisely because they are so central in bestowing subjectivity and identity' (Douzinas, 2007: 7). Importantly, Douzinas argues, rights processes and approaches vary significantly across space and time. To understand what rights *are* and what they *do* with regard to subjects, we need to study them across jurisdictions and time frames. In a related sense, as John Erni (2019: 37) notes, 'just as positive law has the capacity to produce rights that are differently moral, and governments that are differently political, it also possesses the capacity to render the "subjects" of rights as differently human'. Erni illustrates this point using an example from the World Health Organization's work on sexual health. There, sexual health was defined as 'the integration of the somatic, emotional, intellectual and social aspects of sexual being, in ways that are positively enriching and that enhance personality, communication and love' (World Health Organization, 1975). In this example, the WHO 'embeds this particular iteration of "the human" in the ambit of "positive" sexual health, thereby excluding other ways by which "the human" becomes sexual' (Erni, 2019: 40). Such ways of conceptualising the human give rise to laws and regulations, including those that 'accentuate the rights of people who are humanized through WHO's definition' (Erni, 2019: 40). In other words, 'rights' constitute the human, including appropriate modes of being human, and authorise disciplinary and regulatory practices, including political subjection, control and violence (see Erni, 2019; Esmeir, 2012). In this chapter I read these critical insights on human rights together with STS theory on the making of law and the meaning of legal content. It is valuable to bring these two literatures into conversation because in the process of making law, at least in the jurisdictions I am examining in this chapter, parliamentarians must explicitly 'go through' human rights. Costas Douzinas and John Erni would argue that those practices are likely to be constitutive, producing 'the human', on the one hand, while authorising and enabling processes for the regulation of subjects in particular ways, on the other. Importantly, these scholars approach human rights as fluid and fragile, as both transformative and capable of undergoing transformation. In this they share something with the perspectives of STS scholars who have written on the nature and meaning of legal content, to which I now turn.

As I noted in the introductory chapter, Kyle McGee views legal content as 'fully identical' with its conditions of enunciation (2015b: 64). In a crucial passage on the making of law, McGee explains:

> It is a truism that doctrinal constructs are not self-executing, self-applying creatures, but must be manipulated, balanced, coordinated not unlike a piece of laboratory equipment. Their contours, sometimes appearing very rigid, nevertheless undergo transformation in every case. This is ultimately a lesson imparted by pragmatic semiotics: the doctrinal category, figure or rule does not exist except as a function of its application which varies every time.
>
> (2015b: 69)

By way of example, McGee refers to areas of law that necessitate legal tests of 'reasonableness', as in cases where circumstances are to be viewed from the perspective of the hypothetical construct of the 'reasonable person'. Notions of objective 'reasonableness' have been subjected to detailed scrutiny in the past, including by feminists (e.g. Conaghan, 1996; Cahn, 1992), for their normative and gendered dimensions. Here, McGee makes a slightly different point that is indicative of his overall approach to legal content. Such standards, McGee suggests, turn 'on the court's perception of what is customary or generally expected by participants, or of what "everyone knows" or "should know", as the lawyers present it and the court imagines it' (2015b: 69). Although the content of the standard purports to be flexible and inclusive, this 'forgets that there is only performance' (2015b: 69). Central to McGee's thesis is the concept of the 'jurimorph', and the associated processes by which entities are 'jurimorphised' (2015b). The jurimorph is a 'semiotic tool for capturing the peculiar translation that must precede entry into the trajectory and which results in a new legal figure – a value-object or, in later stages, after certain trials have been met, an obligation' (2015a: 7–8). McGee further explains these concepts as follows:

> Provisionally, we can define legal devices as assemblages of mostly non-legal beings deployed for a legal purpose, namely to give consistency and objectivity, as well as direction, to a specific legal trajectory. The device *formats*, translates the diverse strata bound up in a disputed matter into technical legal discourse, but while this entails certain technical reductions, it entails no ontological reduction of agency. Technically, the various entities and agents at stake are semiotically re-figured – jurimorphised. This, we will see, amplifies their agency rather than (or in addition to) diminishing it. Legal content – or what I will also call *sense* – thus exists only by way of the mediation of jurimorphs (i.e. value objects and devices).
>
> (McGee, 2015b: 64; original emphasis)

McGee demonstrates these points through a detailed analysis of one procedural motion in one case in an American trial court (addressed briefly in the introductory chapter of this book). The case involved residents of a small community in Illinois, several of whom had developed brain cancers in the 1990s and 2000s. The case was not about cancer clusters or the liability of local chemical factories for causing cancer, but a more limited issue – namely, whether those companies could be held liable for the costs of monitoring the health of residents, and for compensating them for decreases in the value of their homes. The specific motion McGee was concerned with was whether the community could be certified as a unified 'class' for the purposes of a class action under US Federal Rules. The case involved more than 1,000 people; hundreds of homes of different sizes, with different designs and locations; domestic and multinational companies; toxicology reports and risk assessments; various other documents, including medical records of a diverse population of individuals, with varying genetic predispositions and mutations; and much more. McGee considered how these 'stratified' issues and 'disjointed enunciative planes' were locked together, 'reintegrated, connected horizontally to form a chain, to construct a specific trajectory of relevant legal grounds' (2015b: 72–73). In a crucial statement on the making of legal truths and legal content, McGee notes that:

> The threads knotted together in the stratified issue will be untangled and reassembled in a distinctive way to arrive at the unmistakably legal truth of the matter. The complex issue will be contorted, simplified and brought into alignment with rules. This transformation of the issue allows the rules to 'apply' – but as we will see, such application also entails a transformation of the rules themselves.

Latour has himself endorsed McGee's explanation of how legal content is made, along with his concept of the jurimorph, explaining that:

> If there are no extra-judicial factors in accounting for legal decisions, it is because everything in law is extraneous! This is exactly why McGee's term jurimorph is so apt for capturing what is going on: *everything in law is extra-legal and streamlined to pave the trajectory* of moving toward the law or being moved by the law [...] Law is what happens to extra-legal features when they are jurimorphed! To give shape to something, that is to 'morph' it, you need this thing there first.
>
> (2015: 340–341; original emphasis)

The law is thusly comprised of unique processes by which a multitude of subjects and objects are connected and transformed, 'operating to bind and unbind, to link and de-link, to release and make secure' (Matthews & Veitch, 2016: 353).

In what follows I read two bills together through the lens of critical human rights theory and McGee's work on jurimorphs. I examine how legal content is generated through processes of articulation and connections, assembly and disaggregation (jurimorphing). Before I get to those bills, I should explain why it is that I have chosen to examine two bills rather than one. The first reason is that the bills are substantively different and ostensibly concern different 'problems'. In examining more than one bill, I argue that we can get a better sense of the kinds of problems parliamentarians attach to alcohol and other drugs. In this way my analysis extends the brief introduction to how addiction features in legislation that I offered in the introduction. Second, the two bills I examine in this chapter were proposed at different points in time and in two different jurisdictions: one at the federal level and the other at state level (Victoria). As I shall explain, the processes in each jurisdiction differ ever so slightly, a factor which is worth considering for reasons I will come to. Third, the bills were proposed by the two major political parties in Australia: one by the Australian Labor Party, which is generally understood as the more socially progressive party, and the other by the Liberal National Coalition, which is viewed as more socially and economically conservative. Although partisan politics are undoubtedly relevant to the kinds of things that politicians prioritise, what they problematise and what solutions they propose to such problems (on which, see: Bacchi, 2009; see also Pienaar & Savic, 2016; Lancaster, Seear, & Treloar, 2015; Seear & Fraser, 2014; Moore & Fraser, 2013), I aim in this chapter to think beyond politics with a capital P. My point is not that Politics does not matter, but that it is not the only factor worth examining in relation to the making of law and legal content. Various procedural and technical factors also play a role. Fourth, as we will see, although the bills concern different subjects and objects there are important overlaps and points of convergence in the central assumptions and objectives of both bills. Moreover, the process of human rights scrutiny is undertaken by both jurisdictions jurimorphs alcohol and other drugs in similar ways. In bringing two bills together as I do here, I also want to make it clear that I am not undertaking a conventional comparative legal analysis. Instead, I aim to give a sense of the kind of legal objects that alcohol and other drugs become during the process of lawmaking, to say something about how the process of human rights scrutiny functions to shape those objects, and to highlight how these human rights processes work to constitute the subject.

## The process of human rights scrutiny

As noted earlier, the content of the bills cannot be separated out from the conditions of their development, including the requisite dialogue between key measures in the bills and ostensibly external legal principles. The nature and form that law takes is intimately bound up with these dialogic conditions. When it comes to assessing the nature of rights, along with whether they might be limited, the Victorian charter makes it clear that international law and the decisions of international bodies are relevant but 'not directive or determinative' (Williams, 2017: 29; see also Charter Section 32(2)). How are 'rights' and 'rights limitations' to be adjudged, then, if not through some external and readily identifiable legal content, simply and easily capable of being 'applied'? I argue that the content of such rights simultaneously appears self-evident and prior to their application but is in fact constituted in the course of their interpretation, application and articulation. In other words, when politicians speak of apparently *legal* questions, such as what a reasonable and demonstrably justifiable limitation of rights looks like, or what a reasonable and proportionate means of pursuing a legitimate objective entails, they are, in the moment of articulation, constituting such things. They are, in Kyle McGee's sense, applying the rules while transforming and constituting them. The content of law is forged through connecting together seemingly obvious or taken-for-granted 'truths' about alcohol and other drugs, what problems they produce and how such problems might be resolved. The process involves linking together various subjects and objects, and jurimorphing them, on the path to establishing 'relevant legal grounds' which justify the measures being proposed (McGee, 2015b: 73).

Take, for instance, the Victorian government's statements on the apparent 'reasonableness' of mandated detention, assessment and treatment under the *Severe Substance Dependence Treatment* bill. The 'reasonableness' of the rights limitations proposed are determined by assessing the measures against the afore-mentioned criteria in Section 7(2) of the charter, which include the nature of the right and the importance of the purpose of the limitation. The minister signals how these issues are going to be framed through an initial overarching comment at the beginning of the statement of compatibility:

> In my view, the bill's objectives are consistent with the principle of personal autonomy. The bill aims to enhance the capacity of persons with a severe substance dependence to make their own decisions about their substance use and personal welfare. The provisions for detention and treatment are designed to give persons with severe substance dependence 'time out' from their substance use, creating an opportunity for the person to engage with services for voluntary treatment.
>
> (Victorian Legislative Assembly, 2009: 4579)

We know, in other words, that human rights will be interpreted through con-cepts such as 'personal welfare', 'personal autonomy' and 'capacity', and that the specific kind of 'autonomy' and 'capacity' the government seeks to promote is narrow; its focus is on abstaining from the consumption of substances, with a view to taking up alcohol or other drug treatment. In other words, human 'au-tonomy' is valued, but only to the extent that one expresses one's 'autonomy' in certain ways. This tension – between the gesture towards 'autonomous' selfhood and the obligations of selfhood – has been the subject of detailed analysis in the social sciences in recent years (see also Rose, 1999, 1996). The minister's com-ments bring to mind Nikolas Rose's classic statement on the nature of freedom as obligation, in which:

> The forms of freedom we inhabit today are intrinsically bound to a regime of subjectification in which subjects are not merely 'free to choose', but obliged to be free, to understand and enact their lives in terms of choice under conditions that systematically limit the capacities of many to shape their own identity.
>
> (1996: 17)

The process of rights assessment is refracted through these priorities and values, including a set of *obligations expressed as freedoms*, such that the process becomes self-referential and circular.

The importance of the purpose does not exist prior to the process of delibera-tion, but must be evaluated, weighed up, arranged and presented. The statement of compatibility, in this sense, is a creative process, which operates to constitute law. Both the 'purpose' of the rights limitation and its putative 'importance' are matters to be determined by the politician who does the speaking. On the proposal to restrict the right to freedom of movement and the right to liberty and security of the person, for instance, the statement of compatibility (Victorian Legislative Assembly, 2009: 4580; original emphasis) notes as follows:

a   *The nature of the rights being limited*
     The nature of the rights to liberty and freedom of movement is the basic principle that every person has a right to physical liberty that can only be interfered with in specific circumstances. These rights are not absolute in international human rights law and may be subject to reasonable limitations.
b   *The importance of the purpose of the limitation*
     It is necessary to limit a person's rights in order to provide urgent treatment to save the person's life or to prevent serious damage to a person's health. This is a very important purpose.
c   *The nature and extent of the limitation*
     The limitation is proportionate. The bill provides that a person can only be detained if a number of criteria are established, and only for up to 14 days. There are a number of safeguards contained in the bill to minimise the interference that the bill may have on a person's human rights.

Other factors are also mentioned. In considering proportionality, the parliament looks at whether 'this thing' is in proportion to 'that thing', how 'this' relates to 'that' and what it would mean for them to relate 'proportionately'. Again, the meaning of proportionality is not self-evident. As each new bill involves novel measures and populations, these issues must be assessed, anew, every time. In order to decide whether *this* is in proportion with *that*, the parliament must balance this and that against each other. But it is not certain, before this process unfolds, how to undertake such a balancing act. What is the 'this' or the 'that' in this scenario? And what would it mean to strike a balance between this and that? These questions persist even though similar balancing acts have been undertaken for different bills before, and even though they will be undertaken again. In this instance, the limitations on movement, liberty and security are said to be 'proportionate' because they are 'only for up to 14 days'. In other words, the proportionality of the proposed measure is judged according to temporality. Those temporal dimensions in turn reveal something important about what the parliament thinks dependence is, and how it can be addressed. Dependence is capable of being 'halted', in other words, through 'pause time'. A person's capacity for apparently rational decision-making is disrupted by severe substance dependence, but not destroyed altogether; it can be revived, because the effects of dependence are only temporary.

On the relationship between the limitation and its purpose, the minister notes that the purpose 'is to protect a person', and that this 'is rationally connected to the purpose of limiting rights – namely, detention is necessary for the treatment to occur'. In these passages, the minister appears to be *speaking legally* – of rights, the 'nature' of rights, the 'importance of the purpose', the 'relationship' between the limitation and the purpose, of 'reasonableness' and 'proportionality'. Notably, there is no detailed exegesis regarding what the law 'is', and no attempt to explain where the law 'comes from', beyond the brief gesture towards the fact that international human rights law permits limitations. This is simply a reminder of what we already know: that rights *may* be limited. The content of the law emerges through the practice of linking subjects to objects and securing connections between them. Dependence is linked to death in that it may lead to death. Life is connected to rights insofar as it is configured as a (or perhaps the) pre-eminent condition of the human. The preservation of health and life is depicted as obviously important purposes, and no attempt is made to explain why this is so. There is no detailed consideration of why preservation of health is an important purpose, whose version of health is being deployed or whether this involves normative or moralising considerations of health and illness. There is an assumption that the dependent person lacks will, or fails to exercise their will validly, and that encouraging a different kind of will is a reasonable objective. There is also no recognition of the inherent irony here (flagged earlier through Nikolas Rose's work) that the call to exercise one's will in accordance with certain, externally imposed priorities is not an exercise of free will at all. It is instead another kind of *attenuated will*, where 'attenuated will' is apparently the hallmark of addiction, and the very 'problem' parliament is trying to address. Further, acceptable limitations on rights (and thus the nature and extent of rights themselves) need almost no explanation, because the limitations are in furtherance of an apparently shared set of aspirations. Importantly, the content of law is also forged by absences. There is no mention, for instance, of other factors that might be implicated in risks to health or death, including poverty, homelessness, the criminalisation of drugs, inadequacies in social policy and economic conditions, or the well-documented shortage of alcohol and other drug treatment in Australia, for those who want it. On the latter point, Alison Ritter has estimated that somewhere between 250,000 and 400,000 Australians are unable to access drug and alcohol treatment (Commonwealth of Australia, 2018). Factors such as these are not explored. Instead, sickness and death are enacted as a product of disordered thinking and disordered habits of consumption. These are the things, above all, that need to be fixed. The process of rights scrutiny thus constitutes both *rights* and *dependence*, along with how rights and dependence 'relate' to one another, legally speaking. In other words, in articulating dependence via rights as if the meaning of those rights is self-evident, the minister *appears to speak legally* and in the act of so doing constitutes the things about which he speaks as *legal*. I am reminded here of McGee's claim that in law 'everything turns on how the issue is articulated', along with his statement that:

> The transformation of a contentious issue into a legal case is monumental, in terms of the arrangement of these many layers. In a sense that merits serious reflection but which lies beyond this chapter's compass, the crossing of that invisible boundary is an entry into a room the disputants are already inside. This signals the paradoxical tautology of the law's totality, according

to which, when one utters a promise, for instance, or declares 'this is mine, that is yours', *the whole of the law passes through her mouth.* That is to say, legal statements – from the lowliest petty appropriation to the loftiest provision of the constitution, charter or international treaty – with which they claim solidarity and kinship.

(McGee, 2015b: 66; emphasis added)

These processes also reveal something vital about the content of law. It is fragile and mutable. It is made manifest through processes of articulation and connection. Here, the meaning of doctrinal constructs, such as 'proportionality', exist only as a function of their application, as McGee (2015b: 69) reminds us, and these applications can vary every time.

Something similar happens with the Commonwealth bill. In that case, the parliament had to consider the possibility that the bill engaged rights under various international instruments to which Australia was a signatory. One of those was the *Convention on the Rights of the Child* (CRC) (1989). The statement of compatibility noted that the bill to drug test welfare recipients 'engages with rights under the CRC as it is applied to people with children' (Commonwealth of Australia House of Representatives, 2018a: 7). Article 3 of the CRC establishes the general principle that 'in all actions concerning children, whether undertaken by public or private social welfare institutions, courts of law, administrative authorities or legislative bodies, the best interests of the child shall be a primary consideration'. Importantly, the child's best interests are *a* primary interest, rather than *the* primary interest. The question of precisely how the proposal to drug test welfare recipients connects to the best interests of the child, if indeed if does at all, is not pre-ordained. It requires consideration and concatenation. Any connections that exist must be 'found', or else, forged. In constructing these connections, the statement of compatibility noted:

> Article 3 provides that in all actions concerning a child, the best interests of the child will be a primary consideration. This measure is intended to achieve the objectives of ensuring appropriate use of welfare payments (including to meet essential living costs for recipients and their families) and identifying drug use and helping people who require it to seek treatment. These objectives are in line with article 3 of CRC. Supporting and encouraging recipients to address their drug misuse issues will improve their capacity to find work and support themselves and their children.
>
> (Commonwealth of Australia House of Representatives, 2018a: 7)

Here, again, the content of law is established through processes of articulation, as well as linking and de-linking, binding and omission. In this example, legislation should be relevantly consistent with the CRC and in particular Article 3, which emphasises the 'best interests of the child'. This is the extraneous legal principle upon which the appropriateness or otherwise of the proposed measures hinges. In being told that the measures 'are in line with article 3 of CRC', there is a tacit assumption that alcohol or other drug consumption by welfare recipients impacts upon a parents' capacity to find work and support their children. By extension, the implication is that being on welfare is itself not in the best interests of the child, and that relying on the state for support is problematic. In connecting these matters together in this way, the 'best interests' provision in Article 3 is given form and purpose, made anew. As I argue in the next section, these specific connections have particular effects with regard to alcohol and other drugs, and the subjects who consume them.

## The subject of rights

As I explained in the previous section, the human rights process requires certain questions to be asked about the measures being proposed. These include questions like whether the measures are 'reasonable' or 'proportionate', or whether the purpose is 'important' and for a 'legitimate objective'. In requiring parliament to turn its mind to these issues in the process of developing the bill, the human rights process makes certain deliberations possible. It allows for certain connections and relationships to be articulated but it does not prescribe what those relationships are, nor what is in relation and what is not. The content of those connections, as I have already explained, is not mandated, nor *a priori* the process of rights scrutiny, but generated through deliberation and articulation. They are forged and stabilised at the point of their pronouncement. Crucially, these connections enact the objects and subjects of rights in particular ways, erasing other possibilities and ways of thinking about phenomena. This is best illustrated by some examples from the Commonwealth bill. That bill estimated that 5,000 welfare recipients would be subject to the proposed drug tests. These would be people of different ages, genders, ethnicities, employment backgrounds and histories, geographical locales and educational levels, united by two things, as far as we are aware: that they were receiving welfare, and that they had consumed illicit substances of some kind. As with the class action motion studied by Kyle McGee (2015b), the sheer volume of subjects and objects involved is noteworthy: multiple people, resident in various locations, various other actors including lab technicians, documents, test results, laboratory facilities, needles, tourniquets, different substances, employers and job markets, consumer behaviours, market trends and the global economy. The process of human rights scrutiny does not highlight or examine variations or complexity as between the multitude of subjects and objects involved, but contorts, transforms and simplifies them. Choices are made about which subjects and objects relate to each other and how. In other words, when the parliament considers how 'this' relates to 'that', there is a need to first settle on what the 'this' and the 'that' are. Through this process, various phenomena including 'substances', 'unemployment' and 'welfare recipients' are morphed into singular categories posing a consistent set of challenges. Diverse individual, familial and communal contexts are largely erased in favour of references to 'welfare recipients', as a singular category. Anything else might have seemed impractical.

To be clear, the bill does not position drug use or even drug 'problems' as the sole driver of unemployment. This is made clear in the statement of compatibility, where it is suggested that 'for some job seekers', at least, 'substance abuse can be a major barrier to social and economic participation' (Commonwealth of Australia House of Representatives, 2018a: 3). Despite this, the process of rights scrutiny has the effect of fixing drug use to unemployment. It also renders 'welfare recipients' as a largely homogeneous category. This is because rights, rights breaches and the reasons for those breaches are conceptualised, for practical purposes, as they pertain to an imagined collective. The way that 'substances' work upon 'welfare recipients' and unemployment also results in 'substances' being enacted as a singular category. There is no differentiation between different substances, doses, levels of consumption or consumptive practices. Importantly, the bill used a range of different terms to describe the problems it sought to address. These included substance 'use', substance 'misuse', substance 'abuse', 'drug misuse issues', 'drug abuse issues' and substance 'dependency'. The confusion in terminology is significant because it represents, at the very least, conceptual confusion and inconsistency about precisely what it was that the bill purported to target. The interchangeable use of such terms has the effect of enacting any kind of drug use as a potential barrier to employment. In isolating alcohol and other drugs as integral to unemployment, and in connecting them together in these ways, other subjects and objects are de-linked. These include other phenomena potentially associated with unemployment, such as labour market conditions, access to education and training, poverty, housing security and homelessness, experiences of sexual assault and sexual abuse, racism, sexism, homophobia and transphobia, family violence, trauma, stigma, discrimination and the impact of criminal records. In addition, the capacity to support oneself and one's family is enacted as an individual responsibility and a product of individual action, will and effort. Other possibilities, including social and economic policy, stigma and discrimination, regional differences in employment opportunities, industry downturns and more, might just as well be implicated in unemployment and poverty. It is worth noting here that people in receipt of welfare payments experience poverty at higher rates than the rest of the Australian population. In 2014, almost 60% of those people below the poverty line relied upon social security as their main income (Saunders et al., 2017). In a statement on people's experiences of welfare and poverty in Australia, the CEO of the Australian Council of Social Service said that:

> People relying on the unemployment benefit Newstart, at less than $40 per day, are choosing between meals and bills, transport and pills. It is near impossible to look for work if you're homeless and hungry.
>
> (Australian Council of Social Service, 2018)

A recent Australian study found that there is only one job for every eight applicants who are unemployed or under-employed, and that when employed people changing jobs are added into the mix, there is only one job for every 16 applicants (Australian Council of Social Service & Jobs Australia, 2018). The report also notes that job growth in Australia was stagnant from the global financial crisis in 2008 to 2017, and that most of the jobs created over that period were part-time jobs. The situation is more difficult for some people, including those with fewer skills or less education. How these factors might relate to unemployment and poverty is never explored in the process of human rights scrutiny. This would have only been necessary if someone had asked different questions, linked things together in different ways and secured alternative relations between objects and subjects.

Following Douzinas, I argue that the process of rights articulation has the effect of enacting individuals as legal subjects, constituting those subjects as the 'bearer of certain attributes and the beneficiary of certain activities' (1996: 127). In other words, the *Severe Substance Dependence Treatment* bill constitutes the 'severely substance dependent' subject as a legal subject as well as a bearer of certain attributes, such as the inability to make 'appropriate' decisions in one's own 'best interests'. This in turn authorises other regulatory measures. The *Social Services Legislation Amendment (Drug Testing Trial) Bill* (2018) (Commonwealth) also constitutes 'welfare recipients' as legal subjects with particular attributes, rights and responsibilities and enables interventions upon them. This includes restrictions on bodily integrity, autonomy and privacy, through the requirement that they submit to medical procedures. Welfare recipients are also constituted as being in a particular and contingent relation to the state, a relationship that is conditional upon the subject of rights avoiding ways of 'being human' that have been designated as self-evidently inappropriate, less viable, or inferior. Like the sexual subjects in John Erni's work (2019), the subjects instantiated in these two bills are granted rights, but the relation between these subjects and rights is fragile and contingent. They are 'conferred', but on the basis that subjects will take up the opportunities ostensibly afforded to them through drug testing and treatment in ways that will make them become 'better' humans. In Erni's example, other ways of being human were 'excluded'; here, other ways of being human figure, but are explicitly disavowed. This process calls to mind Eve Sedgwick's work on the transformation of subjects to objects:

> From being the *subject* of her own perceptual manipulations or indeed experimentations she is installed as the proper *object* of compulsory institutional disciplines, legal and medical, that, without actually being able to do anything to 'help' her, nonetheless presume to know her better than she can know herself – and indeed, offer everyone in her culture who is *not* herself the opportunity of enjoying the same flattering presumption.
>
> (1993: 131; original emphasis)

We might similarly say that the human rights process morphs subjects into objects of institutional discipline, ordering and control. Measures such as the quarantining and control of welfare monies, the regulation of alcohol and other drug consumption, the control of what can be purchased and how, along with associated practices such as forced entry into a person's residence, sedation and restraint, mandated treatment and mandated testing, all become legal practices *not in spite of rights but because of them*. Practices which might otherwise be described as excessive exercises of power upon the person by the state become appropriate and legitimate, properly legal practices, administered to properly legal subjects, via a logic of rights. Income measurement is performed in 'furtherance' of rights. Mandated alcohol and other drug treatment is offered in order to 'assist' people and 'advance' their 'best interests'. As such, the human rights processes I have examined in this chapter treat subjects differently; endorse certain ways of being human as preferable to others; confer rights but in ways that are contingent on becoming certain kinds of subjects; transform subjects into objects; authorise interventions, governance, violence and control; reject other ways of being human (being on welfare, being dependent on the state, being 'dependent' on substances, seeking pleasure in substances); and compel the drug-using subject to become *differently* human. Hannah Arendt might argue that, as with stateless subjects, human rights are not conferred on people merely on the basis of being part of the human race but rather on the basis of the extent to which they embody other values and priorities. Here, I make a slightly different point, which is that the interpretation and application of rights is part of the process by which the human is constituted, and certain ways of being validly human become entrenched. Rights are, at least in the examples studied here, constitutive. They are one of the ways in which substances and the people who consume them come to be understood as problematic, less than human, and proper objects, ultimately, for intervention and control. Crucially, these ways of *doing* rights are also made possible by the objects (substances) and subjects (the dependent, welfare recipients) to which they are being 'applied'. Drugs, in other words, help to make rights, and help justify making them differently. This works in much the same way that nationalism and state power have traditionally worked to confer rights – not universal rights based on one's participation in the human race, following Arendt (1958), but differently constituted rights and obligations, emerging and adhering to a new kind of stateless subject. A subject that is less than fully human.

## Conclusion

This chapter sought to examine the process by which legislation is made. It focussed on an important and somewhat obscure technical aspect of the legislative process in Australia. This process requires parliaments to consider one set of laws (articulating human rights obligations) whenever they propose new ones. In this sense, human rights laws are one of the conditions under which legislation is developed, and form an important context for law's making. The chapter explored how law is interpreted, applied and developed, along with how these processes are co-constitutive when the intersection, application and development of law intersects. In undertaking this analysis I made two main points about the nature and content of law.

First, that practices of articulation and connection are integral to legal content. Law is made when connections are 'identified' or 'discovered', made visible and expressed, or when they are bound, unbound or omitted. Here, various subjects and objects were drawn into the path of 'the law' (or the 'legal trajectory', as McGee (2015b) would say), and connected: formatted, translated and transformed into technical legal discourse. They were, in other words, 'jurimorphised' (McGee, 2015b). These jurimorphs included *subjects* – such as the alcohol- or other drug-dependent person, the welfare recipient, registered medical practitioners, the state, the family and the child – and *objects* – such as drugs, alcohol, cigarettes, pornography, employment and unemployment, job markets, testing laboratories and courts. Second, I argued that the law is more fragile than we might assume. These insights into law's very being in turn reveal something important: that the content of law can be made anew if different connections are articulated, if those links are enunciated differently or if they are disarticulated. Opening law's black box in this way brings us closer to understanding what law 'is'. It also presents opportunities for remaking law, and the subjects and objects shaped by it. Of course, Kyle McGee (2015a, 2015b, 2014) and Bruno Latour (2015, 2013, 2009) have both previously made similar arguments about the inherent fragility and delicacy of law. Both argue that law is fundamentally unstable. The novel aspect of my analysis is thus not in repeating observations they have already made, nor even in demonstrating how the law's fragility is (paradoxically) fortified. Rather, it is about what happens when processes of articulation and connection are *required to be made through recourse to 'human rights'*. This way of making law is unique, and obliges those who would seek to make law to consider how what is proposed intersects with 'rights' and 'the human'. It requires law to be performed via 'the human' and via 'rights', and thus it performs human rights along the way. As this chapter has shown, the content of human rights law is not fixed. Neither its substance, nor how it relates to the specific subjects and objects being proposed in bills is determined prior to processes of deliberation, interpretation and application. In this regard, the meaning and content of human rights is variable and fragile, too, and constituted in the course of articulations purporting to tell us what it is that the bills 'demand'. Through all of this – and this is the crucial point – it becomes possible to say that human rights and alcohol and other drugs *help to make each other*. They are co-constitutive.

In this chapter I also argued that as certain connections are forged, human rights enable the use of particular kinds of state power over subjects. Practices such as forced treatment and quarantining of income become lawful *not in spite of rights but because of them*. As I noted in the introduction to this book, Eve Sedgwick (1993) has previously linked the rise in addiction-attribution to empire. Drawing upon Foucauldian ideas and the work of Virginia Berridge and Griffith Edwards (1987), Sedgwick noted connections between the invention of the addict, the 'newly ramified and pervasive medical-juridical authority of the late nineteenth century', and 'the context of changing class and imperial relations' (1993: 130). The particular configuration of drug use and drug problems that I have identified in this chapter certainly does not emerge because of

(Western) conceptions of rights. Those configurations pre-date modern rights discourses and practices, as Sedgwick (1993) points out. Nevertheless, and notably, these configurations are sustained and stabilised by rights discourses and practices. At least sometimes, human rights constitute the subject as differently human and authorise interventions, governance, violence and control. They produce and reproduce people who use drugs and those characterised as 'dependent' as less than full citizens (Seear & Fraser, 2010a, 2010b; Moore & Fraser, 2006; Fraser & valentine, 2008) that must be 'humanised', or made differently human. Drugs also constitute rights as differently available to subjects. In other words, and building upon Arendt's (1958) critiques of rights for the stateless, I argue that the interpretation and application of rights via drugs is a part of the process by which the human is constituted, and certain ways of being validly human become entrenched. It is important to acknowledge that human rights are sometimes criticised as weak, devoid of substance, and difficult to enforce, potentially making them an easy target for analysis. While these critiques are important, they miss a key point. Whatever their strengths and weaknesses, human rights practices are still practices, and practices are productive. They *matter*. Although they may sometimes operate as a bulwark on state power, they also instantiate particular and limited notions of 'the human', at least in relation to drug use, with material consequences for those subjected to them. Moreover, they instantiate particular relationships between humans, drugs, free will, poverty, suffering, death, health, the state and so on. They help to fix drug use to a range of phenomena, position problematic drug use as fundamental to various forms of harm and enact drug use as antithetical to being 'fully' or 'properly' human. Of course, these connections can also be undone. On this, it is important to acknowledge Costas Douzinas' (2007: 9) point that human rights involve 'diverse practices, languages, institutions, remedies and personnel'. In order to understand what human rights are, or what human rights law means, we need to study local practices for their specificity, for what they make possible and for what they enact. And we must recognise that just as the nature and content of law varies in accordance with the conditions of its enunciation, so does the nature and meaning of 'human rights'. As such, the particular consequences of human rights processes that I identified in this chapter may differ from those at other points in time, under other systems, where different questions are involved. Drugs and human rights may be differently entangled, in other contexts, where slightly different processes are at play, or where different connections between rights and subjects are stabilised. What if, for instance, the right to life were differently envisaged through drugs, not as an obligation to prevent death or refrain from imperilling life, but as a commitment to the value of different ways of living? What if the rights to privacy, conscience, movement and liberty were similarly reimagined, not laden by assumptions about the putative hazards of drugs but by an openness to their affordances? What if a different kind of autonomy were valorised? What if various social phenomena such as poverty and homelessness were reimagined, not as the artefacts of consumptive regimes but as the failings of social policy? And what if the right to be free from policy failings were instead prioritised? In other words, what if rights were no longer 'driven, ever more blindly, by its own compulsion to isolate some new, receding but absolutized space of pure voluntarity?' (Sedgwick, 1993: 134). In other words: might we find new ways of articulating the links between drugs, rights and other phenomena, and in so doing, find new and more generous ways of making the human?

# References

Arendt, H. (1958). *The Origins of Totalitarianism*. Cleveland and New York: Meridian Books.

Australian Council of Social Service. (2018). *Getting a job on Newstart is harder than you think, September 14*. Available at: www.acoss.org.au/media_release/getting-a-job-on-newstart-is-harder-than-you-think/ (accessed 22 January 2019).

Australian Council of Social Service & Jobs Australia. (2018). *Faces of Unemployment*. Strawberry Hills: Australian Council of Social Service.

Bacchi, C. (2009). *Analysing Policy: What is the Problem Represented To Be?* Sydney: Pearson.

Berridge, V., & Edwards, G. (1987). *Opium and the People: Opiate Use in Nineteenth-century England* (2nd edn). New Haven: Yale University Press.

Boughey, J. (2017). The scope and application of the charters. In M. Groves & C. Campbell (eds.), *Australian Charters of Rights a Decade On* (pp. 36–52). Sydney: The Federation Press.

Brett Young, M. (2015). *From Commitment to Culture: The 2015 Review of the Charter of Human Rights and Responsibilities Act 2006*. Melbourne: Victorian Government Printer.

Cahn, N. (1992). The looseness of legal language: The reasonable woman standard in theory and practice. *Cornell Law Review, 77*(6), 1398–1446.

Clarkson, C., Jacobs, Z., Marwick, B., Fullagar, R., Wallis, L., & Smith, M., et al. (2017). Human occupation of northern Australia by 65,000 years ago. *Nature, 547*, 306–310.

Commonwealth of Australia. (2018). *Report of the Community Affairs Legislation Committee: Social Services Legislation Amendment (Drug Testing Trial) Bill 2018 [Provisions]*. Canberra: Commonwealth of Australia.

Commonwealth of Australia. (2017). *Report of the Community Affairs Legislation Committee; Social Services Legislation Amendment (Welfare Reform) Bill 2017 [Provisions]*. Canberra: Commonwealth of Australia.

Commonwealth of Australia House of Representatives. (2018a). *Explanatory Memorandum to the Social Services Legislation Amendment (Drug Testing Trial) Bill 2018: Statement of Compatibility with Human Rights*. Canberra: Commonwealth of Australia.

Commonwealth of Australia House of Representatives. (2018b). *Explanatory Memorandum to the Social Services Legislation Amendment (Drug Testing Trial) Bill 2018: Schedule 1 (Amendments)*. Canberra: Commonwealth of Australia.

Conaghan, J. (1996). Gendered harms and the law of Tort: Remedying (sexual) harassment. *Oxford Journal of Legal Studies, 16*(3), 407–432.

Davis, M. (2006). A culture of disrespect: Indigenous peoples and Australian public institutions. *University of Technology Sydney Law Review, 8*, 137–154.

Donnelly, J. (1989). *Universal Human Rights in Theory and Practice*. Ithaca: Cornell University Press.

Douzinas, C. (2007). *Human Rights and Empire: The Political Philosophy of Cosmopolitanism*. Milton Park: Routledge-Cavendish.

Douzinas, C. (1996). Justice and human rights in postmodernity. In C. Gearty & A. Tomkins (eds.), *Understanding Human Rights* (pp. 115–137). London and New York: Pinter.

Erni, J. (2019). *Law and Cultural Studies: A critical Rearticulation of Human Rights*. Abingdon: Routledge.

Erni, J. (2012). Who needs human rights? Cultural studies and public institutions. In M. Morris & M. Hjort (eds.), *Creativity and Academic Activism: Instituting Cultural Studies* (pp. 175–190). Hong Kong: Hong Kong University Press.

Esmeir, S. (2012). *Juridical Humanity: A Colonial History*. Stanford: Stanford University Press.

Fraser, S., & valentine, k. (2008). *Substance and Substitution: Methadone Subjects in Liberal Societies*. Basingstoke: Palgrave.

Gans, J. (2009). *Scrutiny of Bills under Bills of Rights: Is Victoria's Model the Way Forward?* Paper presented at the Australia–New Zealand Scrutiny of Legislation Conference: Scrutiny and Accountability in the 21st Century, Parliament House, Canberra, Australia, 6–8 July. Available at: www.aph.gov.au/About_Parliament/Senate/Whats_On/Conferences/sl_conference/papers/gans (accessed 8 January 2019).

Groves, M. (2017). Interpreting the effect of our charters. In M. Groves & C. Campbell (eds.), *Australian Charters of Rights a Decade On* (pp. 2–21). The Federation Press: Sydney.

Gutwirth, S. (2015). Providing the missing link: Law after Latour's passage. In K. McGee (ed.), *Latour and the Passage of Law* (pp. 122–159). Edinburgh: Edinburgh University Press.

Lancaster, K., Seear, K., & Treloar, C. (2015). Laws prohibiting peer distribution of injecting equipment in Australia: A critical analysis of their effects. *International Journal of Drug Policy*, 26(12), 1198–1206.

Latour, B. (2015). The strange entanglement of jurimorphs. In K. McGee (ed.), *Latour and the Passage of Law* (pp. 331–353). Edinburgh: Edinburgh University Press.

Latour, B. (2013). *An Inquiry into Modes of Existence: An Anthropology of the Moderns*. Cambridge: Harvard University Press.

Latour, B. (2009). *The Making of Law: An Ethnography of the Conseil D'Etat*. Cambridge: Polity Press.

Mathew, P. (2017). Taking stock of the audit power. In M. Groves & C. Campbell (eds.), *Australian Charters of Rights a Decade On* (pp. 53–68). Sydney: The Federation Press.

Matthews, D., & Veitch, S. (2016). The limits of critique and the forces of law. *Law Critique*, 27, 349–361.

McGee, K. (2015a). Introduction. In K. McGee (ed.), *Latour and the Passage of Law* (pp. 1–16). Edinburgh: Edinburgh University Press.

McGee, K. (2015b). On devices and logics of legal sense: Toward socio-technical legal analysis. In K. McGee (ed.), *Latour and the Passage of Law* (pp. 61–92). Edinburgh: Edinburgh University Press.

McGee, K. (2014). *Bruno Latour: The Normativity of Networks*. Abingdon: Routledge.

Moore, D., & Fraser, S. (2013). Producing the 'problem' of addiction in drug treatment. *Qualitative Health Research*, 23(7), 916–923.

Moore, D., & Fraser, S. (2006). Putting at risk what we know: Reflecting on the drug using subject in harm reduction and its political implications. *Social Science and Medicine*, 62, 3035–3047.

Pienaar, K., & Savic, M. (2016). Producing alcohol and other drugs as a policy 'problem': A critical analysis of South Africa's 'National Drug Master Plan' (2013–2017). *International Journal of Drug Policy*, 30, 35–42.

Rose, N. (1999). *Governing the Soul: The Shaping of the Private Self* (2nd edn). London: Free Association Books.

Rose, N. (1996). *Inventing Our Selves: Psychology, Power, and Personhood*. Cambridge: Cambridge University Press.

Saunders, P., Bradbury, B., Wong, M., Dorsch, P., Phillips, J., & Crowe, C. (2017). *Poverty in Australia 2016*. Sydney: ACOSS and the Social Policy Research Centre, UNSW Sydney.

Sedgwick, E. (1993). Epidemics of the will. In E. Sedgwick (ed.), *Tendencies* (pp. 130–142). London: Routledge.

Seear, K., & Fraser, S. (2014). The addict as victim: Producing the 'problem' of addiction in Australian victims of crime compensation laws. *International Journal of Drug Policy*, 25(5), 826–835.

Seear, K., & Fraser, S. (2010a). The 'sorry addict': Ben Cousins and the construction of drug use and addiction in elite sport. *Health Sociology Review*, 19(2), 176–191.

Seear, K., & Fraser, S. (2010b). Ben Cousins and the 'double life': Exploring citizenship and the voluntarity/compulsivity binary through the experiences of a 'drug addicted' elite athlete. *Critical Public Health*, 20(4), 439–452.

Spivakovsky, C., Seear, K., & Carter, A. (2018). *Critical Perspectives on Coercive Interventions: Law, Medicine and Society*. Abingdon: Routledge.

Victorian Equal Opportunity and Human Rights Commission. (2008). *First Steps Forward*. Melbourne: Victorian Equal Opportunity and Human Rights Commission.

Victorian Legislative Assembly. (2010). *Hansard: Thursday, 11 March*. Melbourne: Victorian Government Printer.

Victorian Legislative Assembly. (2009). *Hansard: Thursday, 10 December*. Melbourne: Victorian Government Printer.

Williams, G. (2017). The distinctive features of Australia's human rights charters. In M. Groves & C. Campbell (eds.), *Australian Charters of Rights a Decade On* (pp. 22–35). Sydney: The Federation Press.

Williams, G. (2007). *A Charter of Rights for Australia*. Sydney: UNSW Press.

World Health Organization. (1975). *Education and Treatment in Human Sexuality: The Training of Health Professionals. Technical Report Series, No. 572*. Geneva: World Health Organization.

Zucca, L. (2016). The fragility of international human rights law. *Ethics and International Affairs*, 30(4), 491–499.

## Case

*Mabo and Others v Queensland (No. 2)* [1992] HCA 23.

## Legislation

*Alcoholics and Drug-Dependent Persons Act* (1968) (Victoria).

*Bill of Rights* (1789) (United States of America).

*Charter of Human Rights and Responsibilities Act* (2006) (Victoria).

*Charter of Rights and Freedoms* (1982) (Canada).

*Commonwealth of Australia Constitution Act* (1900) (Commonwealth).

*Human Rights Act* (2004) (Australian Capital Territory).

*Human Rights Act* (1998) (United Kingdom).

*Human Rights (Parliamentary Scrutiny) Act* (2011) (Commonwealth).

## *Bills*

*Severe Substance Dependence Treatment Bill* (2009) (Victoria). *Social Services Legislation Amendment (Drug Testing Trial) Bill* (2018) (Commonwealth).
*Social Services Legislation Amendment (Welfare Reform) Bill* (2017) (Commonwealth).

## *Treaties*

*Convention on the Rights of Persons with Disabilities* (2006).
*Convention on the Rights of the Child* (1989).
*International Covenant on Civil and Political Rights* (1966).
*International Covenant on Economic, Social and Cultural Rights* (1966).
*International Convention on the Elimination of all Forms of Racial Discrimination* (1965).
*Universal Declaration of Human Rights* (1948).

# 2 *Advocacy practices*

## On legal strategies, habits and the action of anticipation

## Introduction

This chapter examines lawyers' accounts of their strategies when dealing with alcohol and other drugs in the law. It explores how alcohol and other drugs surface in various areas of legal practice, how lawyers understand and constitute the relevance of alcohol and other drugs to legal issues, and how, along the way, they enact 'addiction' in legal advocacy. The overarching theme of this chapter is that a crucial part of legal practice involves *anticipating* what decision makers might do and expect, and that these anticipatory practices shape both lawyers' strategies and the subjects and objects in their work. Here, I draw upon Serge Gutwirth's (2015: 130) observation that 'a thing becomes legal when it is processed or thought from a position that anticipates how a judge could or should do it'. Focussing on this idea – of legality as anticipatory – I explore what lawyers anticipate decision makers such as judges will think about alcohol and other drugs, how anticipation shapes lawyers' strategy and practice, and, in so doing, how anticipation works to materialise and stabilise addiction as a (certain kind of) legal object. Lawyers' practice is shaped and constrained by anticipation, including the notion that alcohol and other drug use will invariably constitute a legal 'problem' and that it thus must be managed in specific ways (or 'solved'). In undertaking this analysis, I argue that the ontology of addiction is an effect of legal strategy. I consider the implications of these accounts for Gutwirth's claim that law is simultaneously 'autochtonous' (already there) and 'anticipatory' (not yet stated), suggesting that addiction is shaped via shared and anticipated understandings. I read lawyers' accounts of what they do alongside Judith Butler's (1997) work on interpellation and Moore and Fraser's (2013) work on problem formulation, in order to demonstrate some of the ways that anticipatory practices matter. Instantiating familiar addiction concepts through their legal practice, lawyers 'perform' people who addicts and enact addicts in ways that are devalued, as non-agentive and irrational. This is of particular concern, I argue, given that people who use drugs are often already highly stigmatised and marginalised for both their lack of volition and claimed irrationality. There are also important gendered and affective dimensions to this work, which has implications for men's and women's legal outcomes. These practices also shape the nature and

scale of 'addiction' and constitute it as causally linked to a range of social problems and phenomena (such as criminal offending). Finally, I contrast lawyers'
accounts with those of decision makers. Somewhat surprisingly, decision makers
afford themselves less agency in the enactment of legal addiction than we might
assume them to have. Whereas lawyers enact addiction in ways they anticipate
will accord with decision makers' conceptualisations, decision makers claim to
be constrained in their enactments, with their judgements contingent upon the
ideas that lawyers put to them. When lawyers' and decision makers' accounts are
read alongside one another, it becomes clear that addiction is a co-production,
and that anticipation plays a central role in its emergence. In the conclusion, I
consider what this means for the future of legal practice, including the possibility
of new strategies emerging. In order to explore what may be possible, I turn to
Gutwirth (2015) again, and his notion that law is a 'mode of habit'. I consider
what this means for legal advocacy pertaining to alcohol and other drugs, going
forward.

## Anticipation, hesitation and the making of law

As I explained in the introductory chapter, an STS account of law emphasises,
among other things, the central role played by mediators (both human and
non-human) and practices in the production and stabilisation of law. In the previous chapter, I examined the role of practices in the form of enunciation, articulation, linking and de-linking, noting that those practices were particularly
integral to the making of legal content (see also McGee, 2015a). These are not
the only practices, however, that work to make law. Serge Gutwirth has offered
a particularly rich account of the role of *anticipation* in law. Gutwirth's central
idea is that 'a thing becomes legal when it is processed or thought from a position that anticipates how a judge could or should do it' (Gutwirth, 2015: 130).
In order to understand what Gutwirth means by this, and why it matters, we
must first examine his overarching approach to law, including his analysis of law's
'two modes', or the 'two ways' that people tend to speak of law. He explains
these modes thus:

> On the one hand law is referred to as an intertwined whole of statutes,
> rules and regulations, and thus, in one word, as norms (or 'normativity'),
> while, on the other hand, it can well be understood as decision-making or
> as a practice that produces solutions. Thus: norms or solutions, that's the
> question.
>
> (Gutwirth, 2015: 130)

In Gutwirth's view, discussions about law are characterised by an 'incessant
switching' between these two modes. This has the effect of 'blurring our understanding of what the law does, what it produces' and more (2015: 123). In
order to address this problem, Gutwirth proposes a distinction between law's
two modes: what he calls 'Law1' and 'Law2'. Starting with the question 'what

is law?', Gutwirth identifies the various 'formal sources' of law. These include legislation, case law, legal doctrine (especially where *stare decisis*, discussed in the introductory chapter, applies), customs, general legal principles and (possibly) contracts. Taking these as his starting point, Gutwirth defines 'Law1' as 'what the (continental) lawyers understand as the legal sources' (2015: 127) or 'formal sources' of law. Gutwirth then asks, 'who practices law?' In asking this question, 'the responses given take a completely different turn in comparison with the "What is law?" entry' (2015: 129). Those who practise law include judges, advocates, attorneys, public prosecutors, paralegals, bailiffs and registrars. That is:

> Not the political representatives that populate the representative assemblies nor the members of bodies with legislative powers, but all those who are involved in the production not of rules but of decisions, among which the judges and the members of courts are the most emblematic examples.
>
> (2015: 129)

These legal professionals are unmistakably involved in the making of law and yet, as Gutwirth points out, would not be captured within the category that he calls 'Law1'. Thus, 'Law2' is needed. Law2 'provides for decisions/solutions under the form of judgments, where no other way or mode succeeded in making and respectively finding them' (Gutwirth, 2015: 132). Law2 emphasises 'law as a practice, which again and again, case by case, is reactivated to produce, state or 'draw' the *vinculum iuris*' (2015: 132; original emphasis). For Gutwirth, Law1 'isn't really law at all' (McGee, 2015b), but a political and organisational phenomenon (Gutwirth, 2015); what Latour (2013) might call [POL:ORG]. He continues:

> It is thus only from the perspective of law2 that an unequivocal and consistent understanding of the relation between the 'sources of law' and the law itself, which 'springs' from them, can be built. Consequently, only legal practice – the coping with things in anticipation of what a judge can do or does – extracts or derives law from its sources.
>
> (Gutwirth, 2015: 134)

This brings us back to the point at which I started this discussion, then, and to Gutwirth's focus on the function of *anticipation*.

Legislation's force is 'co-produced by case law' and depends on 'how the judges will interpret, concretise and give consequences to' it (Gutwirth, 2015: 142; see also Ewick & Silbey, 1998). What a judge will decide is 'never completely predictable'; 'the only thing that is certain is *that* she will decide' something, bringing closure and stability to the issues at hand (Gutwirth, 2015: 131; original emphasis). It is the process of anticipating what a judge might do, and being *moved* by that anticipation, that in turn moves the law forward, or makes the law (Gutwirth, 2015: 130). But what does it mean to anticipate something in law? What, precisely, does this anticipatory process involve? How does it manifest, and what does anticipation do? Gutwirth argues that legal approaches are characterised by a series of 'distinctive operations' including qualification, distinguishing, subsumption and imputation. The processes of 'hesitation, pondering and tinkering' (Gutwirth, 2015: 133) are particularly important. The concept of 'hesitation' comes from Latour and requires some explanation. In *The Making of Law* (2009), Latour identified ten 'value objects' implicated in 'the ordeal' of judicial decision-making. One of these is what he calls 'hesitation', which he defines in this way:

> Those who enunciate the law seem almost to measure the realization of their performances by their capacity to have hesitated well, extensively and sufficiently, to have crunched and crushed the content of their files by making them react with a sufficient number of texts. It is in fact only in this moment of abeyance, slowness or preliminary unlinking that they seem to find a proof of their freedom of manoeuvre, before then proceeding to the work of linking, knitting or deciding.
>
> (2009: 193–194)

The process of hesitation is a 'winding path' (Latour, 2009: 151), through which the decision maker is pulled in one direction, pushed in another, dragged back and forth by texts and precedents, before a decision is reached. Other aspects of law's singularity are also manifest, such as the 'detachment' of

> jurists coping with facts, their singular obligation to *hesitate*, to de-bind and re-bind, to reassemble and disassemble, to redo the hermeneutical loop again and again, until the issue is ripe for a decision, and thus for the law to be 'solemnly' stated or put down, for a *dictum*, a ver*dict*.
>
> (Gutwirth, 2015: 133; original emphasis)

In these passages, the focus is on the process of judicial decision making itself. But this does not mean that lawyers don't engage in similar practices, including hesitation, linking and so on. Rather than being mere bystanders to this process, passive witnesses to the judicial method, lawyers in fact participate in it (and thus, in the making of law). As Gutwirth explains,

> Lawyers or advocates do indeed play a very important role here, since they will try to pre-structure and prepare the claims, means and files in order to build a *dispositif* and to set the scene in anticipation of the hermeneutical trajectories they wish the judge to take (and indeed the other parties will do the same).
>
> (2015: 132; original emphasis)

In other words, although part of the lawyers' role is to anticipate what judges and other decision makers might do, they are moved to action in response to that which they anticipate. This movement to action means that they become involved in the production of law through practices of pre-structuring; preparation; building; anticipating; and, ultimately, of course, advocating. The significance of this is twofold. First, it means that decision makers such as judges are not the only legal professionals with a vital role to play in the making of law. Second, the way in which lawyers pre-structure, prepare, build, anticipate and then advocate in cases will have material implications for what might be decided. This also leads us to one of the central paradoxes of law, in that its 'omnipresent possibility' explains why 'paradoxically [it] is both "autochtonous" ("already there") and anticipatory ("not yet stated by a judge")' (Gutwirth, 2015: 131). These might seem like obvious points, especially to lawyers. Textbooks and articles on legal practice are replete with references to the practical and strategic importance of anticipation. Lawyers are told to anticipate matters, including potential dilemmas in conflict resolution advocacy (e.g. Macfarlane, 2008), admissibility issues with evidence and the arguments that their opponents will make (e.g. Hampel, Brimer, & Kune, 2008) as well as how different audiences will receive the narratives they construct (Johnson, 2017).

Gutwirth's analysis works with these seemingly 'common sense' observations of law and connects them to law's ontology. His framework gives explicit recognition to the role that lawyers can play in the making of law and legal content, even as law paradoxically appears to pre-exist such practices. Gutwirth's analysis of anticipation also opens up other possibilities for understanding the ontological power of legal practices. I want to draw attention to two possibilities here, in order to set the scene for the analysis that follows. The first involves the possibility that legal practices of anticipation shape the nature and scale of problems. This idea comes from research on alcohol and other drug policy and service provision, and was flagged briefly in the introductory chapter (Moore & Fraser, 2013). Challenging conventional understandings of policy making as a process by which social problems are simply identified and addressed, Moore and Fraser (2013) adopted a critical approach to policy processes, combining ideas from French philosopher Gilles Deleuze (1994), feminist theorist Paola Marrati (2006) and poststructuralist policy scholar Carol Bacchi (2009). Their research examined the state-based 'episodes of care' system for the funding of addiction treatment. Under the system, service providers were tasked with identifying 'addicts' and providing them with alcohol and other drug treatment. The government funded each episode of care. Moore and Fraser argued that although the policy generally understood 'addiction' as an object that precedes attempts to identify or manage it, addiction was in fact made through policy and practice. Drawing upon qualitative interviews with policymakers and service providers, they found that:

> alcohol and other drug treatment policy in Victoria does not merely identify and respond to a pre-existing condition called 'addiction'; instead, it is one of the processes through which addiction is produced.

> (2013: 922)

They continued, arguing that:

> the problem of addiction emerges as an effect of treatment service provision as well as a precursor to it, largely as a result of policy and budgetary imperatives governing the provision of treatment.
>
> (2013: 916)

Systems, that is, work 'to produce "addicts" as an effect of policy' and as this work happens, 'the scale of the problem appears to be growing rather than shrinking' (Moore & Fraser, 2013: 916). As I explain later, these ideas can also be mobilised to understand actions undertaken *within* law and the consequential action *of* law. The second possibility I flag briefly here comes from Judith Butler's work on interpellation (1997), which itself draws upon writings by Louis Althusser (1971). For Althusser, 'interpellation' signals the process by which subjects are enrolled into discourse. He argues that individuals are transformed into subjects, or come to recognise themselves as subjects, through processes of 'hailing' and 'calling', as when a police officer calls out 'Hey, you there!' The process of turning around in response to the call is one through which we recognise ourselves as the subjects and objects of regulatory discourse. Building upon these ideas, Judith Butler points out that 'the interpellative name may arrive without a speaker – on bureaucratic forms, the census, adoption papers, employment applications' (1997: 34). In other words, these processes may be bureaucratic in nature, and may arise in different forums and formats. These ideas have previously been applied to the study of alcohol and other drug 'recovery' discourses by Fomiatti, Moore and Fraser (2017). They argue that the 'recovering addict' is a socially produced category made possible by therapeutic technologies, treatment logics, counselling practices and injunctions to overcome one's 'problem'. In what follows, I read Butler's (1997) work on interpellation and Moore and Fraser's (2013) work on problem formulation alongside Gutwirth's (2015) work on anticipation and its role in the constitution of law. I argue that lawyers' accounts of their work emphasise the central role of anticipation in legal strategy. Through examples drawn from interviews with lawyers, I consider what lawyers anticipate and predict courts will do, how this shapes their advocacy strategies, what these practices make possible and what they do with subjects, objects and problems. Towards the end of this chapter, I contrast these data with data from decision makers, revealing that they afford themselves less agency in the making of law than we might assume. These findings have implications for the way lawyers anticipate and strategise in relation to alcohol and other drugs, and open up new possibilities for the making of law.

## How do alcohol and other drugs feature in law?

Drug use appears in a wide range of legal realms and there is no single or consistent approach either across or within different areas of law (Seear & Fraser, 2014a). As I explained in the introductory chapter, alcohol and other drugs feature in law in various ways. Sometimes, the language of 'addiction' or 'dependence' figures in legislation, as with legislation that mandates treatment for those experiencing a 'severe substance dependence'. Sometimes, alcohol or other drugs are the subject of an offence, as where a person has been charged under the criminal law with possession of an illicit drug, or with drug trafficking. In most circumstances, however, alcohol and other drugs surface not because they appear in relevant legislation or are the objects of an offence. Instead, they appear as an effect of legal strategy or advocacy, sometimes *proactively* asserted by a party to a legal proceeding in circumstances where it is considered useful or necessary to make such assertions as a means of pursuing a legal argument, or seeking a legal remedy. Sometimes they are *reactively* asserted: as where drug use becomes known in a legal proceeding and a strategic decision is made to respond to that revelation by developing an argument designed to manage or mitigate that drug use as an 'addiction'. In this section, I explain these processes in detail. I have previously given an account of how this works in one area of law. Working with Suzanne Fraser (2014b), I examined how alcohol and other drugs and 'addiction' surface in the area of crimes compensation law. Our research considered the operation of a remedial, statutory compensation scheme in the state of Victoria, designed to benefit victims of crime. Under that scheme, individuals are entitled to compensation if they can establish, on the balance of probabilities, that they were the victim of a crime. Section 54 of the relevant legislation (*Victims of Crime Assistance Act* (1996) (Victoria)) sets out a series of matters to which the presiding tribunal must have regard when considering an application for an award of compensation. That section states that the tribunal must consider:

> the character, behaviour (including past criminal activity and the number and nature of any findings of guilt or convictions) or attitude of the applicant at any time, whether before, during or after the commission of the act of violence.

Although Section 54 makes no explicit reference to alcohol or drugs, our research found a number of cases where a victim of crime's past history of alcohol or other drug use was found to be relevant to the question of whether they should be compensated. As we explained:

> Section 54 offers no guidance as to what might be a relevant consideration, what weight should be given to relevant considerations in deciding whether or not to make an award, and how those considerations impact on decisions about the kind or size of award to make. The upshot of this is that judges have considerable scope for determining what is both 'relevant' and 'problematic', notions that have the potential to be taken up in subsequent case law as self-evidently relevant and problematic [...] It is telling, therefore, that drug use and 'addiction' were understood to be [...] a potential obstacle to the provision of compensation [...], although the apparent relevance of drug use and addiction varied.
>
> (Seear & Fraser, 2014b: 830)

Typically, lawyers acting for victims in crimes compensation matters would be familiar with Section 54 and these previous cases involving alcohol or other drugs. In pre-empting those issues, lawyers might plan for the possibility that an applicant victim's character would be impugned under Section 54, by asking their clients about their past history of alcohol or other drug use. The victim's alcohol or other drug use might also become known in some other way – as where, for instance, they were assaulted whilst under the influence of alcohol or other drugs, the details of which appeared in a police or hospital report. In a case like this, lawyers would learn to anticipate that alcohol or other drugs might be thought of as relevant under Section 54, and plan on how to manage the fact of alcohol or other drug use, accordingly. In this example, even though alcohol or other drug 'addiction' appears nowhere in the relevant legislation (law1), it appears in the case law (law1) and thus becomes a proper object for deliberation and management through advocacy (law2).

Most of the time, lawyers I interviewed reported alcohol and other drug issues surfacing in their work in similar ways. It didn't necessarily appear in legislation, that is, but was known to be relevant, or potentially relevant, to the area of law in which they worked because of past cases, past experience, 'common sense' or other anticipatory processes. By way of example, Australian lawyer Erin explained how these issues might surface as potentially relevant within the context of family law:

> So the *Family Law Act* [(1975) (Commonwealth)] basically says, you've got two primary considerations and [...] the prime consideration that needs to be referred is that the children are protected from harm. [...] So I mean if [alcohol or other drug use] comes up in a family law matter, it primarily comes up by way of either [an] allegation by the other party, or allegation by our client about the other person being 'drug addicted' or a drug user and [that there is a] risk of harm, basically.

In the previous chapter, I argued that processes of connection and articulation are foundational to law, and to the constitution of subjects and objects through law. Contained within Erin's account are a series of forecasts about how things might link together (drugs and addiction to risk, risk to harm, harm to one of the primary considerations in the Act). In other words, even as Erin explains how alcohol and other drugs surface in the area of law with which she is most familiar, we can see that processes of anticipation, theorising and pondering are underway. Her description also reflects Gutwirth's (2015: 131) paradox, noted earlier, in which the law is understood to be both 'already there' and 'not yet stated'. The legal 'relevance' of a matter also does not pre-exist the process by which lawyers speculate about both what the matter 'is' and how its relevance might be interpreted. Is the fact of alcohol or other drug use relevant to a case? If so, how? What legal significance, in other words, might attach to it? Which legal principles, if any, might it be connected to, or capable of being connected to? What are the various challenges that consumption poses? What legal arguments can be made? To what ends? And given all of this, what is likely to be the best way to proceed? In other words: where alcohol or other drug use becomes known, is alleged or is admitted in a case, what should be done about it? As Olivia explained, the answer to these questions is often simple: it is all about 'how that [drug use] might be *perceived* by a court' (emphasis added). Alcohol and other drugs were often assumed to be relevant because of ideas that lawyers anticipated that decision makers would hold about them, including that substances were always already problematic. Importantly – and this is a key point – even though alcohol or other drugs may feature in legal settings, 'addiction' often does not often feature in law *unless or until a strategic decision is made to introduce the language of addiction or key concepts of addiction into law.* In this sense, *legal strategy is central to the emergence of addiction in law.*

In Australia, lawyers described working intuitively when alcohol or other drugs are concerned, and in the absence of an overarching decision such as the one in the *Insite* case (*Canada (Attorney General) v PHS Community Services Society* [2011] 3 SCR 134). Several anticipated that the location of the forum where the case is to be heard would be an important factor when determining how to manage alcohol or other drugs. In these instances, lawyers try to anticipate how a particular jurisdiction and/or judge might respond to drug use. For example, as Maxwell explained:

> Also, it depends, it varies on the magistrates as well. There are magistrates out there who are far more understanding than others, obviously, so yeah that all changes as well.

As Melanie, an Australian lawyer explained:

> It's just 'Judge Lotto'. Like it's just really, you have certain [judicial figures] and certain [jurisdictions] that a culture grows up in and who are very unsympathetic [to drug use ...] It really is a judgment call on a case by case basis and primarily the first question I ask [clients] is: 'Where do you live?' Because it'll depend what tribunal we're in and I know that if we're, you know presently we're at [a particular location] and this person's got addiction issues that may translate to a lengthy prior history, so we're in all sorts [of difficulties]. Whereas with other clients I hardly look into it at all because I know we're likely to have a sympathetic tribunal. But it's just sort of on a case by case basis really. Like I can't say that I don't handle [addiction] consistently but *it's just what's required which basically is from my past experience and judgment.*
> (emphasis added)

Similarly as Fern noted:

> you make a call with the particular magistrate or judge to what extent, if at all, you bring up information, whether it becomes a mitigating factor or something that they would see as an aggravating factor. [...] And that's often either because you know [from experience] that the particular magistrate will ascribe a certain approach or have a particular gut instinct reaction, or sympathy.

Lawyers saw this work, and the process of being able to guess how courts would want drugs and addiction to be constituted, as one of the core skills of being a lawyer.

As Maxwell, Melanie and Fern's comments reveal, lawyers often rely on their own experience and knowledge of the law, including how particular decision makers might react, when deciding how to handle drug use. Their approaches may vary by the location of the forum, but also by the particular area of law involved. In some jurisdictions, lawyers believe that it is essential to acknowledge past drug use and frame it as a 'problem', in part because there is an assumption that all forms of illicit drug use will be perceived as harmful, and that to not acknowledge that use as a problem is itself a risky strategy. In these cases, refusing to account for drug use as a problem for which one is seeking help might be just as problematic as the use 'itself'. This is one of the ways that the practical process of lawyering can work to enact drug use as drug addiction. In the Family Court, for example:

> that always will be a strategy to absolutely admit that you have a 'drug problem', be honest about the extent of it and what you are doing to fix it, because if you can't convince the Court that you admit it was bad and you are going to do things to fix it, then you are just dead in the water, so that will always be a strategy [...] I think there's this real culture that if you don't have insight into your flaws as a parent and how you might rectify those, I guess it goes towards maturity and ability as a parent, but if you don't have insight into your flaws and problems, then you potentially are facing sort of change of residence for the children and really serious consequences if you can't establish you have insight [...] We have had cases where the other side is, where there's allegations of drug or alcohol use and they've denied them or downplayed them and said they don't impact the children. And that sort of continual denial and refusal to admit the extent of the impact that we are arguing, will damage them in the end because they'll be seen as having no insight, so not to be trusted. And probably [they will end up with] no unsupervised time [with their children], probably supervised time only, so I think it would be a dangerous strategy.
>
> (Erin, Australia)

In contrast with the account Erin gave about the family law, lawyers working in the criminal law had a mixture of opinions about how to handle drug use. Betty, a Canadian lawyer, was unequivocal. In her experience, it was always a sound strategy to position use as addiction in a bid to mitigate (reduce) a client's criminal sentence. She explained:

> There was never a time where you would downplay the addiction in my mind because in the criminal justice system the addiction piece is the ultimate I think. Maybe not the ultimate, but it's a huge mitigating factor,

because it's part of a larger systemic problem that I always felt should be addressed in the criminal court. Saying, 'Look, we have problems out there and this person ended up in here for whatever it was', stealing a steak from the store or whatever petty crime that they were alleged to have done and they probably did do. So the addiction piece was critical to [the case] strategically.

On the other hand, Anne Marie had trouble knowing whether to raise drug use in criminal cases and if so, what to make of it. She anticipated a 'philosophical contradiction' where prescription drugs and illicit drugs were concerned, with those consuming prescription drugs being viewed more compassionately by magistrates. Moreover, Anne Marie had to sometimes represent clients who had legal problems in more than one area of law at the same time (e.g. criminal and civil) and make decisions about how to approach them. The anticipatory work lawyers do thus sometimes stretches to having to assess how decision makers in multiple legal realms will think about drug use, as well as how processes unfolding in one area of law will intersect with those unfolding in another.

> I think for me it's, there's no consensus on how to deal with these issues necessarily. [...] Is it a criminal matter for which you can be charged or is it a mitigating factor in a civil claim or a criminal matter? [...] You might find difficulty in raising it before a magistrate if you've got a civil debt matter and you are in negotiations with the Ombudsman [about that civil debt matter] or something. Do you raise this drug issue? Or is that going to make [the criminal magistrate] prejudiced against your client because that's a legal issue and they're breaking the law? And that's what's challenging from a lawyer's point of view, because *you are guessing whether you raise these matters or not*. That's what I see as a most challenging thing for a lawyer there.
>
> (Anne Marie, Australian lawyer; emphasis added)

Although their views and expectations differ, Erin, Betty and Anne Marie's perspectives on the court process remind us of the situated, unstable and unpredictable nature of drug use's 'relevance' to legal proceedings. Drug use, in other words, is typically enacted as a 'problem' in the form of addiction only where lawyers anticipate that it is necessary to do so, and even then, approaches to it are carefully crafted and managed. The relevance of drug use/addiction to parenting, for example, is not a given, essential or intrinsic function of drug use 'itself'. Instead, its relevance is at least partially an effect of legal strategy and the judgements that lawyers make about it. Its 'relevance' may also differ with different substances, or across different areas of law, and sometimes in ways that are directly contradictory. It also seemed inherently paradoxical that a person could be charged for drug possession, on the one hand, but then mitigate their sentence or other civil matters by arguing they had a 'problem' with drug use, on the other. Lawyers are often 'guessing' how to approach challenges such as these. This is important, I suggest, because it undermines realist assertions about the ontology of drugs and addiction – at least in certain legal contexts – where drugs might be viewed as established objects with particular, stable attributes and intrinsic 'effects'. In law, those 'effects' are even less stable and predictable, contingent on multiple factors, including strategy and expectations. Instead, those attributes and effects, as I shall explain, take shape and form through legal strategy, rather than preceding it. As part of these overarching anticipatory and strategic decisions, lawyers must decide how, precisely, to articulate a client's alcohol or other drug use, including whether to frame it as an addiction, and how to characterise addiction itself.

## How lawyers constitute alcohol and other drugs

Once alcohol or other drugs feature in a case, the question becomes 'how you will get over the line and presenting it, packaging it and presenting it to best serve [the client]' (Melanie, Australia). In Canada, lawyers acknowledged that it was best, 'as a legal strategy, [to] sort of align [drug use] with an illness and that disability framework' (Simone, Canada). Canadian lawyers' approaches were strongly influenced by findings from the Supreme Court of Canada's decision in *Insite*, noted earlier. As Amy explained, the significance of that case is that:

> The trial judge finds, and the courts above confirm it, that addiction is non-volitional and whatever brought you to use in the first place once this progresses to the point of addiction – and addiction in the narrow way that the court understands and not really on the ground understanding – no matter what brings you to it, once you are addicted you are working on a kind of compulsion.
>
> (Amy, Canada)

The implications of the *Insite* decision were far-reaching. Canadian lawyers in a wide range of legal realms saw it as enabling, insofar as they could (and should) now advocate for the rights of people who use drugs in much the same way that one might advocate for people living with any other illness, disability or disease. In other words, as Canadian lawyer Janine explained, lawyers could subsequently argue that 'addiction is a disability [that] might [be] recognised as such under human rights laws' (Janine, Canada). Lawyers in Canada have subsequently adopted this approach to argue for clients' access to medical care. This includes the right to receive opioid replacement therapies including methadone in prisons, or the right to receive diacetylmorphine (heroin) treatment for opioid dependency where other assisted withdrawal treatments have not worked, as in the 2014 Canadian case of *Providence Health Care Society v Canada (Attorney General)* [2014] BCSC 936 (for a discussion, see Boyd et al., 2017).

In examples like these, the process of framing drug use as addiction is a means to an end: a way of ensuring access to basic health care rights and harm reduction services for people who use drugs, but who are not, by virtue of conservative political approaches to drugs, otherwise able to access them. According to Simone:

> I think that it's a sort of a 'necessary evil', if you will, that there is a need to have some framing, that there needs to be discussion of addiction in cases involving drugs.
>
> (Simone, Canada)

In other words, although the process of framing drug use as addiction and clients as ill, sick and lacking in agency might be problematic, lawyers felt they had few other options or that it was the option most likely to get the best result for their client. As noted earlier, this is so at least partly because lawyers anticipate that judges will expect them to frame their client's behaviour in such a way. Legal addiction-attribution is a 'necessary evil'; in Simone's words: it is simply 'how [we] advocate for harm reduction in health services'. In these cases, there is a perceived need to collapse drug use and addiction, in order to achieve structural reforms:

> It is strategic to frame many people's drug use [as addiction...] even if many people are not using drugs because of addiction.
>
> (Simone, Canada)

These processes are repeated across a wide range of legal realms, including the criminal law. In criminal law settings, for instance, lawyers sometimes positioned their clients as addicts in order to help them gain access to basic services and medical care that their clients might want, but which was otherwise not readily accessible. One way to access support services was to admit to a drug 'problem', plead guilty to charges in the drug court and undertake rehabilitation. According to Canadian lawyer Michelle, this was how lawyers often got things done, but it was an approach that had problems:

> When I say many people dispute the model, you know, the whole idea in order to get addiction services, you have to plead guilty to a crime to get services that are otherwise honestly not available here. So, the landscape of how you go about meaningfully addressing these issues in the context of social policy, how they intersect with kind of the criminal justice system, [it's] problematic. Again, we've decided to funnel a whole lot of people through the criminal justice system in order to get them addiction services, which I think ordinarily sensible people might argue would be better served at the front end of the funnel and not the back end of the funnel.
>
> (Michelle, Canada)

Importantly, as this excerpt from my interview with Michelle reveals, these approaches can be ethically fraught. Clients might plead guilty and forego basic legal rights in order to access health services that should otherwise, in her mind, be available to them. Clients who do so are also being encouraged to take up the framework and language of addiction, regardless of whether they understand themselves in that way. I will return to this issue shortly.

In Australia, lawyers were not as explicit about utilising a disability or disease framework. Although lawyers might use the language of disease, disability or illness when describing what they did, their specific approach was often more responsive to perceived challenges.

Take, for example, this excerpt from my interview with Australian lawyer Maxwell:

> *It seems to me* that I'm dealing with a court that believes that drugs are a scourge, that's very clear. So, you have to present your clients in a way that they're willing to accept that what they do is 'wrong'. So, in a sense you want to – you know what the Court likes – so you say, 'Oh yes, drugs are bad', as well, like because *you just have to*. Even though underneath it all, I'm screaming and thinking this is actually a ridiculous concept [...] But before that, [I think] drugs aren't bad, that's why they use them, because they're the only good thing going on in their life. [...] You'd want to have something more. [Laughs]. 'Drugs are good, Your Honour'. Yeah. So, yeah, it's always that tactic to try to see how they're dealing with their 'battle', you know. 'Addiction is very, very ugly, and it's very, very lonely'.
>
> (emphasis added)

Here, Maxwell's strategy is shaped by what he anticipates courts will think of drugs (i.e. that they are a 'scourge'). Because he expects the court to react this way, he believes it is necessary to position drug use as 'wrong'. Implicit in Maxwell's account is a need to downplay any benefits associated with drugs (including pleasure), regardless of his client's lived experience. His clients will also need to account for the decision to take drugs, or otherwise problematise the extent to which those choices were made freely. It is here that we see a shift in nomenclature in Maxwell's account: from drug 'use' to drug 'addiction'. Anticipating that the magistrate will take pity on his client by framing it this way, Maxwell depicts his client as an addict fighting a 'battle', where addiction is 'ugly' and 'lonely'. As he explained:

> having an 'addict' is better than having someone who has used methamphetamines just on a weekend occasionally, and then gone and beaten up their partner.
>
> (Maxwell, Australia)

In other words, 'addiction' is a strategic device deployed to engender sympathy and to justify his client's use of drugs as non-volitional. Thus, there are affective dimensions to Maxwell's thought process and resultant strategy. He is assessing what kind of emotional response is most likely to flow if he positions his client as addicted. As Maxwell later explained, his approach was shaped by the perception that:

> drugs are evil, you know, in the eyes of the court. But if you can say: 'Oh, they are evil, and look how evil they've been to my client, my client has been completely whipped to the gutter with these drugs, and can't get up, but he's trying – he's on this, he's on a methadone program, or he wants to be on there'. You know that's more of a sob story than: 'Oh yeah, my client likes to get on it on the weekend, and Your Honour, and in a state of mania from the methamphetamines, he hit his girlfriend'.
>
> (Maxwell)

In these excerpts, Maxwell draws no distinction between use and addiction. Through his advocacy practices, shaped by what he anticipates will be the best strategy, *use becomes addiction*, in a similar sense to the way that Canadian lawyers described earlier. This is a process that resonates with Fraser, Moore and Keane's (2014) analysis of policy approaches to methamphetamines. There they argued that policy guidelines about methamphetamines frequently collapsed 'dependence and episodic intoxication into a single category – or, at the very least, a blurring of the differences between the two' (2014: 96). Use was frequently equated with harm, with psychosis repeatedly mobilised as a means of sustaining these blurred lines, therein stabilising the object of 'methamphetamine addiction'. Legal practices similarly stabilise use as addiction, driven by perceptions about the strategic utility of addiction concepts and the affective dimensions of those concepts.

## Interpellating 'addicted' subjects

When lawyers decide that alcohol or other drug use is relevant to a proceeding, it becomes necessary to secure the client's cooperation to whatever approach is going to be taken. The need to secure the client's cooperation moves us into the territory of legal ethics, in that lawyers are bound by formal ethical obligations that require them to act only upon the instructions of their client (for more, see Chapter 5). Australian lawyer Erin, who spoke earlier about the importance of constituting drug use as a 'problem' in Family Court proceedings, explained that the process of providing information and securing cooperation often begins at an early stage of the lawyer-client relationship:

> So, it's just sort of saying right at the start, 'Look I'm sorry about this, but *this is what the Court is going to say* and I accept that you don't think [drug use] is a problem, but if we argue that, we'll lose'.
>
> (Erin, Australia; emphasis added)

A similar process unfolds across other areas of the law, including the criminal law. As another lawyer explained, the process of negotiation is sometimes a delicate one, in which lawyers try to convince their clients to think differently about alcohol and other drug use and the utility of framing it in certain ways:

> Well just to say, 'Oh look, from what this summary reads and how it reads, you know *our courts probably will think you might have a drinking problem*. I'm not saying that you do, it's not really my call, but *that's how the judge is going to look at* it, so if you are engaged in counselling or something like that, that will make them feel more confident that they don't need to give you a heavier penalty'. So, *I'll kind of put it on the court* and just say that 'Magistrates, some of them are so conservative', and you know try and push it onto them rather than make the judgment.
>
> (Anne Marie, Australia; emphasis added)

Lawyers sometimes described a 'strategy [of] trying to take the worst-case scenario' (Niamh) when explaining to clients how they might be perceived by a court and why, therefore, they were recommending a particular strategy. Sometimes this meant telling the clients that 'the kids are going to be removed' (Niamh) if they didn't comply with the strategy that they were recommending. As another lawyer, Olivia, explained, lawyers often characterise these strategies as ones that arise from the court, rather than from lawyers themselves:

> I mean you do have to talk with them about how that is going to be. I mean, I think the way the lawyers tend to get around it to some extent is that we talk to clients about *how that might be perceived by a court*, or by the Department of Child Safety.

Of course, this obscures the central role that lawyers claim to play in strategically constituting the addicted subject. Lawyers such as Olivia are in fact centrally engaged in processes of 'hailing' and 'calling', both when they speak with their clients and when they rise in court to speak for *and about* them. Despite this, some lawyers felt compelled to reassure their clients that their own view of them might differ from that of the court. In other words, lawyers deliberately distanced themselves from their own interpellative practices, including processes of anticipation, pondering, hesitation, hailing and calling through advocacy. As Australian lawyer Maxwell explained:

> Yeah, and it goes back to that just doing what the court wants you to say. It's not necessarily what you believe, and there's been times afterwards I've said: 'Look, you know, that was for the court. You know that I think you're a great guy, and all the rest of it, but you have to paint this picture that the court wants to hear in order to get the result that you want to get'.

Here, lawyers' accounts of their practices are striking insofar as they mostly did not engage with or ask clients about what this way of narrating their lives would mean for them. Some lawyers assumed that the process of interpellation was meaningless or just for show: as if utterances made in the courtroom were not 'real' and could be separated out from the client's 'real' life, and thus from how they might come to understand themselves. This discounts the interpellative function of legal discourse, and the potential for clients to 'recognise' themselves as something other than 'great guys' (Maxwell) in these accounts. It also overlooks the multiple other processes that might be set in motion once clients are sentenced, or otherwise dealt with by decision makers. This includes being required to undertake addiction treatment or counselling, parenting courses for their addiction, being asked to undergo (and pay for) regular alcohol or other drug tests, and so on. Subjects who are ordered to undertake treatment or other 'therapeutic' processes such as counselling will likely be exposed to the same discourses they have encountered in law, further instantiating 'addicted' identities (see Fomiatti, Moore, & Fraser, 2017). Whether they are able to resist those interpellative processes or not, these practices raise ethical and political questions about what the law does with subjects. I will explore these in more detail in Chapter 5.

As Suzanne Fraser (2016: 12) has recently shown, policymakers and service providers across Australia and Canada hold internally contradictory views on addiction, marked by a 'dissonance between perceptions of the true complexity and variability of experiences labelled addiction, and the strategic indispensability of the term and its stabilising tendencies'. Lawyers accounts are also marked by a kind of internally contradictory dissonance, albeit of a slightly different kind to the one in Fraser's (2016) study. Lawyers saw addiction as both a constructed, strategic device, largely devoid of meaning, deployed for purely instrumental purposes, *and* a lived, material reality, rich with inherent meaning, that affected the lives of those they represented. For instance, Australian lawyer Iris was at times doubtful that addiction had any intrinsic value, and later described it as 'the underlying cause for bad judgement which leads people to be engaged with the law'; the cause, that is, of 'impaired judgment leading to impulsive actions [and] poor decision making'. In another similar example, Canadian lawyer Amy explained:

> I will use the language of [addiction in] the court if it will help. And if a 'user' needs to be an 'addict' when I am talking to a judge that's okay. That might sound mercenary, but that's what we are doing. We are keeping the state from locking people up because they are sick.

Later, Amy told me that she did not 'see [addiction] as a – it's not a switch, it doesn't just come on and suddenly you are an "addict"'. In other words, Amy here articulates a complex conception of addiction, both as a device imposed upon a 'user' as part of a purely instrumental legal strategy and as a material reality or state of being ('they are sick') that pre-exists legal practices. As Amy noted earlier in this chapter, the notion of addiction as 'non volitional' figures centrally in the *Insite* decision, shaping subsequent legal approaches. I asked her whether addiction had any inherent meaning for her. She explained:

> I recognise that it has meaning for other people and it is helpful to engage in a rhetoric or language that they understand using their words. If I would like my client to not go to jail and it's ok with my client, I will say 'addiction': 'My client stole this thing from this car because she was addicted and she's made some efforts to deal with her addiction and so she should get community service and not go to jail'.

In spite of Amy's seemingly flexible approach, lawyers often assumed and thus re/produced a particular conception of addiction as disease or disability, characterised by lack of agency. Indeed, the process of advocating for clients as addicts often involved performing them as non-agentive, even though lawyers often claimed this was itself a mere trope that did not reflect people's lived reality. As Simone, a Canadian lawyer, explained: 'you go to all drug policy conferences and people will go "it's rational to use drugs, it makes you happy", [but] you never want to have that out there in a legal case' (Simone, Canada). A more appropriate strategy is instead to focus on the seemingly irrational nature of the client's behaviour, and to emphasise that:

> They are making a genuine effort to address their addiction problems and they know what they did was wrong, to be accountable for their actions but also to recognise that it is illness that needs treatment and relapse is part of the recovery.
>
> (Janine, Canada)

Importantly, Janine's language is clearly consistent with a familiar and internally contradictory disease model of addiction, in which the individual addict is positioned as sick, non-agentive and irrational, at the same time as they are responsible, autonomous and agentive. These paradoxical conceptualisations of addicted subjectivity arguably complicate the lived experience of people who use drugs. In this sense, lawyering has a clear potential to stigmatise and marginalise people who use drugs, especially where those approaches involve recourse to and a reiteration of common addiction tropes. It may also be confusing to them, however, particularly where they are involved in multiple legal proceedings across different jurisdictions, and the advice they receive is contradictory or differently tailored to the expectations lawyers have about what different legal realms will require. As Canadian lawyer Yannick explained:

> One is that first of all it puts [the clients] through the wringer, just what they have to go through in order to get benefits. Also often our clients are involved in multiple legal proceedings at the same time and it can be difficult for them to conceptualise that for example, for purposes of disability, we've got to emphasise the effects of the addiction, but maybe in a family law case or a criminal case, they want to de-emphasise that.

There is also a gendered dimension to these processes of interpellation. For some, the anticipated strategic value of addiction is that it has the potential to generate compassion among decision makers, in circumstances where compassion is considered to be beneficial. In the criminal law context, for instance,

> You're trying to engender sympathy from a magistrate and making the magistrate feel like addictions and anything else in their life is beyond their control. And therefore they're less culpable and shouldn't be punished as much.
> (Fern, Australian lawyer)

Fern also believed there was a gendered dimension to this process, however. She explained:

> I think because so many of the decision makers, like judges and magistrates, a lot of judges – less over time – but still the culture is old, white male decision makers. They have a different approach to vulnerable young females coming before them and this sense of 'poor young things' being overwhelmed and 'isn't that tragic?' And wanting to help them or protect them or whatever. Whereas young men won't ever engender that kind of response in them, even if their backgrounds are very similar to the females.

Fern believed that there were thus two types of 'addict' constituted in legal advocacy, being the:

> client [who] presents as a sympathetic substance user versus an unsympathetic substance user. They were driven to it by trauma and they're a victim of family violence and all of these other things then it becomes mitigating, but if they're young, male, single, not a positive factor. Even if there's a history of trauma and other things, there's a lot of judgements.

Here, Fern raises a number of important questions about the potential for gendered assumptions to shape legal outcomes. At its most basic, Fern is concerned about 'unjust' outcomes for men, particularly if men do not have a 'sympathetic' background, or cannot construct a sympathetic narrative regarding their background. She also seems concerned about a kind of injustice for women, though, especially if decision makers impose patronising and paternalistic gendered tropes on the women who come before them. Later, Fern raised concerns about the role of lawyers in these processes. She noted that based on these assessments, lawyers often 'make a call with the particular magistrate or judge to what extent, if at all, you bring up information, whether it becomes a mitigating factor or something that they would see as an aggravating factor'. In other words, regardless of what magistrates *actually do*, lawyers' anticipation about what they *might do* shaped their legal strategy and what they were prepared to say. They might decide to underscore the putative importance of trauma or family violence to their client's 'addiction', or to emphasise the 'tragedy' of their lives in a bid to render them more 'sympathetic'. Assuming women to be better-suited to such narratives, lawyers might avoid performing their male clients in such a way, thereby instantiating ideas about what addiction 'is', where it originates from and how it manifests. Importantly, constituting 'addiction' as an effect of trauma or suffering is not without problems (Seear & Fraser, 2014b; valentine & Fraser, 2008). Similarly, constituting addiction via the feminine can also be problematic, given that processes of mutual co-constitution can render both as abject (see Fraser & Seear, 2011; Fraser & valentine, 2008). There are risks, in other words, when mobilising trauma and gender to 'explain' addiction. The choices lawyers make thus have implications for justice, broadly conceived.

## Problem formulation

In the strategic deployment of addiction language, lawyers do not necessarily require clients to 'prove' that they are addicts, as I noted earlier. Rather, if clients agree to being portrayed as 'addicts' or (come to) understand themselves as experiencing an addiction, and there is strategic utility in framing their use in such a way, lawyers will proceed accordingly:

> if you need access to health services, it doesn't really matter, like we don't interrogate what addiction [is] and how that plays out for people who use drugs.
> (Simone, Canada)

This is not to say that a formal 'diagnosis' of addiction, however achieved, will not sometimes be necessary or useful. In some areas of the law, it might be required. In some jurisdictions, legal rules allow only expert witnesses to give evidence of such (for example in criminal cases in higher courts such as the Victorian Supreme and County Court, practice directions outline who is an 'expert' and how expert evidence is to be given; for more, see Seear, 2017). In many instances, however, and especially in busy tribunals and lower courts, where rules of evidence may be less stringently applied, it was often irrelevant whether a client 'really' had a problem with alcohol or other drugs, or whether they had ever been diagnosed with one. In all likelihood – according to some lawyers – they would be seen to have one, and it was this perception that mattered most of all. This is another important feature of legal practice and its approach to subjects and objects; because it is a problem that you might have a problem, anticipating and responding to such a perception is crucial. In legal practice, lawyers are thus predisposed not only to think about problems in unique ways but to act upon those thought processes in ways that have distinct material consequences. Distinctions between 'perceptions' of drug use and 'realities' of drug use, if indeed such boundaries exist, are not blurred, but immaterial. These processes have implications for clients, who must then respond to the 'problem' their lawyers have identified:

> The best answer most of the time is be seen to do something about it, rather than in denial, rather than sort of argue, 'No, no, no, no, no, it's

not a problem. Not a problem. Not a problem'. That's where that strategic judgement comes in. Maybe it's best just to swallow it a bit and go and see a counsellor. Cut down a bit. It won't do any harm. What harm is it going to do? Well, maybe some [cost]. What harm is it going to do if you cut down a bit? You might save a few bucks. You might just save yourself a bit of grief. And in particular, you should get a better outcome in this particular case that we're dealing with if we can do something about it.

(Vaughan, Australian lawyer)

Several lawyers said that all of this meant it was not necessary for them to know about different theories of addiction, nor for clients to obtain a formal diagnosis of addiction. As Vaughan further explained:

I'm also aware of that debate about addiction theory, about what the latest ideas are about how to approach it. And my view would be the happily ignorant one of: don't know about that. Not my field. I don't care. In a sense, don't care. You've either got a problem or you don't or more importantly you are seen to have a problem or you're not seen to have a problem. And whenever you're seen to have a problem it's a matter then of making some further judgement about whether it's important enough to worry about. Often the answer to that question will be well, yes, it is and let's do something, as in you do something, I'm not. You do something.

There are some parallels with these legal practices, and Moore and Fraser's work (2013), noted earlier. In the present context, that is, law and policy work together to produce addiction. Addiction emerges in part as an effect of constraints in service provision governing health care for people who use drugs, and in part as an effect of legal strategy, with each responding to and shaping the other. Here, as with Moore and Fraser's work (2013), the 'problem' of addiction appears to grow bigger, rather than to shrink. The 'nature' of both drug use and addiction, as well as the putative 'scale' of its role and relevance to social problems and other phenomena (such as criminal offending) are also constituted as effects of legal strategy and advocacy practices.

## Judging addiction and anticipation

Things become especially interesting when we contrast lawyers' accounts of what they do and why they do it with accounts from decision makers. Whereas lawyers' enact addiction in ways they anticipate will accord with decision makers' conceptualisations, some decision makers claim to be constrained in their approaches, with their judgements contingent upon the ideas that lawyers put to them. As one decision maker, Henry, explained:

Look, I have to say [...] magistrates are led, and judges, by lawyers, in the sense that the argument that is before us in an adversarial system is the argument we deal with. The cases that are handed up are the cases we consider. The amendments to law that we're alerted to are the ones that we apply.

Henry went on to say that he was frustrated that more creative and daring arguments were not put to him:

Well, lawyers have a vested – they love the drug laws, the drug wars – because there's an industry. They love the drug-driving laws because it's $1,000 a pop. And say, for example, after Mardi Gras, there's 200 drug-driving matters being listed on one day. So, you know, we average, I think – it's gone down recently – but it was running at 50 a week. That's a lot of money for lawyers [...] Mind you, there are lawyers pushing for changes. [Some lawyers] see it as ridiculous, so.

There is thus a kind of circularity to how addiction is enacted in law. Lawyers constitute alcohol and other drug use and addiction based on their 'feel' for what decision makers will want or conclude, while some decision makers describe their decisions as responsive to what lawyers say and do. Some decision makers were suspicious of these processes, expressing an underlying uncertainty about lawyers' motives and scepticism about whether addiction was 'real', or 'genuine'. As decision maker Quentin said, for instance:

I'm cynical about the claims made about addiction. Mere claims about addiction – you hear them so often, but there's never any proof. It's the easiest thing in the world to say [...] For example, a person might have been sexually abused as a child and then they'll claim later that it explained [the addiction and the] offending. I don't believe it.

(Quentin)

Later, however, Quentin explained that:

If someone is genuinely addicted though, I will give them the benefit of the doubt, as long as they are trying [to get better].

I asked Quentin how he could tell if addiction was 'genuine'. What is a judge looking for in such cases? He said that it was partly based on experience, noting that it is: 'Often your experience in life. I tend to think people who have had more experience in law have a much greater feel for it'. By way of explanation, Quentin offered examples from his own time as a lawyer, before he was appointed to the bench, which he said shaped his thinking:

Years ago, a client I acted for had a pethidine addiction because he'd had migraines. He became addicted and then lost his job, family, wife, started forging prescriptions. There was no doubt he was addicted because he'd never done anything wrong before. I also acted for a doctor who'd experimented with himself with drugs, but regrettably he became addicted. He wanted to plead guilty but the magistrate wouldn't let him because he had so much to offer and because we knew the guy didn't understand how serious it'd been. Luckily in that case, the magistrate was sympathetic.

Quentin went on to say that 'Very rarely does someone come before you, aged 45, with no criminal history, and then have an addiction'. Gendered factors were also important, as was the 'look' of the person appearing before him in court:

Sometimes [you can tell] merely by looking at them. Sometimes it's their criminal histories. With women, you look for a history of prostitution. It's hard to produce a list, because you inevitably leave things off.

In all of these examples, Quentin's understanding of whether addiction was 'genuine' or 'real' depended upon factors deliberately mobilised by lawyers in their practice. These included gendered stereotypes about clients, the affective dimensions of the case and the possibility of 'sympathy', the availability of a narrative which might 'explain' the emergence of an addiction and the extent to which the person appeared willing to address their 'problem'. In other words, Quentin's account of 'genuine' or 'real' addiction closely resembled the account of 'addiction' lawyers claim *they make* through their advocacy practices. Other decision makers offered similar accounts of addiction, or reported addiction as emerging from the narratives lawyers deliver to them. This, in turn, becomes something *decision makers anticipate*. Their work was marked by both particular, familiar accounts of addiction from lawyers, in which the client's 'path is predictable' (Caitlin, judge) and the expectation of the direction in which those accounts would lead. As one decision maker, Linda, explained:

After I'd been sitting on criminal appeals for some years, you'd see the nature of the offence and you'd see the individual and you'd see the age and you'd just think to yourself: I can anticipate what this person's life story broadly speaking is going to be. And it's the sort of scenario that I describe, which is tragic in our society.

Decision makers became used to hearing these narratives so often that 'from the first paragraph of [the client's] story, the writing is on the wall' (Celeste, decision maker).

In other words, decision makers' approaches to addiction are partly an artefact of what is said to them. In this sense, anticipation by lawyers concretises addiction and stabilises its 'effects', while solidifying judicial thinking. These processes fold back into one another, repeatedly, so that it becomes impossible to say who 'initiates' its ontology or how. Lawyers and decision makers share responsibility, in any event, for the version of addiction that is ultimately produced. It is a co-production. Crucially, both parties appear to be unaware of the complex, circular and hermetically sealed nature of these co-constitutive practices, and of their respective (or perhaps more accurately, *joint*) roles in the making of addiction.

## Conclusion

This chapter has explored lawyers' accounts of how alcohol and other drug issues surface in law. Concentrating on how lawyers perceive the relevance of alcohol and drugs to the work that they do, I examined, first, how they assess the potential significance of alcohol and other drugs in different areas of law, what they anticipate decision makers such as judges will think about alcohol and other drugs, and what strategies, consequently, they employ in their work. Importantly, even though alcohol or other drugs may feature in legal settings, 'addiction' often does not often feature in law *unless or until a strategic decision is made to introduce the language of addiction or key concepts of addiction into law.* Lawyers often utilise the language of addiction because they believe it will be beneficial to their clients to do so; for them, addiction is a means, in other words, of tempering the role that 'choice' might be perceived to have played in otherwise problematic conduct (such as criminal offending), and of engendering sympathy in the minds of decision makers. Drawing upon Serge Gutwirth's work (2015) on legality as anticipatory, I argued that lawyers' accounts of their strategies are underpinned by what they anticipate decision makers will think, want or do. Lawyers anticipate that decision makers will disapprove of alcohol or other drug use (especially illicit drug use) when they hear about it, or that they will lack sympathy for people who use such substances, especially where certain subjects (e.g. children) are involved, or where certain offences are concerned. They thus strategise that it will be necessary to frame or explain away use as an addiction. Lawyers also see themselves as 'responding' to legal framings of alcohol and other drugs (and law), as if they pre-exist their practices, at the same time as they constitute themselves as central to the constitution of 'addiction', law and legal content. This accords with Gutwirth's (2015) observation on the paradox of law: seemingly 'already there' and 'not yet stated', as prior to practices and emergent through them. Typically, lawyers constitute addiction as a sickness, chaotic, non-volitional, or in other ways they believe will attract sympathy (thus adjudging sympathy to be important). As these processes make clear, advocacy strategies and practices have potential effects, including the potential to interpellate (Butler, 1997; Althusser, 1971) clients as 'addicts' and stigmatise and marginalise them. Instantiating familiar addiction concepts through their legal practice, lawyers 'perform' addicts in ways that are devalued, as non-agentive and irrational. This is of particular concern, I argue, given that people who use drugs are often already highly stigmatised and marginalised for both their lack of volition and claimed irrationality. One other potential effect of lawyers' advocacy and strategy is that it shapes the nature and scale of the 'addiction problem', through constituting various phenomena as the effects of alcohol and other drugs. Along the way, the scale of the addiction 'problem' appears to grow, rather than shrink (following Moore & Fraser, 2013). This may shape understandings of how addiction works, what it does and how centrally it is involved in social problems. Later in the chapter I explored decision makers' own accounts of addiction and advocacy practices. They accorded themselves less agency than we might have otherwise assumed, noting that their approaches to addiction emerge in response to the accounts lawyers put to them, or that they expect to hear. In this way, anticipation by lawyers concretises addiction and stabilises its 'effects', while solidifying judicial thinking. Lawyers and decision makers ultimately co-produce addiction. Crucially, both parties appear to be unaware of the complex, circular and hermetically sealed nature of these practices, underplaying their respective (joint) roles in the making of addiction.

In law, then, addiction is not simply bound up with strategic imperatives (whether perceived or otherwise), but *forged through strategy*. Addiction's ontology is achieved and maintained through the deployment of multiple strategic, political and affective concerns, as tactical counterpoint to otherwise punitive and dehumanising policies and laws. This also suggests that the ontology of addiction has the potential to be remade through law, *as different strategic imperatives emerge or are anticipated*. But how might this happen? On this it is worth going back to where I began this chapter, and to Serge Gutwirth's work on the nature and meaning of law. Returning to the paradoxical tension between law as 'already there' and 'not yet stated', Gutwirth (2015) wonders: how is it that we can be bound by the 'force of law' if law has not yet been decided? Gutwirth suggests that it is generally because of a 'mode of habit' (2015: 144). On this point, Gutwirth is taking his cue from Latour's observation (2013: 265) that much of what we do is habit, and that of the modes of existence, habit is 'the most common, the most familiar of all'. Interestingly, 'habit' is a phrase with special resonance in the field of alcohol and other drug research. Eve Sedgwick (1993) famously proposed 'habit' as an otherwise to addiction-attribution. She described habit as 'not opposed to [addiction] or explanatory of it, but rather one step to the side of it' (1993: 138). It was 'a version of repeated action that moves, not toward metaphysical absolutes, but toward interrelations of the action – and the self acting – with the bodily habitus, the apparelling habit, the sheltering habitation' (1993: 138). According to this approach, habit is neither compulsion nor free will, good nor bad, 'something to be overcome or [...] automatically embraced' (Seear & Fraser, 2010a: 450; see also Seear & Fraser, 2010b). Taking up Sedgwick's ideas, Fraser, Moore and Keane (2014: 242) call for a remaking of addiction as habit. They also call for a recasting of reality 'itself' as habit, noting:

> What are realities, if we are to accept them as multiply made and remade, performed and enacted, dependent upon repetition for stability, for their very existence, if not habits? This is no idle speculation. If accepted, it would mean a fundamental shift in the status of habit from at best a way of modulating or refining reality, at worst of diminishing or obscuring it, to that of reality's very foundation.
>
> (Fraser, Moore, & Keane, 2014: 23)

The accounts of lawyers and decision makers in this chapter also speak to the centrality of habit to law's ontology. Lawyers are in the habit of anticipating alcohol and other drugs as always already a problem. They are also in the habit of constituting use as addiction. Decision makers are in the habit of expecting lawyers to account for alcohol and drug use in precisely these ways. One lawyer, Fern, even described lawyers' practices as a habit:

> As lawyers, we probably fall into the habit of either using the language described in an Act, so even say in [certain legislation] there's particular terminology about substance use that you use that language when you're talking to a magistrate. So then your habit would be to just use that language all the time.

If lawyers and decision makers co-produce addiction via anticipation, as I have argued in this chapter, then this is at least partly because these anticipatory practices have become habit. Habit is what we do when we 'follow' a well-trodden track; it is what we 'do next […] without reflecting' (Latour, 2013: 265). If we were to reflect on legal practices in relation to alcohol and other drug 'addiction', we might ask: *are these just habits, and are those habits just?* Crucially, Latour (2013) makes the point that without habit, or through different habits, we might make new mistakes or forge new pathways (for good or bad). Because of this it becomes possible to say that law is marked by boundless possibilities, for the making of new mistakes and the carving out of new pathways. For things to be otherwise in law, therefore, a new critical orientation to habituation is needed. This might begin with the recognition that habit plays a vital role in law's ontology, and that habit's potential can be harnessed to generate new realities with regard to alcohol and other drugs.

## References

Althusser, L. (1971). Ideology and ideological state apparatuses (notes towards an investigation). In L. Althusser (ed.), *Lenin and Philosophy and Other Essays* (pp. 127–186). New York: Monthly Review Press.

Bacchi, C. (2009). *Analysing Policy: What Is the Problem Represented to Be?* Sydney: Pearson.

Boyd, S., Murray, D., SNAP, & MacDonald, D. (2017). Telling our stories: Heroin-assisted treatment and SNAP activism in the Downtown Eastside of Vancouver. *Harm Reduction Journal, 14*(27), 1–14.

Butler, J. (1997). *Excitable Speech: A Politics of the Performative*. New York and London: Routledge.

Deleuze, G. (1994). *What Is Philosophy?* New York: Columbia University Press.

Ewick, P., & Silbey, S. (1998). *The Common Place of Law: Stories from Everyday Life*. Chicago and London: University of Chicago Press.

Fomiatti, R., Moore, D., & Fraser, S. (2017). Interpellating recovery: The politics of 'identity' in recovery-focused treatment. *International Journal of Drug Policy, 44*, 174–182.

Fraser, S. (2016). Articulating addiction in alcohol and other drug policy: A multiverse of habits. *International Journal of Drug Policy, 31*, 6–14.

Fraser, S., Moore, D., & Keane, H. (2014). *Habits: Remaking Addiction*. London: Palgrave Macmillan.

Fraser, S., & Seear, K. (2011). *Making Disease, Making Citizens: The Politics of Hepatitis C*. Aldershot: Ashgate.

Fraser, S., & valentine, k. (2008). *Substance and Substitution: Methadone Subjects in Liberal Societies*. Basingstoke: Palgrave.

Gutwirth, S. (2015). Providing the missing link: Law after Latour's passage. In K. McGee (ed.), *Latour and the Passage of Law* (pp. 122–159). Edinburgh: Edinburgh University Press.

Hampel, G., Brimer, E., & Kune, R. (2008). *Advocacy Manual: The Complete Guide to Persuasive Advocacy*. Melbourne: Australian Advocacy Institute.

Johnson, L. D. (2017). Redefining roles and duties of the transactional lawyer: A narrative approach. *St John's Law Review*, *91*, 845–881.

Latour, B. (2013). *An Inquiry into Modes of Existence: An Anthropology of the Moderns*. Cambridge: Harvard University Press.

Latour, B. (2009). *The Making of Law: An Ethnography of the Conseil D'Etat*. Cambridge: Polity Press.

Macfarlane, J. (2008). The evolution of the new lawyer: How lawyers are reshaping the practice of law. *Journal of Dispute Resolution*, (1), 61–81.

Marrati, P. (2006). Time and affects: Deleuze on gender and sexual difference. *Australian Feminist Studies*, *21*(51), 313–325.

McGee, K. (2015a). *Latour and the Passage of Law*. Edinburgh: Edinburgh University Press.

McGee, K. (2015b). Introduction. In K. McGee (ed.), *Latour and the Passage of Law* (pp. 1–16). Edinburgh: Edinburgh University Press.

Moore, D., & Fraser, S. (2013). Producing the "problem" of addiction in drug treatment. *Qualitative Health Research*, *23*(7), 916–923.

Sedgwick, E. (1993). Epidemics of the will. In E. Sedgwick (ed.), *Tendencies* (pp. 130–142). Durham: Duke University Press.

Seear, K. (2017). The emerging role of lawyers as addiction 'quasi-experts'. *International Journal of Drug Policy*, *44*, 183–191.

Seear, K., & Fraser, S. (2014a). Beyond criminal law: The multiple constitution of addiction in Australian legislation. *Addiction Research and Theory*, *22*(5), 438–450.

Seear, K., & Fraser, S. (2014b). The addict as victim: Producing the 'problem' of addiction in Australian victims of crime compensation. *International Journal of Drug Policy*, *25*(5), 826–835.

Seear, K., & Fraser, S. (2010a). The "sorry addict": Ben Cousins and the construction of drug use and addiction in elite sport. *Health Sociology Review*, *19*(2), 176–191.

Seear, K., & Fraser, S. (2010b). Ben Cousins and the "double life": Exploring citizenship and the voluntarity/compulsivity binary through the experiences of a "drug addicted" elite athlete. *Critical Public Health*, *20*(4), 439–452.

valentine, k., & Fraser, S. (2008). Trauma, damage and pleasure: Rethinking problematic drug use. *International Journal of Drug Policy*, *19*(5), 410–416.

## Cases

*Canada (Attorney General) v PHS Community Services Society* [2011] 3 SCR 134 ('*Insite*').
*Providence Health Care Society v Canada (Attorney General)* [2014] BCSC 936.

## Legislation

*Family Law Act* (1975) (Commonwealth).
*Victims of Crime Assistance Act* (1996) (Victoria).

# 3   *Negotiation practices*

## On addiction veridiction and the gendering of agency in family violence and child protection cases

## Introduction

In the previous chapter I examined lawyers' accounts of their advocacy strategies and considered how those strategies were implicated in the content of law and the stabilisation of addiction realities. When reflecting on how addiction surfaced in their work, lawyers spoke primarily about their advocacy practices in adversarial contexts. Their accounts were of their advocacy work as it unfolds in court, in front of magistrates, judges and other decision makers. Of course, lawyers can advocate for their clients in other ways, too, including in less formal settings. In fact, a large proportion of the work that many lawyers undertake is not done in court at all. They spend much time negotiating over the phone – in writing or in person, as well as in court – sometimes with the opponent's lawyer or another party (such as an insurer), and sometimes with the unrepresented opponent directly. This chapter focusses specifically on lawyers' accounts of their approach to negotiation and the role that negotiation practices of varying kinds can play in stabilising addiction 'facts'. In this respect, the focus of this chapter differs slightly from the previous one, in that although it is still concerned with legal advocacy and strategy, it is about how advocacy strategies manifest in the context of lawyers' attempts to reach agreement on issues in dispute, without adjudication or judicial determination. These subtle differences in setting and focus are important, for reasons I will explain. In exploring these practices, I consider how certain 'truths' about addiction materialise and are then stabilised within two areas of law: family violence and child protection. I also focus on an area to date largely ignored in the literature: the gender dimensions of legal addiction-attribution. Using the work of Bruno Latour (2013), in particular his anthropological analysis of scientific and legal 'modes of existence', I explore legal processes of 'veridiction' – or the specific processes by which law distinguishes truth from falsity – associated with addiction and gender. To this end, I examine lawyers' understandings of the role of legal practices of negotiation in the production of addiction as a disease, the related stabilisation of 'addicts' as lacking volition for the violence they perpetrate, or as having heightened responsibility for crimes committed against them, the putative links between alcohol, other drugs and child welfare, and the place of gender in these processes. As my focus in this chapter is on the work lawyers do when negotiating addiction and resolving matters without adjudication, I do not draw upon decision maker data here. Lawyers' accounts of their own roles in negotiations are worthy of attention on their own, because they illuminate in-depth how they encounter addiction in their work and understand truth-making practices to unfold, almost entirely absent of decision makers. Building on previous work on the limits of disease models of addiction, and on the impressions articulated by my participants, I argue that, when brought to bear on issues of addiction, legal processes of veridiction may operate to marginalise and oppress women – particularly when they experience family violence at the hands of men, or where risks to child safety, welfare and well-being are concerned. These processes, rarely subjected to public scrutiny, require more critical analysis, particularly by feminist scholars, socio-legal scholars and experts in alternative dispute resolution (ADR).

## Background

As I noted in the introductory chapter, litigation is a 'key site for the production of the sense or truths of law' (McGee, 2015: 67), but it is not the only one (see Silbey, 2005). Indeed, the vast majority of legal disputes are not resolved through litigation, jury verdicts or judicial pronouncements, but through less formal processes. Estimates suggest that around 2% of contested civil matters initiated in the Supreme Court of Western Australia are resolved by trial (Supreme Court of Western Australia, 2017). According to former Chief Justice of the Supreme Court of Western Australia the Honourable Wayne Martin, this 2% figure is 'fairly typical of Australian courts' (Martin, 2018: 3). Similar estimates can be found in other parts of the world. It is likely that less than 2% of civil disputes commenced in the United States are decided by adjudication by a court, for instance (Murray, 2011), and an empirical study of all class action proceedings filed in the Federal Court of Australia from 4 March 1992 to 3 March 2016 found that only 9.7% of cases proceeded to a post-trial judgement (Morabito, 2016). Lawyers thus spend a great deal of their time trying to resolve matters, and often this work is done outside of court. This work includes negotiating over the phone, in writing or in person, as well as in court. Sometimes these discussions unfold with an opponent's lawyer; sometimes with the unrepresented opponent directly; and sometimes with an insurer, government department, Ombudsman, service provider or corporation.

There are several reasons why most matters resolve without the need for a decision maker's adjudication or determination. In part, it has to do with a growing commitment to ADR (see Weinberg, 2018). ADR is an umbrella term used to describe a set of practices designed to resolve disputes, including mediation and negotiation (see Sourdin, 2016). Buoyed by a realisation that adjudicative processes are more rigid, complex and costly, as well as inaccessible to all but a few, legal practice has undergone significant change, especially over the last three decades, including a shift away from adversarial processes (Weinberg, 2018; Susskind, 2013). These ADR processes are sometimes mandated by courts and sometimes voluntarily undertaken by parties in a bid to resolve disputes. In recent years, courts all over the world have begun to implement processes of 'managerial judging', whereby 'judges or judicial officers [...] control the movement of cases through a court [...] managing the time and events involved' (King et al., 2014: 218). One of the main initiatives of managerial judging is that of 'case management', where the aim is to:

> encourage the parties to identify and reach agreement on as many issues as possible that are not in dispute and thus reduce the length of a trial or obviate it altogether.
>
> (King et al., 2014: 218)

In most instances, this happens via multiple formal meetings (such as mediations) between the parties, where the court has ordered them to try and narrow or resolve the issues in dispute (see Australian Centre for Justice Innovation, 2013). In other instances, these processes happen less formally, as courts invite or encourage parties to reach agreement on key facts and points of law. Although there is a considerable literature on the use of ADR techniques and strategies in numerous areas of law, including many studies that speak to its impact on women (e.g. Field, 2016, 2010, 2006; Alexander, 1999, 1997; Bryan, 1993), little attention has been paid to what negotiation practices do with alcohol and other drugs. This chapter represents an initial attempt to explore these issues.

## Legal veridiction

As I explained in more detail in the introductory chapter, my analysis is inspired in part by Bruno Latour's work, including his book *An Inquiry Into Modes of Existence* (hereafter *AIME*) (Latour, 2013). Latour's book synthesises several decades of scholarship to consider what he terms modernist 'modes of thought' across various 'domains' including law, science, politics, religion and economics. Drawing on Latour's key observation that the law is a 'highly distinctive world' (2013: 54), with its own processes of veridiction – or truth making – I argue that the law has particular ways of establishing truth, allowing non-expert deliberations that frequently rely upon commonsense assumptions, for example about gender. The nature of these processes of veridiction also means that such deliberations remain largely immune to scrutiny. Latour's book is in many respects the culmination of a life's work. Bringing together ethnographic research on science, law and other domains of knowledge and practice including politics and economics, *AIME* is concerned with exploring 'modern' – developed late capitalist – societies, how their institutions understand and make sense of the world, and the claims they make in the process of producing knowledge about fundamental phenomena such as nature, culture and truth. *AIME* builds upon and extends Latour's earlier works, including his first major foray into the study of law, the detailed ethnography of a French administrative court, discussed in earlier chapters (Latour, 2009). This anthropological project has led him to conceptualise these institutions as each positing and working from a particular 'mode' of existence with an 'exclusive manner of demanding truth' (2013: 366). The law, for example, is a 'highly distinctive' (2013: 54) structure that mobilises 'its own [system of] explanation' (2013: 359). In this sense:

> law has its own separate place; it is recognized as a domain that can be isolated from the rest; it has its own force, as everyone would agree; and above all [...] it has its own mode of veridiction, certainly different from that of science, but universally acknowledged as capable of distinguishing truth from falsity *in its own way*.
>
> (Latour, 2013: 358–359; original emphasis)

According to Latour, the law is the only mode of existence 'to have offered [...] resistance to the demand for explicitness' (Latour, 2013: 359–360), in that it is dominated by a simultaneously 'obscure' and 'respectable' method of establishing truth and falsity that is distinct from other modes of veridiction.

In *The Making of Law*, Latour argues that one of the key characteristics of legal processes of veridiction involves the setting of parameters for the issues to be resolved. He explains that judges have specific, defined tasks, and these separate them from other knowledge-makers, notably scientists. Judges, he says, have to:

> answer each of the arguments invoked [...] and *only* those arguments (imagine how horrified a scientist would be if she were asked to address only those questions asked of her by others rather than the hundreds she has asked of herself), to add as few innovations as possible to the knowledge established by their predecessors [...] and to do all of this in such a way as to close the discussion once and for all.
>
> (Latour, 2009: 205; original emphasis)

In this way, legal processes of veridiction are fundamentally distinct from those of science. Law is intended to be an internally coherent total system of logic through which lawyers 'can indulge a power to invent fictions' or to introduce 'constructive solutions', precisely because – unlike science – 'they have no object, or no objectity, to deal with' (Latour, 2009: 240). According to Latour,

> we should distinguish 'objectivity' as the basis of a mood of indifference and serenity as to the solution, from what might be termed 'objectity': the ordeal by means of which a scientist binds her own fate and that of her speech to the trials undergone by the phenomenon in the course of an experiment. Whereas objectivity, paradoxically, pertains to the *subject* and his *interior state*, objectity pertains to the *object* and its peculiarly *judicial* role.
>
> (2009: 236; original emphasis)

Processes of veridiction play out differently between different courts, tribunals and jurisdictions (there are, for example, differences between how lawyers operate in the French administrative tribunal that was Latour's focus in *The Making of Law* and how they operate in the jurisdictions I analyse for this chapter). Nevertheless, there are important connections too. In many areas of law, legal professionals are not simply *empowered* to engage in processes designed to result in constructive solutions, but *required* to do so, as I noted earlier.

The differences between two of modern societies' most influential systems of veridiction (law and science) raise important questions about what happens when they come into contact, as they do more and more frequently where scientific evidence is used in deciding cases. Because of the law's distinctive approach to veridiction,

> When an expert gives evidence in court, the judge and the law take all precautions to ensure that what the expert says should be neither a judgment nor a warrant for judgment, but that it should serve only as a form of testimony which does not usurp the role of the judge.
>
> (Latour, 2009: 206)

In other words, the law takes into account but does not necessarily defer to scientific knowledge, nor to claims of scientific 'objectivity' and 'truth'. Legal officials retain the power to determine for themselves the meaning of specific scientific findings or assertions, to determine their relevance or otherwise to legal issues and to incorporate these assessments into a distinctly legal framework for distinguishing truth from falsity.

As Latour points out, legal conceptualisations of 'truth' and 'falsity' often make little sense to people other than legal experts. Importantly, legal conceptualisations of what is (and is not) legally possible often depend upon whether there is a *legal means* for a particular course of legal action. The existence of a legal 'means' depends upon a combination of obscure and highly specific factors including the existence of legislation, regulations and other legal procedures, rules of evidence and case law, details of how these have or are likely to be interpreted, and how these have been connected (as I explained in Chapter 1). These are factors generally understood only by lawyers. In what follows, I mobilise Latour's insights to consider lawyers' impressions of the contact between science and the law in the specific case of addiction. In particular I examine how lawyers perceive these processes, including their perceptions of the effects of the encounter between medico-psychiatric modes of conceptualising addiction and the legal processes of veridiction noted above. Drawing on interview data with lawyers, I explore how, in their view, debates about the 'nature' of addiction play out in law, focussing on what has to get resolved, how boundaries are drawn, what arguments are invoked in the process of negotiating matters and how all of this concretises both addiction 'problems' and 'solutions'. As I shall explain, lawyers' descriptions of these processes suggest that lawyers have considerable power when setting the parameters of disputes and when stabilising quasi-scientific, quasi-expert accounts of how addiction 'functions'. I argue that legal practices may often reinforce and compound existing inequities, especially for women. Because of this, I argue, these processes demand further attention from researchers, and that more work needs to be done in areas of law other than those I study in this chapter.

## Stabilising the legal 'fact' of addiction as a disease

The starting point for my analysis is the examination of how legal processes secure or stabilise particular notions of addiction. A key exemplar of how this happens is the aforementioned landmark decision of the Canadian Supreme Court in *Canada (Attorney General) v PHS Community Services Society* [2011] 3 SCR 134 (known as the 'Insite' case), which instantiated the idea that addiction is a 'disease'. The case was concerned with the legality of Vancouver's supervised drug consumption facility ('Insite'), a clinic designed to allow on-site consumption of illicit drugs such as heroin and crystal methamphetamine so as to support illicit drug consumers in avoiding blood-borne virus transmission, overdose and other harms that can be associated with illicit drug use. Established as a pilot facility in 2003, Insite operated at first through a special government exemption from the *Controlled Drugs and Substances Act* (1996). By 2007, however, the Federal Minister for Health had decided not to grant further exemptions beyond the middle of 2008. In effect, the operation of Insite would be illegal after that time. Clients and advocates of the facility issued legal proceedings, with the case eventually making its way to the Supreme Court of Canada. The Supreme Court concluded that drug addiction was an 'illness', and that although some addicts retain the 'power of choice', addiction was ultimately 'a disease in which the central feature is impaired control over the use of the addictive substance' (*Canada (Attorney General) v PHS Community Services Society* [2011] 3 SCR 134). Based in part on this assessment, the Supreme Court concluded that the Federal Government's intended closure of Insite limited the rights of 'addicts' under Section 7 of the Canadian *Charter of Rights and Freedoms* 1982, which protects the right to life, liberty and security of the person. The court found that in limiting access to health care services, the government's intentions would have created a risk to the health and the lives of people who inject drugs, thereby depriving them of the protections afforded under Section 7. The facility therefore remained open.

Although scientific evidence about the nature of addiction had been gathered for the case, and was for a time a live issue, these debates were resolved at a critical point of the trial not by scientific experts, nor even the judge, but by the opposing lawyers. As the trial judge, Judge Pitfield, explained, 'The plaintiffs and Canada agree on one thing: drug addiction is an illness' (*PHS Community Services Society v Attorney General of Canada* (2008) BCSC 661 at para. 47). One of my Canadian participants, Erica, was an observer to these proceedings. Erica works across a range of different areas of law, although her work often focusses on disadvantaged and marginalised groups. Her perception of how this agreement was reached aligns with Latour's observations on the way key figures in litigation set parameters about what issues are relevant and need to be re-solved, and the ways courts deal only with arguments invoked before it. As Erica explained:

> I was in court just watching one day and there was something going on in the courtroom that was kind of disturbing, which was that the judge in the course of submissions whenever he used the words 'addiction is an illness' he put like scare quotes around it.
>
> KATE: He actually did that – in gestures?
> ERICA: Yes, he used the bunny ears and so on. You know: 'if addiction is an "illness"' etc, etc. And [the lawyer] rose and said 'You know my Lord, I think everyone in the room is in agreement that addiction is an illness in the way that we are talking about it and my friend [the opposing lawyer] I hope will rise if I'm not right about this'. And so the lawyer for the Crown who is […] a very good lawyer in Vancouver and he is a stalwart lawyer, he's very conservative but he is extremely professional, he was on as an ad hoc lawyer for the Crown, and he rose and he said 'No my Lord, quite right. We all agree that addiction is an illness'. So […  the case was no longer] about that, and from then on everything changed. You know the tone of the room changed, the judge's approach to what they were talking about changed. So when I say that that find-ing was key, it was key […] from the moment that the judge understood what they were after, which was, you know, people who have an illness, their compulsion is, you know, it's not their own volition that they have to do this. It's that they are – for a lack of better word – *infected* with something. You know, his understanding that that was at play was everything to that case.

Viewed from the perspective offered in Latour's analysis, the process Erica de-scribes forecloses debate about the meaning of addiction, resolving it *legally* as a disease. It seems lawyers played a key role in fixing this particular legal truth, in that their agreement alone meant no further argument was needed on the point. Once addiction was defined without contest as a disease, responses to it became subject to particular legal considerations, and from this point onwards the Court's decision-making scope narrowed significantly. In Latour's terms, the legal discussion distinguished 'truth from falsity *in its own way*' and debate was subsequently closed off, 'once and for all'. Like Erica, other participants discussed legal processes by which addiction was, in their estimation, given par-ticular, decisive, meanings in court decisions. Some of these occur in less for-mal ways in legal settings, or with slightly different emphases and implications. In the next section I explore this process, through an analysis of the explana-tions given by one lawyer (Carl) about how debates about addiction play out in family violence negotiations, even before lawyers enter the courtroom. I argue that Carl's account raises important questions about legal understandings of ad-diction, in particular about the connections made between addiction, illness, agency, responsibility, violence and gender. After analysing Carl's account, I turn to the account of two lawyers who work in the field of child protection.

## Veridicting family violence

Carl is a lawyer who works in a wide range of Australian legal realms, but regularly represents female victims of family violence who are seeking protection from their former partners through an intervention order. A family violence intervention order is a civil court order designed to protect a victim of family violence from experiencing further violence. Where granted, an order may have the effect of preventing a person from approaching, harassing or stalking another person, from carrying a gun (if they have a licence to do so) and from perpetrating family violence against them. Family violence is defined broadly under some legislation. In the State of Victoria, for example (which is where Carl is based), family violence intervention orders are governed by the *Family Violence Protection Act* (2008) (Vic). Under Section 5 of that Act, 'family violence' is defined as including:

a   behaviour by a person towards a family member of that person if that behaviour –

    i   is physically or sexually abusive; or
    ii   is emotionally or psychologically abusive; or
    iii   is economically abusive; or
    iv   is threatening; or
    v   is coercive; or
    vi   in any other way controls or dominates the family member and causes that family member to feel fear for the safety or well-being of that family member or another person; or

b   behaviour by a person that causes a child to hear or witness, or otherwise be exposed to the effects of, behaviour referred to in paragraph (a).

The Act provides for the making of both interim (temporary) and final orders. A final order is defined in Section 74 of the Act, and may be made where a 'court is satisfied, on the balance of probabilities, that the respondent has committed family violence against the affected family member [the victim] and is likely to continue to do so or do so again'. Although the exact wording of similar legislation differs in other states and territories, the general principle – that courts may make orders to protect family violence victims from experiencing further violence – is broadly the same.

In my interview, Carl offered details on processes I have already described in this chapter, including those where courts enjoin or order parties to engage in a dialogue in a bid to narrow the issues in dispute or resolve them altogether. This might be understood, in Latour's terms, as an example of lawyers participating in the process of formulating 'constructive solutions' with ontological effects. When one party applies for an intervention order, the presiding magistrate typically begins by setting the application to one side, encouraging the lawyers representing both parties to first try and negotiate an amicable solution. Four main possibilities are available here: the parties reach an agreement for a comprehensive intervention order, they reach agreement for a limited order, they fail to reach an agreement or the victim withdraws the application. If an agreement is reached, the parties go back before the magistrate, set out the terms of the agreement and ask the magistrate to approve it, thus giving it effect as a court order. If no agreement can be reached, the matter will be set down for another court date (a 'mention') where the process is generally repeated. On that occasion, if no agreement is reached, the matter will be set down for a contested hearing, either on the same day or on a later day. Typically, the process of obtaining a final order can take months. One of the main incentives for reaching an agreement is that it negates the need to go back before the magistrate and risk an unfavourable decision. In other words, both parties have pragmatic reasons for accepting alleged facts and finding a way to resolve the dispute without the participation of the magistrate. Naturally, lawyers understand the tensions and incentives at play as these strategic informal discussions unfold. Evidence suggests that a large proportion of these matters are resolved by agreement (i.e. by agreement between the parties, without admissions, with the outcome endorsed by the court) (State of Victoria, 2014–2016). The family violence jurisdiction is heavily reliant upon negotiations and consent to reduce the volume of contested intervention order matters that the court has to deal with (State of Victoria, 2014–2016). Often, the informal negotiations that courts ask the parties to engage in happen in the hallways of the courthouse, or – for those few courts that have them – in 'safe' rooms where victims are seated away from respondents. Frequently, these negotiations occur within earshot of other lawyers, police, court staff and clients waiting to have their matters called before a magistrate. They may be hushed, or rushed. The parties may be in sight of one another. There may be children around. In courts that have safe rooms, a stockpile of toys is available to help keep the children occupied during the long hours of negotiation. There is a television, a pile of magazines. In these spaces it is common to overhear gruesome allegations of family violence, sometimes only hours after an assault has taken place, shared fairly publicly, as an injured victim sits nearby. There is no independent judicial oversight of the nature or content of these discussions. Beyond the professional conduct rules that govern the work of Australian lawyers (explained in more detail in Chapter 5), there are no special rules that govern what can be said and done during these negotiations. In general terms, the parties will be exploring whether they can agree that a family violence intervention order is needed, and if so, what terms it will comprise.

For Carl, addiction (or what is often referred to as 'dependence' in Australia) often plays an important role in these family violence proceedings, especially for lawyers acting for the respondent. As he explains:

> What we know about family violence is that it's very gendered in its nature [… and] the research sort of supports the idea that it's actually about a choice to use violence against partners. The push-back [from other lawyers]

for that is often around saying: 'Well you know the person has addictions, there are drug and alcohol issues, they experienced family violence as a child, it's inter-generational sort of stuff'. So in that sort of context we often see addiction bandied around.

Here, Carl is explaining that because violence has been defined in law as a choice, lawyers acting for respondents often seek ways of casting doubt on their respondents' ability to make choices, turning to addiction to do so. In Carl's view, lawyers' uses of addiction in these negotiations often reproduce very 'gendered approaches and gendered responses' to family violence. In one part of the interview he explained that lawyers often make claims that addicts lack agency:

Yeah, so we have a scenario where we might be looking after Mum. Dad's been removed from the home by virtue of an intervention order. The lawyer comes up and is trying to argue [...] that 'actually he's got an alcohol addiction, he's an alcoholic and he recognises that and as an alcoholic he has limited control over his aggression because of the nature of his addiction. And as a resolution type thing, he has undertaken to get drug and alcohol counselling to address that and on that basis, we [propose that you] withdraw the intervention order or make it a limited order so that he can come back home'. So immediately the cause of the family violence is not actually about him choosing to beat up his wife, it's actually this insidious alcohol addiction that's controlling his behaviour and causing him to beat up his wife.

Carl goes on to offer his assessment of this strategy and its logic:

Now in a family violence context, you know [this] is an absolute misnomer on so many different levels because, for example, if he goes to the pub and gets pissed there because he's an alcoholic, the chances are he doesn't turn around and punch the crap out of everybody that's in his immediate vicinity. He doesn't walk down the street and beat up anyone that looks at him funny. He actually goes home with a belly full of grog and then lashes out against his partner. [... It] only seems to happen when he's in the home, against his wife.

Here Carl's scepticism about the way addiction is 'bandied around' by lawyers extends not just to the way key concepts of the 'disease' (such as agency) are conceptualised but to lawyers' selective approaches to them. Despite his scepticism, however, he must engage in a process of 'unpicking ... those excuses' through negotiations with other lawyers. These negotiations task them with evaluating the veracity of the evidence, if any, of addiction, along with what Carl considers 'very complex' scientific debates about its nature and effects. In many instances these assessments are made by duty lawyers, whose primary role is to assist unrepresented litigants in court, and whose training is, like that of most other lawyers and magistrates, in the discipline of law. In a Latourian sense, these lawyers appear to be playing a key role in establishing and settling 'facts', including medico-legal and scientific 'facts' about the nature and effects of addiction.

Where an agreement is reached (or, in Latourian terms, particular 'truths' are established), as Carl explained, lawyers go back before the court, outlining the nature of any agreement reached (with respect to an order) along with the reasons for it. According to Carl, how this information is received will depend heavily on the individual magistrate:

> Different magistrates have actually talked about getting some anger management, getting drug and alcohol counselling in a family violence context. And on the one hand when you've got a 'Do not drink clause' included [as part of the order], you actually are almost signing up to that understanding that it's actually alcohol that's the problem, not the family violence. But then the flipside is that if the parties have reached agreement on that, then the magistrates are usually reluctant to interfere with that, particularly if there's legal advice all round and it's providing that measure of safety [for the victim].

As with my earlier example of the *Insite* case, Carl's example suggests that officials of all kinds take part in processes of legal veridiction pertaining to addiction. Courts appear to hand over power to legal officials trained only to know what is required in order for legal tests to be satisfied, leaving it to them to establish the 'truth' or 'falsity' of a claim. Significantly, judges may have very limited involvement in the process of evaluating medical evidence and/or the veracity of claims made about the nature and consequences of addiction and key addiction concepts. While these claims are sometimes tested in court (in contested proceedings), much is not. This means that the lion's share of work done to stabilise addiction – to define it, decide what it causes and how it can be addressed – is undertaken by other players hidden from public scrutiny, and with potentially major implications for those affected. Importantly, Carl also notes that even though magistrates have some oversight on the agreements reached, they will be reluctant to interfere if both sides have obtained legal advice. In his experience, magistrates see this as providing a degree of 'safety', perhaps overlooking other ways the agreement might be thought of as unsafe (e.g. for what it suggests about agency and responsibility, for what it leaves unsaid or untouched regarding the 'causes' of violence, and for its practical implications – including allowing the perpetrator back into the home).

Although Carl's view is that lawyers deploy (and ultimately often constitute) 'addiction' in their work in part for strategic reasons, others I interviewed were more sceptical. Alexandra, a Canadian lawyer, believed that lawyers' approaches to addiction were shaped by a combination of factors, including naivety about their clients' lives, a lack of knowledge about drug use and addiction, and moralising about their clients' behaviour. Lawyers often made assumptions and judgements about their clients and the nature of their 'problems'. Speaking about illicit drug use and 'addiction', Alexandra explained:

> I think there is a tremendous class divide between people who use drugs – at least in my neighbourhood – and most lawyers, so if they know anything about addiction it's a drinking aunt or a classmate who does lots of coke. And it's not this unknowing and this space between these two groups isn't restricted to ideas about drug use, but it's caught up in almost Victorian morality about how you conduct your life and what is proper conduct. And I think that's part of the problem and that's part of the harm that lawyers do when they bring ideas from a different place and a different class and pose them in a place where they don't belong. And there's too much lawyers talking to clients and not enough lawyers listening to clients and saying, 'Yeah okay, so you're using this much, what does that mean for you, what impact does that actually have on your life?', instead of thinking, 'Oh how could you possibly use?' I think the same kind of shame that middle class people see around a pregnant women having a glass of wine in a restaurant, it gets amplified by lawyers and imposed on clients.

Alexandra's account raises questions about the making of drug 'problems' and addiction realities as well as the reasons why drug use and 'addiction' concepts are deployed in legal contexts and stabilised in the particular ways they are. In signalling a gender dimension to lawyers' thinking and practices (via the symbolic figure of the pregnant woman), Alexandra also touches upon the potentially gendered nature and effects of lawyers' practices: a subject to which I shall shortly return.

Returning to Carl's account, and the broader literature describing the court processes to which he refers, I see four important questions raised. First, are decision makers such as magistrates, widely thought to be our central legal decision-making figures, involved in the decisions the public believes they are? Second, do the court officials who *are* making decisions have any expertise in, or knowledge of, addiction? Third, is there sufficient independent oversight – even from judges – of the dialogue that unfolds privately between lawyers so crucial to the stabilisation of addiction 'facts' and to the fortunes of victims and respondents? Given much of this decision-making is not open to scrutiny, what do we know of its equity? In particular, how does it withstand scrutiny from the point of view of gender? Although these processes are not inherently gendered and indeed may affect anyone who is understood in a legal setting to be experiencing an addiction, they do have particular implications for women in that it is widely accepted that women experience family and sexual violence at disproportionate rates to men (Department of Families, Housing, Community Services and Indigenous Affairs, 2011). Wherever addiction is used to explain, excuse or mitigate against this violence, women are necessarily disproportionately affected as victims. In this sense, legal conceptualisations of health and illness, and the veridiction processes that allow these conceptualisations to take form as legal 'facts', help shape the way traditionally gendered forms of violence come to be understood, potentially entrenching assumptions about, and material effects of, male violence, agency, the male and female body, and gender along the way.

While these gendered effects could be considered inadvertent, other ways addiction concepts are said to play out in such proceedings suggest that gendered assumptions shape rather more directly than this the arguments made. Carl also spoke of ways key issues of addiction (agency, responsibility and volition) were inverted – with perverse results – where the female victim of violence was the claimed 'addict'. While alcoholism, for example, may serve as a useful defence for male perpetrators of violence,

> 'female alcoholic' will often be used *against her* by an abusive partner. You know: 'She's an alcoholic, she's always drinking, you know she lashes out at me so I lash back'. And in that instance [...] she's turned into the perpetrator or she's actually causing the trouble within the relationship. So then [the court will] question mark whether or not she's a fit parent or whether she needs an intervention order to protect her because she's the one getting pissed and lashing out.

According to Carl, such portrayals may even occur where the female partner is acknowledged to consume alcohol or other drugs as a response to trauma experienced as a result of her partner's violence:

> Research will point to that as her coping mechanism. So her living in a violent relationship and her coping strategy is to drink or take drugs, or whatever. So now suddenly she's a 'junkie', 'alco' mother who is unsafe for the kids to stay with, whereas Dad, who's actually been committing horrendous violence, is an upstanding sober sort of person. The court will more often than not put the kids with Dad at least on an interim basis, which then feeds into the trauma of Mum, which can escalate her drinking or substance abuse.

As with the previous examples, these very serious, complex issues are often first debated outside the formal court setting. Significant, even definitive, aspects of the case are frequently agreed upon there, including those involving key concepts of addiction. According to the accounts given by the participants in my study, then, it appears that lawyers and the processes in which they are engaged play a vital 'veridicting' role in relation to drug use and addiction, and in the process to related concepts such as agency, responsibility and culpability.

## Veridicting child protection

The second example I analyse for this chapter comes from the field of child protection law. It involves a very different set of concerns and practices to those described by Carl, but once again it highlights the work of figures other than judicial decision-makers, both in stabilising 'addiction' and addiction concepts and in initiating actions to address its legal 'significance'. Niamh was a lawyer who undertook publicly funded work for disadvantaged people in a regional centre, several hours from any of Australia's major cities. The area she worked in was socially and economically disadvantaged, with many of its residents living in poverty. Much of her work was in the field of child protection. In this work, Niamh typically represented poor mothers whose children were being taken away, or were at risk of being taken away by a government department, because of concerns for the child's welfare. In New South Wales, where Niamh worked, the protection of children was governed by the *Children and Young Persons (Care and Protection) Act* (1998). The Act details a series of circumstances in which a department might intervene to protect the safety, welfare or well-being of a child. These include where a child or young person is at risk of significant harm. The meaning of this is defined in Section 23 of the Act, as follows:

1   For the purposes of this Part and Part 3, a child or young person is 'at risk of significant harm' if current concerns exist for the safety, welfare or well-being of the child or young person because of the presence, to a significant extent, of any one or more of the following circumstances:

   a   the child's or young person's basic physical or psychological needs are not being met or are at risk of not being met,

   b   the parents or other caregivers have not arranged and are unable or unwilling to arrange for the child or young person to receive necessary medical care,

   b1   in the case of a child or young person who is required to attend school in accordance with the *Education Act 1990* – the parents or other caregivers have not arranged and are unable or unwilling to arrange for the child or young person to receive an education in accordance with that Act,

   c   the child or young person has been, or is at risk of being, physically or sexually abused or ill-treated,

   d   the child or young person is living in a household where there have been incidents of domestic violence and, as a consequence, the child or young person is at risk of serious physical or psychological harm,

   e   a parent or other caregiver has behaved in such a way towards the child or young person that the child or young person has suffered or is at risk of suffering serious psychological harm,

   f   the child was the subject of a pre-natal report under section 25 and the birth mother of the child did not engage successfully with support services to eliminate, or minimise to the lowest level reasonably practical, the risk factors that gave rise to the report.

The Act establishes a system for reporting concerns about a child or young person's safety, welfare or well-being (e.g. Sections 24 and 27), along with a process for assessing such a report, and acting upon it. The department has a range of options once a report has been made. It may do nothing, or it may remove a child or young person, including on an emergency basis and without a warrant (Section 43 of the Act). It might arrange for the family to receive support services, it may develop a 'care plan' designed to meet the needs of the child or young person, or it may develop a 'parental responsibility contract' with the primary caregivers (Redfern Legal Centre, 2016: 218). This may include requirements for the caregiver to attend alcohol or other drug counselling or treatment, or to undergo alcohol or other drug testing.

Niamh described a lot of her work as 'early intervention', which is work that takes place 'prior to the removal of the children, negotiating with the department about care plans' for children who might be at risk. Another lawyer I interviewed (Vaughan) did the same kind of work as Niamh. As Vaughan explained, much turned on the initial assessment of the department regarding what needed to be done.

> Typically in a care matter, the kids are removed by the department [...] But within a week or two of the case beginning, you've got a pretty clear idea about what the problem is with the family from the department's point of view [...] So, the department in a care matter [...] would/should/does provide pretty early on, within the first few weeks, a summary of what they think should be done. A summary of the plan [of required action] basically.

At this stage, lawyers often learned that the department had concerns about their client's consumption of alcohol or other drugs. In Niamh's experience, alcohol or other drug issues might intersect with or be accompanied by family violence. On occasion, a woman's (violent) former partner might have notified the department about the mother's use of alcohol or drugs. This phenomenon is widely documented in Australia and elsewhere and can be an extension of family violence (Department of Child Safety, Youth and Women, 2018) or a form of 'legal systems abuse' (Douglas, 2018) in and of itself. Niamh described a typical case she might be dealing with in this way:

> Dad's violent, has been hitting her, so mum's caring for the kids. The department will be involved because the mother is failing to protect the kids from the violence, because dad keeps turning up unexpectedly and mum also has an addiction problem. So in the care and protection field, it generally is the department removing the children from mum's care as a result of her: A, failure to protect [the children from the father's violence], and B, her failure to deal with her addiction problems in an appropriate manner. [Or] what the department considers an 'appropriate manner'. And normally because she's too overwhelmed and stressed and her addiction to alcohol is her crutch and gets her through the day.

Crucially, much turns, in Niamh's experience, on what *the department* deems will be an 'appropriate manner' to deal with one's alcohol and other drug problems. In other words, the department plays a major role in assessing what kind of a 'problem' the client appears to have, whether it should be treated or how it should be dealt with, and how all of these matters intersect with the legal test for 'risk' (e.g. what degree of risk the consumption of substances poses to the child). Adjudging Niamh's client to be an 'addict', the department might then ask the mother to undertake rehabilitation.

Decisions made by the department as described by Niamh and Vaughan are of a 'quasi-expert' nature (Seear, 2017), and involve a kind of 'hybridisation' of medico-legal power (following Vrecko, 2009). As with Carl's work on family violence, putatively medical or scientific decisions are being assessed by legal figures, and the law allows for these matters to be decided 'in its own way' (Latour, 2013: 358–359). Of course, unlike Carl's example, lawyers are not always involved at an early stage, and thus it is the department that does the crucial, initial work of 'veridicting' addiction. This is a distinct kind of legal veridiction in that it is performed by departmental employees who may be bureaucrats or lawyers rather than decision makers. Lawyers representing parents often become involved soon after, however, and can play a vital role in further shaping addiction. How this happens is itself revealing, according to Niamh. On occasion, the initial assessments made by the department introduced new problems and challenges. One way this happens is when the department makes an assessment of an alcohol or other drug 'problem' and how it should be addressed, and this is at odds with the assessments of alcohol and other drug service providers. She explained the process in this way:

> So if your client's been a victim of [domestic violence] and you want the other party to go to a program [they can easily go to an] anger management course. We have an accredited specialist, men's behaviour change program here. It's 32 weeks' [duration]. [But it is different if we] shift that to what we need with substance abuse and addiction issues [...] because it's been a real shock to me with different programs, who they'll admit, who they won't. So you send your client off to such and such and it's like, 'Oh no, they said I can't go because I'm not addicted enough'.

In cases Niamh has dealt with, local rehabilitation and treatment providers might not consider episodic drinking to be an addiction. According to Niamh, 'binge drinking: you won't get in. So you have to be what they consider to be "an addict". So what is that, I'm not sure'. Adjudged by the department to be 'addicts' in need of rehabilitation, but considered by service providers not to be, Niamh's clients are deemed ineligible for the service. There is a clash, in other words, between medico-psychiatric modes of conceptualising addiction and legal-bureaucratic ones. Rather than this being a simple 'difference of opinion', I argue that this is a manifestation of different modes of existence and their distinct concerns and methods for determining 'truths'.

This is where negotiations over what course of action is required become especially important. Ideally, if Niamh is involved in the case from an early point in time, and becomes aware of these systemic challenges, she can advocate for her client. She explained:

> So even if the children have been removed, you have the opportunity to ring [the department] and say, 'Look, might as well document it and write a letter confirming it. The client went to [the rehabilitation or treatment facility] where you wanted them. They want to go to rehab but [the rehab] said she's not eligible. This is what we're proposing she does: A, B, C, and D. Would you agree? Please respond within 14 days.' So you get a response back, tying [the client] into an alternative proposal.

In this account, Niamh and the department *together* determine what course of action is needed to treat the 'problem' her client has. This may involve agreeing upon another kind of alcohol or other drug treatment, with a different philosophy, approach or conceptualisation of 'the problem'. An agreement is often reached for clients to be sent off to Alcoholics Anonymous, even though, in Niamh's experience, 'not everyone is great with AA', and even though 'that doesn't work for a lot of women [...] certainly Aboriginal women'. AA nevertheless becomes the solution to an eligibility/systems problem, seemingly without regard for what this shift to a new treatment modality might mean for clients. As Karasaki et al. (2013: 195) remind us, 'existing theories or models of addiction vary significantly in their underlying concepts'. They point out that different treatment modalities thus employ different ideas about how addiction works and what it is, including whether it is shaped by irrational thought processes or behavioural patterns, maladaptive responses to unconscious emotional needs, abnormalities in the brain's structure or the product of environmental and contextual factors, among other things. The 12-step programme at the heart of AA has a strong religious component, moreover, that may be at odds with the personal belief system of some clients. More than this, however, the treatment modality taken up concretises particular ways of understanding habitual alcohol or other drug use. In this sense, the work that lawyers and departmental figures do together has the potential to shape how individuals understand themselves and their supposed 'problems'.

As with Carl's account of family violence work, Niamh's account of child protection demonstrates that law is a 'highly distinctive world' (Latour, 2013: 54) with an ability to manufacture its own addiction 'truths'. When individuals undergo treatment, for example, it may be that treatment was decided upon or negotiated between public servants and lawyers, based on their assessment of 'the problem' and what the problem 'requires'. When problems emerge, lawyers work to develop what Latour calls 'constructive solutions' (2009: 240). Law is undeterred by the major disjuncture between legal and scientific accounts of problems. It does not prompt a crisis, nor wholesale reassessment, but a recalibration. A fresh assessment is made, and new and different 'truths' about alcohol and other drugs are stabilised. Lawyers and the department do this work together. This process of reassessing and remaking calls to mind Latour's observations on the apparent 'contrasts' between law, science and judging. He explains:

> If *res judicata* are not to be (mis)taken for the truth, the point is not that this justifies some form of cynicism, but that it has *better things to do* than mimic or approximate to the scientific truth: it has to produce justice, and declare the law, in accordance with the existing state of the texts, taking into account the precedent, with no arbiter other than the judges, who have no one to judge for them.
>
> (2009: 240–241; original emphasis)

Even though Latour is here speaking of processes of judicial decision-making, I argue that the same points hold for processes of legal negotiation. In other words, where apparent tensions between law and science (or medicine) emerge, as in the example offered here, the law does not always try to reconcile them. It matters little that the department's initial assessment was not endorsed by the service provider. Law has 'better things to do', which include making its own assessments of what alcohol and other drug use means, and how it should be addressed under the legal mode. Here again, then, lawyers describe themselves and other non-judicial figures as centrally involved in decision-making and in stabilising facts about addiction. As with Carl's account of family violence, lawyers play a 'veridicting' role in relation to alcohol and other drugs.

Importantly, this work also has implications for agency and responsibility, and, in the accounts of both Niamh and Vaughan, has some troubling gendered dimensions. Niamh has already flagged some of these gender dimensions in her account of how child protection cases sometimes play out. Women were often enjoined, we will recall, to take steps to address their alcohol or other drug consumption *as well as* the violence perpetrated against them. They were required to protect their children from violent partners and to protect the child against the risks that emerge from their substance use. In both instances, risk adheres to the woman. This seemingly disproportionate attribution of agency was not always or only due to decisions made by the department, but could also be secured through negotiations between lawyers and the department about what was 'needed' to protect the child. In other words, lawyers' negotiation strategies concretise links between alcohol and other drugs, family violence, agency, responsibility and risk, in ways that impact intensely on the lives of women, men and children. I asked Niamh what would happen if there was an expectation on the part of the department that a client undertake a specific kind of alcohol and other drug programme (such as in-patient rehabilitation) and her client was unable to because she was deemed ineligible. Niamh's answer was simple. Unless the client could adequately explain away her 'failure' to follow the course of action initially recommended, or unless her lawyers could negotiate a satisfactory resolution, she would be deemed a risk to her children. Simply put, Niamh explained: 'They lose their kids'.

Vaughan's account of child protection also raised vital questions about the way that agency and responsibility was allocated between women and men. Mirroring Niamh's account of child protection care plans, he explained that:

> The key issue in [this work] is the realistic possibility of restoration of a child to their parent or parents. And the realistic aspect of it is judged against some kind of real reality, not the parents' view of reality. And in many cases [...] the department has identified two, three, four, five issues, do something about that, do something about that, do something about that. And then [the client has] got some kind of footing where they can say to [the department], 'Well, I've done everything they said I should. I've done parenting courses. I've left my violent partner. Been to some support around domestic violence counselling in a sense of avoiding future violent relationships as best I can. I think I know what I'm looking for now maybe. And I've also dealt with my drug use. I've either cut down or cut it out altogether'.
>
> (Vaughan, Australian lawyer)

Two things are striking about Vaughan's account. The first is the distinction he draws between the 'real reality' of what is required and the 'parent's view of reality'. He draws this distinction between 'reality' and 'perception' at the same time as he acknowledges the department's crucial role in determining such a 'reality'. In other words, even as Vaughan reflects upon how processes of addiction veridiction play out, including the powerful position departmental figures and lawyers are in to constitute addiction realities, he positions those realities as prior to veridiction practices. The second and more striking aspect of this account is how the onus to take action plays out in Vaughan's experience; the victim of violence is enjoined to leave her partner, learn how to avoid violent relationships in the future, and expected to reduce her substance use. Importantly, both Vaughan and Niamh believed that women's consumption of alcohol and other drugs (their 'addiction') was a consequence of the violence to which they had been subjected. As Niamh explained:

> A lot of my clients who have been victims of domestic violence have addiction problems as a result I'll say, but that's just my observation. To deal with the violence they often have secondary addiction issues themselves.

In other words, 'addiction' was not, for Niamh, a word 'bandied around' (as it was for Carl, whose work was discussed in the previous section). It was not a device cynically deployed by lawyers for strategic purposes. Niamh saw addiction as both a lived reality and a consequence of the abuse that many of her female clients had experienced. I do not discount the possibility that this is the case for some women. My point here is not to minimise, challenge or trivialise women's lived experiences of family violence or the realities of alcohol or other drug use. The point, rather, is to draw attention to the tensions and paradoxes in lawyers' accounts of the work they do. As we saw in Chapter 2, lawyers simultaneously cling to an account of addiction as 'real' at the same time as they suggest addiction is an effect of material-discursive practices. Moreover, Niamh's suggestion that addiction is an effect of violence does not flow on to the care plans she sees the department impose, nor to the plans she is able to negotiate with them. In her experience, that is, it matters little where addiction 'comes from'; it matters only once it is deemed to exist. Lawyers are not motivated, nor perhaps empowered, in their negotiations with departments, to examine such questions. If addiction is adjudged to be at work, it is something the 'addict' is now obliged to address. These accounts are particularly troubling for how they see law as distributing agency and responsibility for risk and violence. These practices appear to have enormous potential to disadvantage women, rendering them as central to phenomena including family violence, and as responsible for protecting themselves (and others) against it. Even where lawyers instantiate addiction as an effect of abuse for which women bear little or no responsibility, their strategies enjoin and responsibilise women. These accounts thus raise questions – at the very least – about the extent to which lawyers and others they negotiate with are alert to the gendered implications of the work they do, and whether other ways of attributing blame and distributing agency are possible.

## Further reflections on gender

Several participants were concerned about the gender implications of the addiction-attribution practices I have described in this chapter. These included Erin, whose work was in Australian women's rights, primarily in the areas of family law and family violence. According to Erin, these processes (and in my terms, the modes of legal veridiction they entail) posed major 'ethical' dilemmas for lawyers, especially where alcohol and other drug consumption or addiction was being asserted and directly tied to questions of witness credibility, agency and legal responsibility or moral culpability for gendered violence. As she explained:

> It's almost like the thing we talk about with sexual assault, that sort of blaming victim thing, comes in to play. And so, being a women's lawyer, I don't want to encourage that, but then also the client is determined they don't want the intervention order because they were drug or alcohol affected also. That is difficult and I don't know what the answer is to that.

Other lawyers I interviewed raised related concerns, especially where the implication of that is that violent conduct is compulsive. For example, Australian lawyer Melanie feared that existing legal processes could have far-reaching implications for forms of sexual violence that traditionally impact on women more than men:

> I do find it quite perplexing, just the notion of being enslaved to behaviours [...] because for a compulsive paedophile, they are enslaved to those behaviours, that's a sexual preference that's grown up from, usually, adolescence. And I wonder, it's funny, just the judgment calls that we put on particular

behaviours and 'this is controllable' and 'this is deplorable' and 'this is repugnant', whereas 'this is an addiction'. And I wonder whether that's – I'm just thinking out loud really – but I just wonder whether that's been looked at.

Melanie's question is well founded. More research is certainly needed to establish how common the processes of veridiction she describes are, and in what settings and with what effects.

Speaking in a very different context – the rights of sex workers – Canadian lawyer Erica also raised concerns about the use of addiction in legal processes, in particular, the use of claims that addiction is a disease to justify coercive and paternalistic policies, or to deny the rights of women. She argues that since the *Insite* decision, conceptualisations of addiction as a disease have been combined in Canadian legal settings with questions about sex workers' agency to launch renewed criticism of the practice and a push to ban it:

> the idea is that the 'illness' of addiction removes your actual ability to make choice. The same idea is imposed on sex workers not just because of the fact that many are addicted in the group of people that I work with, but just by [virtue of] the idea that nobody could possibly choose doing this work.

Here, prevailing understandings of drug use, addiction and sex work appear to converge to shape gender and agency in ways that pose significant issues for women's rights. We know very little about how these processes of veridiction unfold, nor how they might differ across jurisdictions, different legal settings and different areas of law. It is also unclear how conscious lawyers and other key stakeholders (such as departmental figures or others with capacity to participate in the veridiction of addiction) are aware of these implications. As in my previous examples, given the significant stakes here, more research is needed on how these practices play out.

## Conclusion

This chapter has aimed to illuminate the role of legal processes of veridiction in defining and responding to addiction, and to consider the effects of these processes. Focussing on lawyers' accounts of negotiation practices in law, I explored how they understand their own role in enacting addiction as a disease, and the gendered implications of these enactments. Using Bruno Latour's (2013) work on modes of veridiction, I argued that lawyers appear to play a very central role in stabilising addiction 'facts' and establishing legal 'truths' about addiction. These legal 'truths' may differ in key ways from scientific truths about addiction given legal requirements for establishing facts differ significantly from scientific requirements and priorities. I also argued that there were gender implications of these processes, observing that legal practices of veridiction risk securing, reinforcing and perpetuating gendered inequalities for women. Specifically, the particular ways the law establishes truth (its processes of veridiction) allow non-expert deliberations that can reproduce existing inequitable relations between men and women. These deliberations are by their nature largely hidden from scrutiny, because they unfold as negotiations. According to my participant accounts, negotiations and conclusions such as these are commonplace in law, making lawyers just as instrumental as judges in defining addiction, its putative links to family violence and child protection, and in gendering agency and responsibility. Yet their work is less well known and less invigilated. In neglecting this apparently key role for lawyers, important opportunities for reform of legal practices and processes might be being missed. This is a significant issue in need of attention.

I want to emphasise that I do not discount the diversity of effects that these legal processes produce, including the beneficial implications they have for individuals labelled 'addicts'. This is a process I have analysed at length elsewhere (see Seear & Fraser, 2014). Yet it is essential to acknowledge the potentially adverse implications such processes can have, and the disproportionate risks they pose for women. Here, I identify five key ways legal processes that stabilise consumption as addiction and/or addiction as disease can impact disproportionately upon women (while acknowledging that there may be more, and while acknowledging that these can impact on men). These are that:

- Alleged perpetrators can be said to lack agency and/or to have *diminished* responsibility or culpability for violence they commit, including family violence and sexual violence against women;
- Victims can be said to exercise agency and/or *increased* responsibility or culpability for the acts of violence committed *against* them, including family violence;
- Victims are constituted as lacking agency and are unable to make rational decisions in their own best interests, justifying potentially paternalistic policies concerning the rights of women to make decisions about their own bodies;
- Individuals may be enjoined to address their 'addictions' in ways that are difficult or impossible, putting them and their families at heightened risk of stress, anxiety and separation; and
- The steps individuals are enjoined to take distribute agency and responsibility for social phenomena in ways that may be unnecessary, lacking in efficacy, counterproductive or inequitable.

In identifying these tendencies in the interview data I collected, I have drawn attention to the central role of legal processes of veridiction in them, noting that legal ways of establishing truth often proceed in the absence of expertise on central issues, and do so in ways that render them inaccessible to scrutiny. As I have noted, this chapter draws primarily upon accounts from lawyers about their roles in addiction veridiction, and their perceptions of events and motivations. I recognise that these processes might be more complex and nuanced than perceived by my participants. However, the broad structures on which these accounts are based, the opportunities and/or legal requirements for alternative forms of dispute resolution, the role of lawyers in deliberations and their lack of visibility are well established, as are central empirical matters such as the disproportionately gendered incidence of family violence and the use of child protection processes to further abuse of women. Together, these accounts and the broader circumstances in which they are said to have occurred warrant further research. Indeed, in 2015, the Victorian government instigated a landmark Royal Commission into Family Violence. The Commission handed down its final report in March 2016 (State of Victoria, 2014–2016). That report contained 227 recommendations for comprehensive reforms to Victorian laws, policing practices and much more. One of those – Recommendation 77 – dealt specifically with negotiations for family violence intervention orders. The Commission noted that little was known about the process of negotiation in these matters. These processes carry inherent risks, not simply because there may be imbalances in power and capacity as between the parties but also because the very matters that are the subject of discussion and negotiation are allegations of family violence. One of the Commission's recommendations was to explore how negotiation processes unfold and might be improved. I suggest that there is a need for research in the form of direct observation of legal processes, if access to them can indeed be secured, along with an exploration of lawyers' strategic decision making processes and motivations in the construction and deployment of addiction concepts through negotiations in their work.

The deployment of addiction concepts in lawyers' work raises broader ethical questions, too, especially given the potential for processes of addiction veridiction to have disproportionately severe consequences for women. I explore ethical issues in more detail in Chapter 5. Questions must also be raised about whether decision makers should play more of an active oversight role in cases decided by negotiation and if they do, what role they should play and what questions need to be asked. Finally, it bears repeating that in this chapter I have explored only two examples of the ways that lawyers stabilise addiction 'truths' in their work. As I noted earlier, the vast majority of work that lawyers do takes place outside of court, and the overwhelming majority of legal disputes are settled without judicial adjudication or determination. In this sense, the accounts I have presented in this chapter only begin to scratch the surface of law's veridicting of addiction. Those veridicting practices may produce other effects (i.e. effects pertaining not to family violence nor child protection but to other 'problems' and phenomena). It is vital they be traced, too, for what they enable and for what they foreclose.

## References

Alexander, R. (1999). Family mediation under the microscope. *Australasian Dispute Resolution Journal*, *10*, 18–29.

Alexander, R. (1997). Family mediation: Friend or foe for women? *Australian Dispute Resolution Journal*, *8*, 255–266.

Australian Centre for Justice Innovation. (2013). *The Timeliness Project*. Clayton: Monash University.

Bryan, P. (1993). Killing us softly: Divorce mediation and the politics of power. *Buffalo Law Review, 40,* 441–525.

Department of Child Safety, Youth and Women. (2018). *Domestic and Family Violence and Its Relationship to Child Protection, Practice Paper, April.* Brisbane: Queensland Government.

Department of Families, Housing, Community Services and Indigenous Affairs. (2011). *The National Plan to Reduce Violence against Women and their Children 2010–2022.* Canberra: Department of Families, Housing, Community Services and Indigenous Affairs.

Douglas, H. (2018). Legal systems abuse and coercive control. *Criminology and Criminal Justice, 18*(1), 84–99.

Field, R. (2016). A call for a safe model of family mediation. *Bond Law Review, 28*(1), 83–88.

Field, R. (2010). FDR and victims of family violence: Ensuring a safe process and outcomes. *Australasian Dispute Resolution Journal, 21,* 185–193.

Field, R. (2006). Using the feminist critique of mediation to explore 'the good, the bad and the ugly' implications for women of the introduction of mandatory family dispute resolution in Australia. *Australian Journal of Family Law, 20,* 45–78.

Fraser, S. (2016). Articulating addiction in alcohol and other drug policy: A multiverse of habits. *International Journal of Drug Policy, 31,* 6–14.

Fraser, S. (2015). A thousand contradictory ways: Addiction, neuroscience and expert autobiography. *Contemporary Drug Problems, 42*(1), 38–59.

Karasaki, M., Fraser, S., Moore, D., & Dietze, P. (2013). The place of volition in addiction: Differing approaches and their implications for policy and service provision. *Drug and Alcohol Review, 32*(2), 195–204.

King, M., Freiberg, A., Batagol, B., & Ross Hyams, R. (2014). *Non-Adversarial Justice* (2nd edn). Australia: Federation Press.

Latour, B. (2013). *An Inquiry into Modes of Existence: An Anthropology of the Moderns.* Cambridge: Harvard University Press.

Latour, B. (2009). *The Making of Law: An Ethnography of the Conseil D'Etat.* Cambridge: Polity Press.

Martin, W. (2018). *Alternative dispute resolution – A misnomer?* Speech delivered at the Australian Disputes Centre, Perth, 6 March.

McGee, K. (2015). On devices and logics of legal sense: Toward socio-technical legal analysis. In K. McGee (ed.), *Latour and the Passage of Law* (pp. 61–92). Edinburgh: Edinburgh University Press.

Morabito, V. (2016). *An Empirical Study of Australia's Class Action Regimes* (Fourth Report, August 2016). Retrieved from: https://papers.ssrn.com/sol3/papers.cfm?abstract_id=2815777.

Murray, P. L. (2011). The privatisation of civil justice. *Australian Law Journal, 85*(8), 490–503.

Redfern Legal Centre. (2016). *The Law Handbook: Your Practical Guide to the Law in New South Wales* (14th edn). Sydney: Thomson Reuters.

Seear, K. (2017). The emerging role of lawyers as addiction 'quasi-experts'. *International Journal of Drug Policy, 44,* 183–191.

Seear, K., & Fraser, S. (2014). The addict as victim: Producing the 'problem' of addiction in Australian victims of crime compensation laws. *International Journal of Drug Policy, 25*(5), 826–835.

Silbey, S. (2005). After legal consciousness. *Annual Review of Law and Social Science, 1,* 323–368.

Sourdin, T. (2016). *Alternative Dispute Resolution* (5th edn). Rozelle: LBC Thomsons.

State of Victoria. (2014–2016). *Royal Commission into Family Violence: Report and Recommendations*, Parl Paper No. 132.

Supreme Court of Western Australia. (2017). *Annual review 2017.* Retrieved from: www.supremecourt.wa.gov.au/_files/Annual_Review_2017.pdf (accessed 19 February 2019).

Susskind, R. (2013). *Tomorrow's Lawyers.* Oxford: Oxford University Press.

Vrecko, S. (2009). Therapeutic justice in drug courts: Crime, punishment and societies of control. *Science as Culture, 18*(2), 217–232.

Weinberg, J. (2018). Keeping up with change: No alternative to teaching ADR in clinic. An Australian perspective. *International Journal of Clinical Legal Education, 25*(1), 35–78.

## Cases

*Canada (Attorney General) v PHS Community Services Society* [2011] 3 SCR 134.

*PHS Community Services Society v Attorney General of Canada* (2008) BCSC 661.

## Legislation

*Children and Young Persons (Care and Protection) Act* (1998) (New South Wales).

*Controlled Drugs and Substances Act* (1996) (Canada).

*Family Violence Protection Act* (2008) (Victoria).

# 4 *Sentencing practices*

## On assembling 'alcohol effects' and the 'Aboriginal community' in criminal law

### Introduction

Why do some people commit crimes? And how do we understand a violent crime when alcohol and other drugs are involved? What is the link, if any, between 'addiction', 'alcoholism' and violence? In the last chapter I looked at some of these issues, through a focus on how some lawyers conceptualise the links between addiction, family violence, child protection and risk, and stabilise them in their work. Of course, the relationship between alcohol and other drugs and violence is dealt with in other areas of law, too. Each of these areas of law is concerned with different questions, subject to different legislative provisions, procedural minutiae and other legal factors (including relevant precedents). All of these factors shape what kinds of legal questions are being asked about violence, alcohol and other drugs and help shape how addicted realities are constituted. The area of law that deals most explicitly and in the most depth with the putative links between violent crime and addiction is the criminal law. As I will explain, the process of determining guilt and/or sentencing an offender necessitates that courts try to make sense of why the crime was committed, how culpable the offender is, whether they can be rehabilitated and how they – and the wider community – can be deterred from committing similar crimes into the future. This process results in an amalgamation of multiple factors that are thought to be relevant to the criminal act, including an analysis of the behaviour and movements of the victim, the relationship between the victim and offender, the geotemporal dimensions of the crime and the personal history and other life circumstances of the offender. In the process of assembling this information, choices are made about a range of matters, including how the 'social context' within which the offender was brought up might have shaped their agentic capacity, and how geotemporal dynamics shaped the crime. As I will explain, Australian courts have long taken the view that additional factors might be relevant when sentencing Indigenous offenders, given Australia's colonial history and its ongoing legacy. There are also special concerns about the role of alcohol and other drugs in Indigenous communities and how these might interact with historical disadvantage in producing violence. The process of assembling all of these putative criminal antecedents is one deserved of closer scrutiny, both for what such legal processes assume and make possible and for what they efface. This chapter examines these issues. I consider how the criminal law in general and the practice of sentencing in particular assemble the apparent variables involved in acts of criminal violence perpetrated by Indigenous offenders. I ask: what is assembled in the process of criminal sentencing, and what are the political, ethical and material implications of these processes? In order to explore these issues, I offer a detailed analysis of one decision of the Australian High Court – the case of *Munda v Western Australia* [2013] HCA 38. That case involved the sentencing of an Indigenous man who had killed his partner. I argue that the case illustrates the important constitutive work of stereotypes regarding race, addiction, place and time in the criminal law. I then ask: how might the court have proceeded if it were to think through the crime from an STS perspective? In order to do this, I draw on recent work utilising Deleuzian 'assemblage thinking' (Deleuze & Parnet, 1987) on alcohol and other drug events, including those involving violence. I consider how cases like *Munda* might be decided if, instead of 'assembling the facts' of a crime as is currently done, courts approached the process of sentencing through 'assemblage thinking'. I argue that this way of thinking about violent crime offers new opportunities for understanding violence, race, gender and place in Australia, and that it offers new possibilities for preventing forms of harm often ascribed to alcohol and other drugs.

## Background

People who use illicit drugs are heavily represented in the criminal justice system. Research from the Australian Institute of Health and Welfare (Australian Institute of Health and Welfare, 2015) suggests that 67% of prison entrants reported engaging in illicit drug use in the previous 12 months, whereas the figure is just 15.6% for the general population (Australian Institute of Health and Welfare, 2017). There are also differences as between the general population and prison entrants when it comes to alcohol consumption. The Australian Institute of Health and Welfare collects data on 'risky drinking' and found that 58% of prison entrants report drinking alcohol at risky levels prior to prison (a figure that is higher than it is for the general population). Importantly, illicit drug use is more common among Indigenous prison entrants (69%) than non-Indigenous prison entrants (60%) (Australian Institute of Health and Welfare, 2015) and Indigenous discharges report higher rates of 'risky drinking' (71%) than do non-Indigenous discharges (51%). Data such as these routinely prompt questions about the reasons why people who use alcohol and other drugs (but especially illicit drugs) and Indigenous peoples are so heavily represented (even 'over-represented') in prison systems. They also raise questions about whether there might be some link between the two phenomena (consumption and offending). We might expect an overlap of sorts, given the illicit status of drugs and the fact that many people in prison will be there because of drug use, possession or supply charges. Beyond this, there is a range of theories regarding the nature, if any, of a relationship between alcohol and other drugs and other criminal behaviours (Smyth, 2013).

One of the most widely known hypotheses is that substance use *causes* crime (White & Gorman, 2000; Goldstein, 1985). Here, the link between alcohol and other drugs and crime may be *psychopharmacological* (the substances themselves generate physiological and psychological responses that lead to offending), *economic motivational* (crimes are committed to facilitate access to drugs) or *systemic* (engagement in drug markets leads to crime). These theories remain controversial and contested, however, as I noted in the introductory chapter. Despite this controversy, the notion that there is a link between crime, alcohol and other drugs – including, especially, violent crime – persists. Writing about violence in the so-called 'night time economy', MacLean and Moore (2014: 379) note that research has come to be dominated by quantitative epidemiological research,

> in which problems are attributed largely to quantifiable measures [...] In this regard, much research effort has been given to identifying how forms of alcohol-related harm such as violence rise according to two measurable variables – alcohol consumption by individuals and the overall availability of alcohol in specific localities.

MacLean and Moore (2014: 379) suggest that an implicit idea in research of this kind is that alcohol is 'the main independent causal factor in harms such as violence'. Of course, as I noted in the introductory chapter to this book, a growing body of literature raises questions about the tendency to reify and stabilise alcohol and other drug effects as singular, static and predictable (e.g. Race, 2016, 2014; Fraser, Moore, & Keane, 2014; Duff, 2012a, 2012b; Fraser & Moore, 2011; Rhodes, 2002). This includes claims about alcohol's links to violence and sexual violence (Seear & Fraser, 2013). Despite these challenges, the tendency to causally attribute violence to substance use *per se* remains dominant in much research, and plays an important role in shaping policy and legislative responses to crime. A well-known example of this occurred in the city of Sydney in recent years, where a range of measures were introduced in a bid to curb 'alcohol-fuelled violence' in the night time economy. These included lockout laws that prohibited people from entering clubs, pubs and bars after a certain point in time. The special emphasis placed on alcohol was most visible in 2014 when the New South Wales government passed a major reform to the criminal law after two tragic and highly publicised 'one punch' deaths in Sydney's Kings Cross area. These assaults were understood to have been 'fuelled' by alcohol and became the catalyst for the introduction of a new offence of 'assault causing death while intoxicated' (see Sections 25A and 25B of the *Crimes Act* (1900) (New South Wales)). The new offence treated offenders as more culpable and deserving of greater punishment, and introduced a mandatory minimum sentence (see Quilter, 2014). Measures like these have been criticised by some as a knee-jerk policy response (for a discussion, see Lancaster et al., 2012). An important but somewhat overlooked aspect of these reforms was their singling out of alcohol, a process which I argue both stabilised and reified alcohol's 'effects' on violence, and foreclosed other ways of understanding the production of violence.

There is perhaps an even greater tendency to isolate, reify and stabilise the putative links between alcohol and other drugs and violence when 'racialised peoples' (Spivakovsky, 2012) are involved. In Australia, Indigenous peoples are grossly over-represented in the criminal justice system. The most recent available data from the Australian Bureau of Statistics show that although Aboriginal and Torres Strait Islander people account for only around 2% of the Australian population, they account for 27% of the prison population (Australian Bureau of Statistics, 2017). Claire Spivakovsky (2012) identifies two main strands of thought in the criminology literature regarding offending and 'racialised peoples'. The first is that Indigenous peoples are *not* actually over-represented in criminal justice data of the kind I described earlier, but that they are instead imprisoned at rates proportionate to their offending. Scholars who subscribe to this view point to the violent nature of Indigenous offending as one relevant factor (e.g. Snowball & Weatherburn, 2007). The second theory is that they *are* over-represented, and that this is a symptom of Western colonisation. Researchers sometimes single out alcohol and/or other drugs as a cause – and sometimes the main cause – of Indigenous offending. For instance, prominent Australian criminologist Don Weatherburn (2006: 11) has argued that:

> the leading cause of Indigenous over-representation in prison is Indigenous drug and alcohol abuse. [...] Indigenous drug and alcohol abuse is certainly not the sole point of leverage on Indigenous imprisonment [...] Far from being just a symptom of Indigenous poverty and disadvantage, drug and alcohol abuse have become its principal sponsor and cause, ruining Aboriginal lives, destroying Aboriginal families and robbing thousands of Aboriginal kids of their heritage, a decent upbringing and a job.

Claims such as these have important material-discursive effects. On the one hand, they may shape public understandings of the 'nature' and 'origins' of Indigenous offending in Australia, and the apparent risks posed by access to alcohol and other drugs. On the other, as with the New South Wales reforms, they may shape policy and legislative changes, thus reinscribing 'causal' links between substances and violence. Importantly, another assumption is often present in policy and legislative responses to violence: that the 'context' within which alcohol is consumed (e.g. the night time economy of urban Sydney) plays an important function in the production of violence. As I noted earlier, there is a growing body of critical work that raises questions about these claims. Increasingly, this work draws upon 'assemblage thinking', to which I now turn.

## Assemblage thinking

In recent years assemblage thinking has become increasingly influential in the study of alcohol and other drugs (e.g. Dilkes-Frayne & Duff, 2017; Dilkes-Frayne, 2016; Farrugia, 2017; Malins, 2017; Duff, 2016; Fitzgerald, 2015; Hart, 2015). The concept of the 'assemblage' comes from the work of French philosopher Gilles Deleuze. In an interview with Claire Parnet, Deleuze defined the concept in this way:

> What is an assemblage? It is a multiplicity which is made up of many hetero-geneous terms and which establishes liaisons, relations between them, across ages, sexes and reigns – different natures. Thus, the assemblage's only unity is that of co-functioning: it is a symbiosis, a 'sympathy'.
>
> (Deleuze & Parnet, 1987: 69)

'Assemblage thinking' eschews approaches to subjects and objects as having stable, singular and predictable attributes. Instead, it emphasises logics of relations and multiplicities, along with 'processes of emergence, heterogeneity, instability and flux' (Duff, 2014: 633). It means 'harm should be regarded as a property of the assemblage and not of any one discrete body therein [e.g. the drug or the person who uses drugs]' (Duff, 2014: 634). Cameron Duff argues that there are two main advantages to assemblage thinking in alcohol and other drug research. These are:

> First, 'assemblage' dissolves the antinomies of structure and agency in as-serting a relational logic of emergence, association and ordering. Neither structure nor context can be regarded as coherent, distal or remote entities that somehow intervene in the activity of human agents [...] It challenges in particular, the claim that behaviours like illicit drug use, and the problems associated with it, may be distinguished from their nominal social contexts. There is not, in this sense, behaviours and their contexts, but rather an as-semblage of forces in the midst of their associations.
>
> (2014: 634)

The second main advantage to assemblage thinking is 'the attention it calls to the activity of *nonhuman forces* in the modulations of consumption' (Duff, 2014: 634). Given these factors, assemblage thinking requires researchers to pay 'greater attention to the range of spaces, entities bodies, affects, forces and signs that *actually participate* in events of [alcohol and other drug] use' (Duff, 2014: 634; original emphasis) and necessitates 'thick empirical description' (McFar-lane, 2011: 379) of alcohol and other drug events.

Fraser, Moore and Keane (2014) take up these ideas in their work on addic-tion, concluding that addiction, too, is an assemblage. They explain:

> So the assemblage can be seen as an ad hoc cluster of knowledges, technol-ogies, bodies and practices that contingently gather to form a temporary phenomenon, be it abstract or material. *The world is made up of such assem-blages,* not of stable natural objects of self-evident, foundational concepts.
>
> (Fraser, Moore, & Keane, 2014: 19; emphasis added)

In other words, everything is an assemblage. These ideas have major implica-tions for the traditional objects of social science, policy and legal analysis (such as alcohol and other drugs). Assemblage thinking also has major implications for studies involving 'social context', time and place. This is important for the argument that I will make in this chapter and requires some explanation. As I noted earlier, the tendency to reify and stabilise the role of alcohol and other drugs in violence is also true for 'social context'. As Latour (2005) reminds us in *Reassembling the Social*, however, it makes little sense to talk of 'the social' or 'context', since such terms themselves pre-empts decisions about what is central and what is background ('context'). Addressing the question of what sociology is and what it can do, as part of a broader discussion of social constructionism and work on 'the social', Latour calls for a shift away from work on 'social context' in favour of work that allows for a 'tracing of associations', where the 'social does not designate a thing among other things [...] but a *type of connection* between things that are not themselves social' (2005: 5; original emphasis). Working in a similar space, Duff (2014: 636) explains that the

> effort to reconceptualise context in terms of the assemblage should be under-stood as an attempt to return context to the focus of empirical research, rather than to retain it as a heuristic shorthand for the vagaries of power or culture.

Duff calls for a focus on place and time, human and nonhuman actors, affects, material objects, technologies and practice, and how they enter into the assemblage of an event. Developing an appreciation of how these intermingle and coalesce is essential, and will help us eschew the simplistic assumption that structure/context 'determines' conduct. For Duff, 'assemblage thinking' has the benefit of returning 'one's focus to the place and time of drug use; to the array of social, material and affective forces that actually participate in the event of consumption' (2014: 638). He argues that these insights have real implications for policy, research and harm reduction. He suggests that each should be attentive and responsive to the 'real conditions of consumption'. Other scholars have made similar points. For example, Moore et al. (2017: 161) were drawing upon assemblage thinking in their work on consumer accounts of 'addiction' when they asked: 'what would policy and practice look like if assemblages of addiction, health and well-being were taken seriously?' They argue that assemblage thinking may produce more nuanced and effective responses to consumption than those that privilege units of analysis (substances, structure) in the ways I have described. And others have rendered similar insights for improving drug education (Farrugia, 2017), policy in the night time economy (MacLean & Moore, 2014; Duff & Moore, 2015), policing strategies (Race, 2014), harm reduction at music festivals (Dilkes-Frayne, 2014) and more (Bøhling, 2014). It remains to be seen, however, whether these insights can be translated into the law, and what the benefits of doing so might be (although for similar approaches, see Valverde, 2015; Santos, 1987). In this chapter, I take inspiration from these previous studies and examine how they might be extended to the criminal law. I engage in assemblage thinking in two senses. First, taking my cue from Fraser, Moore and Keane's (2014: 19; emphasis added) observation that *'the world is made up of [...] assemblages*', I argue that sentencing is itself an assemblage of moral, instrumental and other dynamics, legislative and common law considerations. I trace how these dynamics relate and play out in the criminal law, and argue that although sentencing is an assemblage it is not truly characterised by assemblage thinking. Second, I consider violence as an event and ask what might happen if sentencing practices reflected assemblage thinking and thus approached violence in new ways. To set the scene, I first provide an introduction to how sentencing offenders in the criminal law works. I then explain what special issues arise in the sentencing of Indigenous offenders. I briefly outline some criticisms of existing approaches before turning to a detailed application of 'assemblage thinking' to a single case from the Australian High Court.

## Sentencing offenders in the criminal law

Sentencing under the criminal law is a complex process, the specific details of which vary across jurisdictions. In general terms, however, the purposes of sentencing are similar, and require courts to weigh a range of considerations including community protection (proportionate) punishment, deterrence and rehabilitation (see, for example, Section 5(1) of the Victorian *Sentencing Act* (1991)). Other factors are also relevant to sentencing, including the presence of aggravating or mitigating factors (see, for example, Sections 6 and 7 of the Western Australian *Sentencing Act* (1995), and Section 5(2AC)(g) of the Victorian *Sentencing Act* (1991)). Aggravating factors are those that compound the seriousness of the offence and might therefore result in a longer sentence. An example of this might be a rape of a young child, where the perpetrator uses a weapon to subdue and threaten them, and the victim suffers particularly serious physical and/or psychological injuries. Here, the age of the victim, the effects on the victim and the use of the weapon might all be viewed as aggravating. 'Mitigating factors' are those 'factors which, in the court's opinion, decrease the culpability of the offender or decrease the extent to which the offender should be punished' (see Section 8(1) of the Western Australian *Sentencing Act* (1995)). Mitigating factors might include the age of the offender; if the offender committed an offence out of need or necessity rather than pure greed or opportunity; and if the offender is contrite, has cooperated and has good prospects of being rehabilitated. The personal history and other life circumstances of the offender become critical, therefore, to determining a sentence. In Australia it is now settled law – by virtue of a decision of the High Court in *Markarian v The Queen* (2005) 228 CLR 357 – that the sentencing of offenders proceeds via a process of 'instinctive synthesis'. As McHugh J explained (para. 51), this is defined as:

> the method of sentencing by which the judge identifies all the factors that are relevant to the sentence, discusses their significance and then makes a value judgment as to what is the appropriate sentence given all the factors of the case. Only at the end of the process does the judge determine the sentence.

The question of how to sentence Indigenous offenders is understood as posing additional challenges (see Edney, 2005). The main issue courts have grappled with is whether one's race deserves special or separate consideration under the criminal law, and if so, how. Similar questions have occupied courts in other jurisdictions, such as Canada (see, for example: *R. v Gladue* [1999] 1 S.C.R. 688; *R v Ipeelee* [2012] 1 SCR 433).

As I explained in Chapter 2, Australia was invaded and colonised by the British over 200 years ago. The impact on the Indigenous people of Australia was, and continues to be, profound. At the time of its colonisation in 1788, it is conservatively estimated that there were at least 750,000 Indigenous peoples living in Australia (Lines, 1991; Butlin, 1983). Through a combination of direct and violent conflict, dispossession of Indigenous land and the introduction of new diseases, the Indigenous population was reduced to just 58,000 by the 1920s (Harris, 2003), with at least 100 of the approximately 250 distinct languages originally spoken by Aboriginal peoples now lost (Australian Bureau of Statistics, 2010). The population of Indigenous peoples only returned to approximate pre-colonisation levels in 2016 (Fitzpatrick, 2017). Australia has never fully recovered from the devastating effects of colonisation and Indigenous people remain disadvantaged on almost every social, economic and health measure in Australia (see generally: Davis, 2015; Sherwood, 2013; Moses, 2004; Mellor & Bretherton, 2003). As noted earlier, courts have grappled for some time with whether and how these ostensibly 'contextual' factors relate to offending. Are they mitigating, for example? As Anthony Hopkins (2012) has explained, there are many ways that one's Aboriginality might be thought to be relevant to sentencing. The circumstances of one's upbringing might be understood to produce the offending, for example, or to shape or constrain one's capacity for choice. It may be relevant to matters such as the likelihood that a person will reoffend or to options for rehabilitation. Hopkins (2012: 39) notes that it may also speak to the 'appropriateness of certain punishment, presenting options where strength of community, reintegration and pride can be harnessed to achieve individual reform and deterrence'. There is both a significant body of case law – including seminal cases such as *Neal v R* (1982) 149 CLR 305, *R v Fernando* (1992) 76 A Crim R 58 (hereinafter referred to as '*Fernando*') and *Bugmy v The Queen* (2013) 249 CLR 571 – and academic literature that examines these issues (e.g. Anthony, Bartels, & Hopkins, 2016; Jackson, 2015; Krasnostein, 2014; Anthony, 2013; Hopkins, 2012; Chesterman & Villaflor, 2000).

## Sentencing Indigenous offenders in the criminal law

The first Australian High Court case to directly consider these issues was the 1982 decision in *Neal v R* (1982) 149 CLR 305. Percy Neal was an Aboriginal man who had been convicted of assault for spitting on the manager of a local store on an Aboriginal community reserve in Northern Queensland. In what came to be understood as an important statement of principle, Brennan J stated that 'courts are bound to take into account [...] all material facts including those facts which exist only by reason of the offender's membership of an ethnic or other group'. In the same case, Murphy J took a slightly different approach, engaging more explicitly with Neal's experiences *as an Aboriginal man*, and the context of colonisation. Murphy J (at 318) characterised this as an 'Aboriginal sense of grievance [...] developed over the two hundred years of white settlement in Australia'. Murphy J (at 317) also said:

> That Mr. Neal was an 'agitator' or stirrer in the magistrate's view obviously contributed to the severe penalty. If he is an agitator, he is in good company. Many of the great religious and political figures of history have been agitators, and human progress owes much to the efforts of these and the many who are unknown [...] Mr. Neal is entitled to be an agitator.

In a later analysis, Anthony Hopkins (2012: 40) noted that the case of *Neal* neither equated Aboriginality with victimhood nor required a 'denial of agency'. In other words, the case acknowledged that Neal was 'an actor in his own history just as much as he is a victim of it' (Hopkins, 2012: 40). As Hopkins' analysis reveals, the sentencing of Indigenous offenders often entails commentary on the nature of Indigenous agency and the legacy of colonialism. This concern – with what sentencing decisions do with race, history and more – has been considered by a number of courts and scholars in the years since *Neal*.

The 1992 New South Wales Supreme Court case of *Fernando* was for many years considered to be the seminal case on the sentencing of Indigenous offenders. The case established eight propositions for sentencing. One of those propositions directly engaged with alcohol, with Wood J stating (at 62–63) that:

> It is proper for the court to recognise that the problems of alcohol abuse and violence that to a very significant degree go hand in hand within Aboriginal communities are very real ones and their cure requires more subtle remedies than the criminal law can provide by way of imprisonment.

Crucially, the judge in *Fernando* did not define 'Aboriginal communities', nor 'alcohol abuse'. Richard Edney (2005) has argued that the *Fernando* propositions reveal an implicit conclusion as to the causes of Aboriginal offending. As he explains it:

> Social and economic deprivation is understood to produce offending in that, owing to the scarcity of resources in Indigenous communities, there is a dissonance between the capacity and the aspirations of Indigenous communities. Also, especially as regards offences against the person, there is considered to be a nexus between offending and alcohol partially due to those deprived social and economic circumstances.
>
> (Edney, 2005: 97–98)

In other words, the court's construction of race and alcohol – as inextricably intertwined via deprivation – stabilised both as being intimately tied to one another and to criminality. In this, there are parallels with criticisms of research and policy that view criminal behaviour as determined by context.

In the aftermath of the *Fernando* case, a trend became evident in the New South Wales case law, in which judges distinguished between Aboriginal offenders who had grown up in rural settings, remote communities or Aboriginal reserves, and those who grew up in urban settings (Flynn, 2005). In *R v Newman; R v Simpson* [2004] NSWCCA 102, for example, it was held that defendants raised in urban settings without a proven link to a discrete Aboriginal community could not be given *Fernando*-style special consideration in the process of sentencing. These cases represented what Richard Edney described as a 'retreat' from *Fernando* in the mid-2000s. Perhaps more importantly, they also signalled a willingness on the part of some judges to draw distinctions between Aboriginal people. Edney (2006) argued that such cases:

> attempt to define the contemporary Indigenous experience and who may be entitled to rely upon Aboriginality for the purpose of sentencing. In effect, the judgments attempt to undercut the position of Indigenous offenders and the benefits that accrue for mitigation of sentence because of a deprived background. The nature and complexity of contemporary Indigenous identity in a post-colonial society such as Australia is ignored and, again, Indigenous identity is defined by the powerful non-Indigenous institution of law.

The question of how Aboriginality is defined and who has the right to define it are not the only areas of concern identified in the sentencing cases. Some have argued, for instance, that the case law has produced and reproduced stereotypes about Aboriginal 'nature' and 'culture'. One example can be found in Caithleen Storr's (2009: 110) analysis of an Aurukun rape case. She found that key players, including the prosecutor and judge, appeared to normalise Indigenous offending, with the sentencing process positioned as 'less judicial procedure than paternalistic management of a degenerate community'. As with Edney's earlier critique, we see in Storr's work a concern about how courts conceptualise and enact 'places', including a tendency to reify Indigenous communities as inherently dangerous.

Extending these ideas further, a number of scholars have considered the gendered implications of sentencing approaches that posit a fixed and/or inherently debased notion of Aboriginality. For instance, Irene Watson (2008: 13) has argued that the courts often:

> contribute to making invisible the harm that is done to Aboriginal women, and while deeming Aboriginal men inherently violent they confirm the 'superiority of white men.' The picture of a 'pathologically violent' race of people emerges, one that absents other narratives and images portraying a fuller range of Aboriginal experiences.

Watson (2008: 3) goes on to note that in the criminal law, the 'history of a violent colonial frontier is given almost no airing in the contemporary analysis of violence in Aboriginal communities.' This includes historic incidents of violence such as sexual assault by white men against Aboriginal women and girls. She notes:

> These and many other historical acts of violence passed without interrogation let alone penalty. What traces might they have left in Aboriginal communities of the past, growing in the present and threatening the future? Where does this violence belong or owe its origins and whose culture might own it? Who holds the power to disown the traces of its past? Who holds the power to construct what 'Aboriginal culture' is and make out its assumed inherent violence?
>
> (Watson, 2008: 4)

In other words, even where violence is constituted as endemic to (or an inherent function of) Aboriginal communities, violence and its potential origins are narrowly construed. As Watson (2007) has elsewhere argued, violence against Aboriginal women is constituted in the criminal law as inherent to Indigenous culture.

In 2013, the High Court of Australia handed down a major and much-anticipated decision (Storr, 2013) on the sentencing of Indigenous offenders: *Bugmy v The Queen* (2013) 249 CLR 571. The case disappointed some, since it did not go as far as they had hoped it might on broader questions about the sentencing of Indigenous peoples (e.g. Anthony, Bartels, & Hopkins, 2016; Bellear, 2013). For example, the court found that the same sentencing principles should apply irrespective of the identity of a particular offender or his or her membership of an ethnic group. (The Court also found that the importance of one's Aboriginality did not diminish over time and thus, in cases involving repeat offenders, could be taken into account on multiple occasions.) Importantly, however, the Court affirmed Wood J's observations in *Fernando* with respect to the role of alcohol abuse in Indigenous communities, and its relevance to sentencing. In particular, the majority judgement stated that:

> Of course, not all Aboriginal offenders come from backgrounds characterised by the abuse of alcohol and alcohol-fuelled violence. However, Wood J was right to recognise both that those problems are endemic in some Aboriginal communities, and the reasons which tend to perpetuate them. The circumstance that an offender has been raised in a community surrounded by alcohol abuse and violence may mitigate the sentence because his or her moral culpability is likely to be less than the culpability of an offender whose formative years have not been marred in that way.
>
> (*Bugmy v The Queen* (2013) 249 CLR 571 at para. 40)

Thus, even as approaches to race, *per se*, have been reappraised in recent years, Aboriginality continues to be constituted via alcohol. Similarly, the relationships between Aboriginality, substances and violence are maintained and stabilised.

I argue that assumptions about the agency of substances, subject positions, place and time are crucial to this. In the next section I explain how the relationships between Aboriginality, substances and violence are maintained and stabilised through a detailed analysis of one case of the Australian High Court. I have chosen to focus on a single case for several reasons. First, it was decided in the same period as *Bugmy*, dealt with similar issues and received considerably less academic and public attention. As a decision of Australia's highest court, it has important precedent value, particularly for what it says about individualised justice. It is also an example of a wider tendency in the criminal law towards the sentencing of Indigenous offenders and conceptualisations of Indigenous and 'addicted' agency. In what follows, I consider how sentencing assembles violence, and what sentencing practices generate regarding race, addiction and 'social context'.

## Introducing *Munda v Western Australia*

In 2013, the High Court of Australia handed down its decision in the case of *Munda v Western Australia* [2013] HCA 38. The case involved an appeal by Munda, an Aboriginal man, over a sentence handed down for the manslaughter of his partner. Munda was 32 years old at the time of the crime. He was educated to year 10, and although he had been employed on and off since leaving school, he was unemployed for four years prior to the killing. The facts of the case were essentially as follows: Munda and his partner had been in a relationship, on and off, for 16 years, and had four children together. In July 2010, they were staying together at the Mindi Rardi community near to Fitzroy Crossing, in the remote Kimberley region of Western Australia. Fitzroy Crossing is about 2,500 km from Perth, the nearest major Australian city. The High Court described the key facts of the case as follows:

> They attended a local tavern on the afternoon of 12 July 2010. Both became intoxicated and the appellant used some cannabis. When the pair returned to their house an argument developed. Each accused the other of being unfaithful. The appellant punched the deceased on numerous occasions, threw her about their bedroom and repeatedly rammed her head into the walls. During the attack the deceased repeatedly screamed at the appellant, telling him to leave her alone. At one stage, the appellant caused the deceased to fall onto a bed mattress. He then stood over her and repeatedly punched her in the face. After the appellant had finished assaulting the deceased, they both went to sleep. The next morning, the appellant had sexual intercourse with the deceased. He then left the house to get some tea. When the appellant returned, he noticed that the deceased had stopped breathing. He called for medical assistance and attempted first aid. The deceased was transported to Fitzroy Crossing Hospital and was pronounced dead on arrival.

The cause of death was traumatic brain injury. Munda pled guilty to manslaughter and was sentenced to a period of five years and three months in prison. The prosecution believed the sentence to be too lenient and appealed to the Court of Appeal in the Supreme Court of Western Australia, which resulted in Munda's sentence being increased to seven years and nine months. Munda then appealed to the High Court, arguing that that sentence was too harsh. The key issue before the High Court, put simply, was whether Munda's sentence was appropriate. To this end a key question in Munda's appeal involved how the deprived background of Munda, including his Aboriginality, should be addressed at sentence. As the High Court stated:

> In particular, it is said [by Munda] that systemic deprivation and disadvantage, including an environment in which the abuse of alcohol is endemic in indigenous communities, should have been, but was not, taken into account by the Court of Appeal.

In the discussion that follows, I draw mainly upon observations by the High Court. However, as we will see, it necessarily references and at times incorporates and endorses passages from both the decision at first instance and the Court of Appeal's decision. As such, I treat those earlier decisions as part of my object of analysis. For ease of reference I sometimes use the singular term 'court' to refer to aspects from the primary judgement, subsequent appeal and final appeal to the High Court.

## Assembling alcohol effects

As noted above, Munda pled guilty to the crime. This meant that a thoroughgoing analysis of the circumstances of the killing was not necessary, since the question of *whether* Munda committed it had been resolved. The sole focus was now on *how* he should be punished. Of course, the *Sentencing Act* and prior case law such as *Fernando* were relevant, but the court was also guided by evidence before it, and submissions made by both the prosecution and defence. Using the 'instinctive synthesis' method described earlier, judges would need to weigh up the various factors relevant to the sentencing exercise. This required the court to consider *who* Munda was, *why* he had committed the crime and *whether* he was capable of rehabilitation, among other things. The specific circumstances of the crime would thus be revisited as these issues were explored. At first instance, Commissioner Sleight took the view that Munda's background had played a role in his offending and was mitigating, stating that:

> it is proper for a court to recognise the problems of alcohol abuse and violence which exist in many Aboriginal communities and the social disadvantages that they create. These social disadvantages often create a conditioning within the community to accept as normal alcohol abuse and violence, as if it were a way of life. In such circumstances, there needs to be a recognition that, although punishment plays a role in personal and general deterrence, to change such behaviour requires a change in the social circumstances. However,

notwithstanding these considerations, the seriousness of an offence must always be given proper weight. Like in all communities, the sentences imposed play a role in trying to protect the vulnerable. This includes, in Aboriginal communities, Aboriginal women, who are frequently subject to violence.

In this passage, two things emerge as especially relevant to Munda's agency, responsibility and level of culpability: alcohol, and the location where the crime took place. This dual focus is made possible by the *Fernando* propositions and other previous case law, but will have also been shaped by the strategy employed by Munda's legal team. In fact, Munda's own submission – including on appeal to the High Court – was that alcohol use/abuse (also at times called 'addiction' in the judgement) was 'endemic' in Aboriginal communities and relevant to the crime. But how, precisely, did the court conceptualise alcohol and the Aboriginal community, and assess their significance?

In the initial sentencing hearing, Commissioner Sleight described the incidents leading up to the crime as being 'largely spontaneous, arising out of [Munda's] suppressed anger, which was released under the influence of alcohol'. Here, alcohol is enacted as the key catalyst and main independent causal factor in the killing. But for the putative effects of alcohol, that is, we are left with the impression that Munda's 'suppressed anger' would never have been 'released' and that he might never have killed his partner. In previous work, Suzanne Fraser and I identified a similar logic at play with respect to the oft-asserted links between alcohol, other drugs and rape. We argued (Seear & Fraser, 2013) that the notion that 'alcohol "unleashes" men's "natural" sexual aggression' is problematic because it naturalises sexuality and rape, positioning it as 'a dynamic embedded in us all' (for a discussion of how similar ideas are inscribed and through drug education for young people, see Farrugia, 2017). A similar dynamic is at work here, as Munda is constituted as having a barely contained capacity for violence that is triggered by alcohol's effects upon him. To be clear, Munda did have a history of violence and had previously been convicted of assaulting his partner. In the court of appeal's decision, Buss JA revisited some of this history, including a particular violent assault that Munda had perpetrated upon his partner in October 2008. I have redacted the more gruesome aspects of the account, as they are not all necessary for the argument I want to make here. Buss JA explained it this way:

On 23 October 2008, the respondent and the deceased were walking between the Kurnangki community and the Mindi Rardi community. The respondent had been drinking at the Crossing Inn for about nine hours. He was angered by the deceased's jealous reaction towards his socialising with other women. [...]

At the sentencing hearing on 4 May 2009, for the offence of unlawfully doing grievous bodily harm, the sentencing judge, Groves DCJ, discussed the offence with the respondent:

GROVES DCJ: This is a very serious offence. No bloke, no man, beats up his missus. You know that is wrong, don't you?

THE ACCUSED: Yeah.

[...]

GROVES DCJ: You get into trouble when you have been drinking too much grog. You know that, don't you?

THE ACCUSED: Yeah.

GROVES DCJ: The grog gets you into trouble. You have to do something about that.

THE ACCUSED: Yeah.

GROVES DCJ: Otherwise if you keep on drinking too much, then you get into more trouble and you end up back here again, back in the prison. You have got to do something about that if you want to keep out of the prison or the gaol for the future. Your wife suffered very, very serious injuries, didn't she?

THE ACCUSED: Yeah.

Crucially, in this excerpt from the earlier hearing, the sentencing judge stabilises alcohol (referred to using the Australian slang term 'grog') as the main driver of violence. This is evidenced, among other things, by the sentencing judge's assertion that it is *the grog that gets Munda into trouble*. Munda is also advised 'to do something about that', with the implication that if he can just address his drinking, he will address his propensity for violence. This raises the question: how should Munda be sentenced, given this? Is he less culpable (because it is the alcohol that acts upon him) or more culpable (because he has the capacity to do something about it, and doesn't)? As I will explain in the next sections, the court's answer to this question depends in part on how it reads race, place and their mutual constitution.

## Assembling the 'Aboriginal community'

As I noted earlier, *Fernando* conceptualised alcohol abuse and violence as going 'hand in hand' in Aboriginal communities. In this sense, just as alcohol is positioned as key to understanding Munda's crime, so is locale. This geographic context is thought to be important in two senses: it is where Munda was raised, and it is where the violent event leading to his partner's death occurred. As in *Fernando* and earlier cases, such as *Neal*, the court is faced with the question of whether the fact that Munda is Indigenous and grew up in a remote Aboriginal community affected his behaviour in some way. In other words, the criminal law necessitates a consideration of place. How 'place' is conceived (whether narrowly or broadly, for instance) is not prescribed in advance, but the court reads it as being about the immediate locale (Mindi Rardi). With boundaries that are never clearly explained, this locale takes the form of what is called, on several occasions, the 'Aboriginal community' (or sometimes, in the plural 'Aboriginal communities'). It is contrasted with and gets its meaning from the 'urban' locale. The mere fact that a person was raised in an Aboriginal community does not automatically result in mitigation, however. Instead, as Buss JA noted in the

Court of Appeal decision, the nature and relevance of background and upbringing, including the geotemporal dimensions of that upbringing, should be the subject of careful analysis:

> Where an offender alleges that he or she has suffered relevant disadvantage, the disadvantage must be established by evidence relevant to the particular offender, even if the disadvantage in question is attributable to the offender's membership of a particular ethnic group.

Here, neither 'race' nor 'place' takes on any inherent, natural or pre-existing meaning. That said, it quickly becomes apparent that the geotemporal dimensions of the Aboriginal community play a vital role in how the court understands Munda's crime. For instance, at all levels, throughout Munda's case, the notion of a distinctive place inhabited by Indigenous peoples emerges (indeed, there are apparently several of these 'communities' across Australia). Aboriginal communities are positioned as geographically, temporally and culturally distinct from 'the rest' of Australia. We can glean this from several passages of the High Court's decision. One of the most important passages deals with the question of how to achieve 'general deterrence' (i.e. how to send a message to the community) when sentencing an offender. The majority judges (French CJ, Hayne, Crenna, Kiefel, Gageler and Keane JJ) explain:

> It may be argued that general deterrence has little rational claim upon the sentencing discretion in relation to crimes which are not premeditated. That argument has special force where prolonged and widespread social disadvantage has produced communities so demoralised or alienated that it is unreasonable to expect the conduct of individuals within those communities to be controlled by rational calculation of the consequences of misconduct. In such cases it may be said that heavy sentences are likely to be of little utility in reducing the general incidence of crimes, especially crimes of passion. That having been said, there are three points to be made in response. First, the proper role of the criminal law is not limited to the utilitarian value of general deterrence. The criminal law is more than a mode of social engineering which operates by providing disincentives directed to reducing unacceptably deviant behaviour within the community. To view the criminal law exclusively, or even principally, as a mechanism for the regulation of the risks of deviant behaviour is to fail to recognise the long-standing obligation of the state to vindicate the dignity of each victim of violence, to express the community's disapproval of that offending, and to afford such protection as can be afforded by the state to the vulnerable against repetition of violence. Further, one of the historical functions of the criminal law has been to discourage victims and their friends and families from resorting to self-help, and the consequent escalation of violent vendettas between members of the community.

In this passage, ostensibly focussing on general deterrence, the court makes some important claims about the 'nature' of communities. Most important among these is the suggestion that particular communities can become dysfunctional to the point that they are no longer 'rational', or capable of being made more rational. In other words, there are occasions where particular communities are so stagnant, dysfunctional and unresponsive to messaging that attempts at general deterrence may be futile. Implicit in this passage, I suggest, is the notion that Aboriginal communities might be so debased, so thoroughly damaged, that they are resistant to change, and that colonial disenfranchisement bears no responsibility for the alternative rationalities operating within them. In other words, although the criminal law claims to make no overarching assumptions about the relevance of upbringing to a crime, it nevertheless stabilises certain racialised and stereotypical ideas about the 'nature' of Aboriginal places in its remarks on the value of general deterrence.

## The mutual force of addiction, race and place

Crucially, the court enacts alcohol effects (along with 'addiction') and Aboriginal communities *relationally*. The operation of Aboriginal communities – what takes place within them, how people behave and interact with one another – is thoroughly dependent upon and thus constituted via an implicit temporality: alcohol use, abuse and family violence are positioned as enduring and endemic to Aboriginal communities, without reference to history or to changes across time, including pre-colonial time. This obscures the possibility of variations between Indigenous persons living in or moving between the bounded locales the court enacts through sentencing, while also obscuring the possibility of differences as between different Aboriginal 'communities'. In other words, the 'Aboriginal community' is enacted as a static and homogeneous 'context' or 'container' (following Barad, 2007), saturated with liquor and dominated by men's violence towards women. This violence is constituted as if perpetrated by nameless, shapeless, timeless subjects whose actions are to some extent determined by this geotemporal 'context'. Following Latour (2005), I argue that the social is mobilised as a way of explaining various phenomena including violence, signalled by a putatively unidirectional causal relationship (where the problem of violence *is caused by the social context*) (see also Seear, 2014). There are some parallels here with MacLean and Moore's work (2014) on the night time economy, and the tendency among those who study urban violence to reify and isolate place and time in ways that instantiate its inherent ('violence-producing') properties. Here the court similarly makes assumptions about context as a *'determinant of encounters'* (Duff, 2014: 636; original emphasis), reifying Aboriginal communal life and its subjects as dangerous, risky, traumatised and potentially violent. Although the court does acknowledge that violence and alcoholism are a function of 'many' Aboriginal communities, rather than 'most' or 'all', there is no other consideration of geographical or temporal variation. There are important parallels between this aspect of the court's approach to violence and its approach to alcohol effects. Earlier, I argued that the court enacts alcohol effects as singular, predictable and stable, and as the main causal attribute in Munda's crime. In Munda's case, it becomes clear that the court enacts place as similarly predictable, stable and resistant to change; as a kind of 'context' for the production of violence and other harms. These enactments are not merely coincidental, however; they are mutually co-constitutive, with each reinforcing and stabilising the other. Importantly, although these 'variables' are presented as relevant to Munda's crime, this is not truly a form of assemblage thinking, since it stems from (and instantiates) a notion of subjects, objects and spacetimes as having pre-existing, stable properties. Moreover, current, active forms of discrimination are rendered as distal (at best) and beyond mention (at worst).

As I noted earlier, at the initial stage of Munda's sentencing, the Commissioner stated, 'there needs to be a recognition that, although punishment plays a role in personal and general deterrence, to change such behaviour requires a change in the social circumstances'. Moreover, we will recall, the Commissioner described 'social disadvantages' as *created by* alcohol abuse and violence (rather than the other way around). Here, the agency of both the offender/'addict' (signalled through the gesture towards *personal deterrence*) and the Aboriginal community as a whole (signalled through the gesture towards *general deterrence*) are enacted as attenuated. Of course, the notion that 'addicts' lack volition, or free will, is both a central concept of addiction (West, 2001) and a controversial one, critiqued by numerous scholars (see, for example, Fraser & valentine, 2008; Keane, 2002). This concept is reiterated in *Munda*, but in a way that takes on a slightly different form. The ostensibly tragic figure of the Indigenous addict is rendered as both the ubiquitous product of Aboriginal society and thoroughly trapped by and within it. This was most apparent in an important passage from the transcript of the argument before the High Court. Here, some consideration was given to how much exposure to alcohol and violence Munda had had as a younger man and to the fact he'd spent periods of time living outside of Fitzroy Crossing, on a 'dry community'. These parts of the appeal hearing shed light on one key component of the High Court's eventual finding – that Aboriginal disadvantage does not diminish over time and may have enduring implications for sentencing. At one stage of the High Court hearing, the lawyer for the prosecution acknowledged as much:

> [LAWYER]: It is certainly the case which we accept that social deprivation of a particular Aboriginal offender does not diminish merely because of the passage of time, nor does the applicability and relevance of social deprivation in respect of an Aboriginal offender diminish merely because the particular offender is a recidivist.

Later in the appeal hearing, one judge asked the prosecution whether it would be appropriate for the court to be 'discounting entirely the significance of the abuse of alcohol because [Munda] was able on occasions to spend time in a dry community'. This exchange between a lawyer for the prosecutor and one of the High Court judges is apposite:

> [LAWYER]: In respect to the background, I note in the pre-sentence report, which was available to both the court below and the sentencing judge,

that under the heading family background, the pre-sentence report noted [that Munda's] family shielded him from the worst aspects of alcohol and violence and that he only saw a violent act once in his childhood. I do not say that to diminish it because he was in the community where this was occurring and Mr Munda is extraordinarily fortunate, but I raise that to give context to her Honour the President's finding, that her Honour correctly considered the available evidence, and Mr Munda in that respect stands somewhat different to many unfortunate persons in his position.

BELL J: But he was a man who had led a tribal life and had then found himself drawn to Fitzroy Crossing from time to time. To discount entirely his difficulties with alcohol might be giving little consideration to the particular circumstances of Aboriginal persons in his situation, surely?

Later in the appeal transcript, one of Munda's lawyers addressed these issues. He explained:

[MUNDA LAWYER]: There was a reference to the personal circumstances concerning the issues of drinking and the bouts of binge drinking. I ask the Court to have regard to what is said at point 6.5 in our written submissions, that in addition to the bouts of binge drinking when he was not living in Mindi Rardi, that there was at least a two-year period where his life had spiralled out of control in the way in which it is described by submissions by counsel before the sentencing judge at 6.5 that we have recorded where both he and his wife were *sucked into the vortex of acute alcohol abuse* such that both of them had been banned from the local tavern, such that his resort to drinking was to drink fast in the time allocated to him, and bearing in mind that there is a direct relationship between the nature of the conflict in the relationship and his and her abuse of alcohol.

(emphasis added)

In these exchanges, we see that substances and places are described in similar ways. Munda is thought to be both drawn back into the Aboriginal community and sucked back into alcohol's web. In other words, both Aboriginal communities and alcohol possess powerfully seductive attributes, which operate separately and together to shape Munda's agency. One of the High Court's eventual findings was that the effects of disadvantage do not diminish over time and thus might continue to be relevant to sentencing. In Munda's case, the High Court seems to have reached this view in part because it understood 'context' and addiction as *continuing to act upon a person* – even after they are no longer present in a geographical location or consuming substances. There is also something telling about the court's emphasis on 'social deprivation' not diminishing over time. What if, instead, the court highlighted the fact that 'social oppression' did not diminish over time? Although this may be an effect of sentencing priorities, it speaks to both the political and performative nature of sentencing, a point I shall return to. The agency of alcohol and 'the Aboriginal community' linger in time and across space. In the next section I consider some of the implications of this.

## The wider effects of the Munda decision

The court's approach to alcohol (including 'alcoholism' and 'addiction'), Aboriginality and Aboriginal communities has a range of implications. One of the most troubling is the implication that Aboriginal communities are thoroughly debased and virtually incapable of reform. The High Court itself recognised the difficulties with its rendering of the Aboriginal community, when it noted that:

> It would be quite inconsistent with the statement of principle in [the earlier case of] *Neal* to act upon a kind of racial stereotyping which diminishes the dignity of individual offenders by consigning them, by reason of their race and place of residence, to a category of persons who are less capable than others of decent behaviour.

Despite this insight, the High Court's approach to addicted agency is of concern. To understand why, we must go back to comments made on appeal. In the court of appeal decision, Buss JA gave the Fernando propositions 'little weight'. He seemed less sympathetic to Munda's background of disadvantage than Commissioner Sleight (at first instance), noting that:

> It is true that the respondent's offence against the deceased was alcohol-related and that alcohol abuse was rife within his extended family when he was a child. However, the respondent had demonstrated a capacity to abstain from alcohol consumption when working at cattle stations for long periods.

As with Groves DCJ in the earlier assault case, Buss JA (at the appeal) took the view that abstaining from alcohol was both possible and relevant. The lead court of appeal judge went even further than Buss JA, noting that Munda's problems with alcohol actually increased his blameworthiness. In particular, McLure P described the crime as a form of 'alcohol-fuelled violence', and noted that:

> Even if it is established that a person's addiction to alcohol and/or drugs is mitigatory because of events in their formative childhood years or otherwise, that does not inevitably reduce the weight to be given to personal deterrence. Indeed, addictions ordinarily increase the weight to be given to personal deterrence (and/or community protection) because of the associated increase in the risk of reoffending.

This last point – on addiction and the risk of reoffending – was one that the High Court described as 'particularly poignant in this case'. It was apparently 'poignant' because Munda had indeed gone on to reoffend (after having assaulted his partner in October 2008), with fatal consequences. Although I do not diminish the tragedy of his partner's death, this observation from the High Court is concerning, for it effectively endorses a version of addiction as largely predictable, where those characterised as 'addicts' are inherently risky/dangerous and criminogenic (see also Spivakovsky & Seear, 2017; Seear & Fraser, 2016). As well as (yet again) rendering the 'addict' as lacking volition and the capacity to change, McLure suggests a degree of inevitability to future activities because of the past. Although this passage is devoid of any explicit reference to race, it needs to be read, I argue, via some of McLure's other comments on general deterrence (to which the above passage relates). In particular, she noted that:

> it is wrong in principle to reduce the weight to be given to general deterrence in circumstances where alcohol-fuelled violence is endemic in the community generally, even if not sufficiently deterred in fact by the prospect of imprisonment.

It is at this point that processes of gathering and connecting the objects of inquiry (race, place and substances) in sentencing becomes most obvious. The notion of endemic and enduring alcoholism/addiction and violence in the abstract temporal-spatialisation of 'the Aboriginal community' now has circularity, becoming a justification for a longer sentence for Munda (or weighing, at least, against mitigation). This appears to be necessary, in part, because of the persistent threat posed by the community context 'itself'.

There are at least three further 'collateral realities' (Law, 2011) produced by the criminal law's approach. The first is gender: a frame that appears curiously absent in the court's enactment of the Aboriginal community. Gender is briefly referenced in both the High Court's decision and those of the lower courts. The court speaks of the special vulnerabilities faced by Aboriginal women, the need to protect them and prevent violence against women, and the importance of sending a clear message to Aboriginal communities about violence against Aboriginal women. These comments must be read, however, within the context of the gender neutral, static and homogenising geotemporalisation of Aboriginal communal life that I have already described. The effect of this rendering is to foreclose discussion about some of the gendered dynamics of Munda's crime. The second involves race: the court effectively obscures the realities of white men's violence towards women. This remains a significant problem in Australia, but one that vanishes in *Munda*. Why, in discussing general deterrence, does the Court focus only on the need to deter 'the Aboriginal community'? The third involves the links between the court's approach and other paternalistic policies in Australia. Put simply, the court enacts – without deviation – Aboriginal communities across Australia as profoundly damaged and violent places. In a way, the criminal law authorises and reinforces a paternalist logic that has long existed in Australia, and which has been gathering pace in Australian government policy in recent years. For example, six years before Munda's case was decided, the Australian government introduced a highly controversial policy known as 'the Intervention' (for a detailed discussion, see Scott & Heiss, 2016; *Northern Territory National Emergency Response Act* (2007) (Commonwealth)). It was based on claims about the seemingly unique problems that attach to Aboriginal communal life. The Intervention resulted in the designation of dry places in Indigenous communities and other coercive measures, such as the quarantining of people's welfare payments and strict controls over how Indigenous people are allowed to spend their money. The momentous nature of the Intervention is reflected in the fact that the government had to suspend its own race discrimination laws (the *Racial Discrimination Act* (1975) (Commonwealth)) to allow the measures to be implemented (because they were racially discriminatory) (Scott & Heiss, 2016). The way the court approaches place, time, race and substances in *Munda* both reflects ideas inherent to these measures and reproduces them, with material-discursive effects that reach beyond the lives of those in question, including Munda, his victim and the people of Mindi Rardi. These ideas have the potential to lodge in the wider public imagination, reflecting and reproducing stereotypes about Aboriginal 'nature' and 'culture', and justifying the need for protectionist and paternalist policies to contain them. The stakes, in other words, are high.

## Reimagining sentencing through assemblage thinking

Here I want to raise a further possibility, which is that the act of sentencing is itself an assemblage of moral, instrumental and other dynamics. As the previous analysis shows, *sentencing is an event*, with various dynamics, priorities and forces in circulation, in the midst of their associations. The purposes and principles of sentencing appear in the *Sentencing Act* (1995) (Western Australia), and are shaped by the common law. As I noted earlier in this chapter, they include mitigating and aggravating factors along with other considerations such as deterrence and proportionality. We will recall that this work might unfold through an 'instinctive synthesis' through which relevant factors are identified, value judgements made and factors balanced (*Markarian v The Queen* (2005) 228 CLR 357). The *Fernando* propositions are also to be weighted and balanced. Although this *sounds* like a kind of assemblage thinking, characterised by openness and emergence, it is not. Sentencing is more prescriptive than assemblage thinking contemplates. It fails to emphasise processes of emergence, instability and flux, or to fully approach harms as the 'property of the assemblage and not of any one discrete body therein' (Duff, 2014: 634). The sentencing processes I have described in this chapter concretise and are sometimes dominated by 'social context', including in ways that can disadvantage Indigenous people. Critical race scholar Linda Tuhiwai-Smith might argue that the very kinds of questions the court asks itself when sentencing – predicated on a seemingly more sympathetic attempt to grapple with the ongoing legacy of Australia's colonial past – nevertheless are underpinned by assumptions of difference, predictability and singularity. In other words, the comparative undertaking that underpins the court's approach is 'predicated on a sense of Otherness' (Tuhiwai-Smith, 2012:

33) rather than emergence and flux. If we return, for example, to the excerpt from the 2008 case where Munda was sentenced for assaulting his wife, we will recall learning that Munda and his partner were out walking, and talking, that they had been drinking, and that she had been jealous of his socialising with other women. The sentencing judge questioned Munda, we will recall, about his alcohol use, noting that 'the grog gets you into trouble' and telling him to 'do something about that'. Even the brief summary of the moments leading up to Munda's violent attack on his partner suggests other possibilities, 'other forces in the midst of their associations' (Duff, 2014: 634). And yet we do not see an account of these associations, the geotemporal dimensions within which discussions unfolded, including whether Munda and his partner were thirsty, hot, hungry or tired. This is not to say that these factors *were* relevant, only that the 'thick empirical description' that assemblage thinking demands is not commensurate with existing sentencing approaches. Instead, the sentencing judge imposed a reading on Munda's crime that both centred and stabilised alcohol effects. This is partly, I suggest, because of the *Fernando* propositions; at the same time as they purport to open up inquiries into offending as a complex phenomenon, they foreclose ways of understanding them, by singling alcohol out as having a likely relevance and force that warrants special attention. Following Farrugia's work on the place of substances and subjects in drug education (2017), I argue that sentencing practices *structure the materiality of Aboriginal lives* whilst purporting to be responsive to them. In Munda's earlier crime, and the later one the subject of the High Court's decision, there was no attempt to submit general concepts such as 'context', 'community', and 'addiction' to detailed scrutiny or to trace other forces in their associations. On this point, I am reminded of Irene Watson's (2008: 1–2) critique of Aboriginal sentencing cases, and her demand to know 'what is really going on in those spaces which purport a recognition of Aboriginality; what is being recognised?' To this I would add: what is not being recognised? What is left untouched or unexplored in these approaches, and what effects might they have?

Earlier in this chapter I asked what the criminal law might look like if it approached the process of sentencing through the lens of assemblage thinking. At its most fundamental, an assemblage approach to criminal violence would require a move away from the deployment of simplistic claims and assumptions about the action of objects, subjects, structures or other forces on bodies in the event being examined. Applied to Munda's case, assemblage thinking would challenge at least the following: that alcohol or other drugs played a straightforward, predictable or causal role in the production of violence absent other forces contingent in their formation; that 'addiction' possesses inherent, stable, predictable attributes that caused or contributed to the violent act; that there is something intrinsic about Aboriginal nature or culture that inevitably or predictably leads to violence; and that the place in which the crime unfolded – a remote Aboriginal community – possesses unchanging or unchangeable characteristics foundational to criminal violence. The key to assemblage thinking, of course, is not to deny that factors such as alcohol, place and time might be relevant to an event, but to pay attention to the range of forces that participate in it. Similarly, assemblage thinking should not involve replacing these 'variables' with simply new or different ones, nor should it lead to assumptions about how other factors might have acted. For example, well-documented problems with employment opportunities in the Fitzroy Crossing area might be relevant in the *Munda* case, but the risk in foregrounding them here is to impose yet another kind of structural reading upon Munda's crime. Problematically, the criminal law steers us towards making assumptions about certain variables, even while it claims that meanings are not pre-empted. A generation of decisions, starting with *Neal*, in fact singles out certain factors and stabilises them, emphasising their likely role in the production of violence. This has the effect of foreclosing a thoroughgoing analysis of how bodies, affects, technologies, human and non-human actors may have actually participated in Munda's act of violence. It also raises questions about how 'just' such outcomes are, given what the assemblage both prioritises and makes material.

## Conclusion

In this chapter I examined how particular objects and subjects are prioritised in the criminal law, how these are understood to relate to one another and produce criminal violence. Although the practice of sentencing in the criminal law appears to start with a blank slate – where courts set out to uncover the 'truth' about how a crime was committed and why – in practice, something else happens. The court in fact elevates certain 'variables' above others, makes assumptions about what is likely to be important in the production of a crime and instantiates problematic notions of how alcohol and race 'work' in relation to violence. In this sense, the particular minutiae, precedents, procedures and practices that adhere to the criminal law are crucial to shaping how violence comes to be understood. Starting with *Neal's* case, successive courts have attempted to grapple with the complexity of Australia's colonial past and its ongoing legacy. Reckoning with our complex past is both welcome and vital. In the criminal law, however, this manifests in a tendency to stabilise and reify race, place and substances, and to foreclose ways of thinking about the complex nature of phenomena such as violence. The sentencing process is thus properly understood as an assemblage, but what is assembled and how is both political and performative. Sentencing practices are not yet truly characterised by 'assemblage thinking'. I considered some of the ethics and politics of these processes, including what happens through the making of both alcohol's agency and the agency of 'Aboriginal communities'. Building upon the work of many Indigenous scholars, I argue that the criminal law renders stable alcohol and other drug effects and race in ways that might lodge in the wider public imagination, reflecting and reproducing stereotypes about the dangers of alcohol and 'addiction', and the perils of Aboriginal 'nature' and 'culture'. The sentencing process also has material-discursive significance well beyond the confines of Munda's case specifically or even the criminal law more broadly, and has the potential to play an important role in justifying the ongoing governance and control of Indigenous peoples. The question then becomes: what can be done differently?

The criminal law poses unique challenges for wholesale reform. The stakes are high, and existing legal practices and technical requirements are constraining. People accused of crime face major implications if convicted and/or sentenced, including loss of their livelihood and liberty. There are thus some obvious strategic benefits to pitching a person's criminal activity in ways that minimise their agency and instead emphasise the role of objects including alcohol, or 'addiction' or 'social context' in crime. The strategic purchase of these arguments was clear at first instance for Munda, when the presiding Commissioner viewed him as less culpable for his crime than he might have been but for those factors being raised. In assembling an account of the offender and their crime (as attenuated), lawyers and clients are incentivised to stabilise the action of social context and structure, objects and subjects. But this cuts both ways. As I argued in this chapter, for example, attempts to attribute agency to alcohol and/or addiction can have the effect of increasing one's culpability, especially if courts adjudge people to have the capacity to abstain from consumption, and if they understand it to increase a person's risk of reoffending. They can also have the effect of instantiating stereotypical notions of addicted agency and Aboriginality. In a very different context, David Moore and Suzanne Fraser (2006) examined the costs and benefits of how subjects are configured in contemporary harm reduction. They argue that harm reduction discourses inscribe a neoliberal subject (as autonomous, rational and calculating). They note that this inscription is potentially empowering for some people who use drugs, carrying benefits such as trust and legitimation. On the other hand, it has costs, including that it is individualising and responsibilising and does not adequately account for constraints on agency. In considering where the neoliberal subject of harm reduction leaves us, they conclude that:

> it is clear that we must reject any dream of discovering a 'pure' location from which to construct the 'ideal' subject of harm reduction. There is no such place. Our intention in this paper has not been to identify and recommend such a location but to spell out the processes of subjectification at work in harm reduction, and the implications of the forms of subject produced. In doing so, we hope to prompt insights into future directions for the subject of harm reduction.
>
> (Moore & Fraser, 2006: 3045)

The point is that there is no perfect subject choice; each carries risks and benefits. The same can be said for the subject in legal practices, including those in the criminal law. Unlike harm reduction, options for producing subjects (and objects) in new ways may seem even more elusive in law, given systemic constraints and lawyers' professional obligations to their clients. And yet, it is important to be attentive to the benefits and costs of rendering the subject in such ways. This is an ethical question for lawyers, clients and other stakeholders, and an issue I take up in more detail in the next chapter.

Of course, lawyers are also working within and responding to existing, somewhat static sentencing assemblages that are less sensitive to emergence and flux than they could be. Can that system be changed? And if so, what comes next? I offer two gestures here. First, we might create new sentencing assemblages with different priorities. In general terms, sentencing processes reflect a set of (apparently shared) societal priorities, underpinned by a belief in individual free will and agency, and operationalised in the form of principles such as blameworthiness, rehabilitation and deterrence. Might we consider remaking these priorities and principles in some way? Such questions have long occupied the minds of sentencing theorists (see generally, Walvisch, 2015). They are complex, and it is well beyond the scope of this book for me to do full justice to them here. That said, the current assemblage is predicated on conventions regarding the value and 'truth' of individual free will, and this remains so even when courts acknowledge that will is capable of being constrained. Where free will is thought to be attenuated, it is addressed in the form (sometimes, not always) of an adjustment to an individual's sentence. Even when criminal courts diagnose free will as constrained, therefore, and even where this appears to be a legacy of state failings including ongoing oppression, this is operationalised via the individual, not the state. Blameworthiness, rehabilitation and deterrence adhere to the individual subject and/or the 'community' in which they were raised but not to the state, which only inadvertently 'pays' for its errors, if at all, via the offender. Can sentencing principles be adjusted so as to compel the state to account for its role in social oppression? Might a differently assembled set of priorities be a way forward? Second, and in a related sense, I question the relevance of the *Fernando* propositions. While they may appear to be helpful, the problem with those propositions is just that: *they are propositions.* They gesture towards inferences and risk mobilising meanings in advance, steering judges in particular directions, in pursuit of associations and connections that are presumed likely to shape behaviour. They open up opportunities for decision makers to approach alcohol, 'the social' and 'context' crudely. Rather than sharpening understandings of Aboriginal lives, in other words, they blunt them. The propositions are, I suggest, inadequate tools for understanding complex phenomena like violence, foisted on events in a bid to 'explain' or 'comprehend' them. In making those choices (and they are choices, to be sure), sentencing practices exclude less predictable, stable and multidirectional approaches to causality. They are paradoxically less responsive and sensitised to flux and flow between bodies, affects, places, times and substances, and between human and non-human forces. How might Munda's case have been decided if, for instance, there was an opportunity for a more open, nuanced and thoroughgoing analysis of the crime as an event (in the sense Duff and others have described)? What if 'alcohol', 'addiction', place and 'social context' were not freighted with meaning (and agency) in advance, as they sometimes appear to be? What if renewed attention was given to violence as an event during the process of sentencing, and if courts were able to resist the rather more stabilising tendencies inscribed by the current assemblage? Here I am suggesting not a set of new, more open, *Fernando*-style propositions, but a thought experiment in which propositions are cast off. This would see a troubling of the present logic of sentencing, and its privileging of the action of 'things' such as alcohol and other drugs. None of this is to say that Aboriginal people are not socially oppressed in Australia or that social oppression is an irrelevant consideration. The truth is that existing approaches work to eclipse the complexities of social disadvantage and oppression, attaching agency instead to the people and communities who experience it, instantiating them as profoundly, perhaps even irreversibly, damaged.

# References

Anthony, T. (2013). Before the High Court: Indigenising sentencing? Bugmy v The Queen. *Sydney Law Review, 35*(2), 451–466.

Anthony, T., Bartels, L., & Hopkins, A. (2016). Lessons lost in sentencing: Welding individualised justice to Indigenous justice. *Melbourne University Law Review, 39*(1), 47–76.

Australian Bureau of Statistics. (2017). *Prisoners in Australia, 4517.0*. Available at: www.abs.gov.au/AUSSTATS/abs@.nsf/Lookup/4517.0Main+Features302017? OpenDocument (accessed 28 February 2019).

Australian Bureau of Statistics. (2010). *Year Book Australia 2009–10, 1301.0*. Available at: www.abs.gov.au/AUSSTATS/abs@.nsf/Lookup/1301.0Feature+Article42009–10 (accessed 28 February, 2019).

Australian Institute of Health and Welfare. (2017). *National Drug Strategy Household Survey 2016: Detailed Findings. Drug Statistics Series No. 31, Cat No. PHE 214*. Canberra: Australian Institute of Health and Welfare.

Australian Institute of Health and Welfare. (2015). *The Health of Australia's Prisoners 2015, Cat No. PHE 207*. Canberra: Australian Institute of Health and Welfare.

Barad, K. (2007). *Meeting the Universe Halfway: Quantum Physics and the Entanglement of Matter and Meaning*. Durham: Duke University Press.

Bellear, S. (2013). Why I won't celebrate the William Bugmy decision. *The Drum*, 10 October. Available at: www.abc.net.au/news/2013-10-10/.-aboriginal-disadvantage-and-the-law/5011950 (accessed 5 March 2018).

Bøhling, F. (2014). Crowded contexts: On the affective dynamics of alcohol and other drug use in nightlife spaces. *Contemporary Drug Problems, 41*(3), 361–392.

Butlin, N. (1983). *Our Original Aggression: Aboriginal Populations of Southeastern Australia, 1788–1888*. Sydney: George Allen and Unwin.

Chesterman, J., & Villaflor, G. (2000). Mr Neal's invasion: Behind an Indigenous rights case. *Australian Journal of Law & Society, 15*, 90–100.

Davis, M. (2015). Closing the gap in Indigenous disadvantage: A trajectory of Indigenous inequality in Australia. *Georgetown Journal of International Affairs, 16*, 34–44.

Deleuze, G., & Parnet, C. (1987). *Dialogues*. London: Athlone Press.

Dilkes-Frayne, E. (2016). Drugs at the campsite: Socio-spatial relations and drug use at music festivals. *International Journal of Drug Policy, 33*, 27–35.

Dilkes-Frayne, E. (2014). Tracing the 'event' of drug use: 'Context' and the coproduction of a night out on MDMA. *Contemporary Drug Problems, 41*(3), 445–479.

Dilkes-Frayne, E., & Duff, C. (2017). Tendencies and trajectories: The production of subjectivity in an event of drug consumption. *Environment and Planning D: Society and Space, 35*(5), 951–967.

Duff, C. (2016). Assemblages, territories, contexts. *International Journal of Drug Policy*, *33*, 15–20.

Duff, C. (2014). The place and time of drugs. *International Journal of Drug Policy*, *25*, 633–639.

Duff, C. (2012a). After methods, after subjects, after drugs. *Contemporary Drug Problems*, *39*(2), 265–287.

Duff, C. (2012b). Accounting for context: Exploring the role of objects and spaces in the consumption of alcohol and other drugs. *Social & Cultural Geography*, *13*(2), 145–159.

Duff, C., & Moore, D. (2015). Going out, getting about: Atmospheres of mobility in Melbourne's night-time economy. *Social & Cultural Geography*, *16*(3), 299–314.

Edney, R. (2006). The retreat from Fernando and the erasure of Indigenous identity in sentencing. *Indigenous Law Bulletin*, *6*(17), 8–11.

Edney, R. (2005). Just deserts in post-colonial society: Problems in the punishment of Indigenous offenders. *Southern Cross University Law Review*, *9*, 73–105.

Farrugia, A. (2017). Gender, reputation and regret: The ontological politics of Australian drug education. *Gender and Education*, *29*(3), 281–298.

Fitzgerald, J. (2015). *Framing Drug Use: Bodies, Space, Economy and Crime*. Basingstoke: Palgrave Macmillan.

Fitzpatrick, S. (2017). Census 2016: Indigenous people return to pre-settlement numbers. *The Australian*, 28 June. Available at: www.theaustralian.com.au/national-affairs/indigenous/census-2016-indigenous-people-return-to-presettlement-numbers/news-story/f9d4a43a92fd72670575af2c3ee1e84e (accessed 28 February 2019).

Flynn, M. (2005). Not 'Aboriginal enough' for particular consideration when sentencing? *Indigenous Law Bulletin*, *6*(9), 15–17.

Fraser, S., & Moore, D. (eds.). (2011). *The Drug Effect: Health Crime and Society*. Melbourne: Cambridge University Press.

Fraser, S., Moore, D., & Keane, H. (2014). *Habits: Remaking Addiction*. London: Palgrave Macmillan.

Fraser, S., & valentine, k. (2008). *Substance and Substitution: Methadone Subjects in Liberal Societies*. Basingstoke: Palgrave.

Goldstein, P. (1985). The drugs/violence nexus: A tripartite conceptual framework. *Journal of Drug Issues*, *15*(4), 143–174.

Harris, J. (2003). Hiding the bodies: The myth of the humane colonisation of Australia. *Journal of Aboriginal History*, *27*, 79–104.

Hart, A. (2015). Assembling interrelations between low socioeconomic status and acute alcohol-related harms among young adult drinkers. *Contemporary Drug Problems*, *42*(2), 148–167.

Hopkins, A. (2012). The relevance of Aboriginality in sentencing: 'Sentencing a person for who they are'. *Australian Indigenous Law Review*, *16*(1), 37–52.

Jackson, L. (2015). Sentencing Indigenous women after Bugmy. *Alternative Law Journal*, *40*(3), 171–174.

Keane, H. (2002). *What's wrong with addiction?* Melbourne: Melbourne University Press.

Krasnostein, S. (2014). Too much individualisation, not enough justice: Bugmy v The Queen. *Alternative Law Journal*, *39*(1), 12–14.

Lancaster, K., Hughes, C., Chalmers, J., & Ritter, A. (2012). More than problem-solving: Critical reflections on the 'problematisation' of alcohol-related violence in Kings Cross. *Drug and Alcohol Review*, *31*, 925–992.

Latour, B. (2005). *Reassembling the Social: An Introduction to Actor-network Theory*. New York: Oxford University Press.

Law, J. (2011). Collateral realities. In F. Rubio & P. Baert (eds.), *The Politics of Knowledge* (pp. 156–178). London: Routledge.

Lines, W. J. (1991). *Taming the Great South Land: A History of the Conquest of Nature in Australia*. Georgia: University of Georgia Press.

MacLean, S., & Moore, D. (2014). 'Hyped up': Assemblages of alcohol, excitement and violence for outer-suburban young adults in the inner-city at night. *International Journal of Drug Policy, 25*, 378–385.

Malins, P. (2017). Desiring assemblages: A case for desire over pleasure in critical drug studies. *International Journal of Drug Policy, 49*, 126–132.

McFarlane, C. (2011). On context: Assemblage, political economy and structure. *City, 14*(3/4), 375–388.

Mellor, D., & Bretherton, D. (2003). Reconciliation between Black and White Australia: The role of social memory. In E. Cairns & M. D. Roe (eds.), *The Role of Memory in Ethnic Conflict* (pp. 37–54). Basingstoke: Palgrave Macmillan.

Moore, D., & Fraser, S. (2006). Putting at risk what we know: Reflecting on the drug-using subject in harm reduction and its political implications. *Social Science and Medicine, 62*(12), 3035–3047.

Moore, D., Pienaar, K., Dilkes-Frayne, E., & Fraser, S. (2017). Challenging the addiction/health binary with assemblage thinking: An analysis of consumer accounts. *International Journal of Drug Policy, 44*, 155–163.

Moses, A. D. (ed.). (2004). *Genocide and Settler Society: Frontier Violence and Stolen Indigenous Children in Australian History*. New York and Oxford: Berghahn Books.

Quilter, J. (2014). One-punch laws, mandatory minimums and "alcohol-fuelled" as an aggravating factor: Implications for NSW criminal law. *International Journal for Crime, Justice and Social Democracy, 3*(1), 81–106.

Race, K. (2016). The sexuality of the night: Violence and transformation. *Current Issues in Criminal Justice, 28*(1), 105–110.

Race, K. (2014). Complex events: Drug effects and emergent causality. *Contemporary Drug Problems, 41*(3), 301–334.

Rhodes, T. (2002). The "risk environment": A framework for understanding and reducing drug-related harm. *International Journal of Drug Policy, 13*(2), 85–94.

Santos, B. (1987). A map of misreading: Toward a postmodern conception of law. *Journal of Law and Society, 14*(3), 279–302.

Scott, A., & Heiss, A. (2016). *The Intervention: An Anthology*. Sydney: University of New South Wales.

Seear, K. (2014). *The Makings of a Modern Epidemic: Endometriosis, Gender and Politics*. Farnham: Ashgate.

Seear, K., & Fraser, S. (2016). Addiction veridiction: Gendering agency in legal mobilisations of addiction discourse. *Griffith Law Review, 25*(1), 13–29.

Seear, K., & Fraser, S. (2013). Mia Freedman et al are wrong: Being drunk doesn't cause rape. *The Conversation*, 12 November. Available at: https://theconversation.com/mia-freedman-et-al-are-wrong-being-drunk-doesnt-cause-rape-19900 (accessed 20 July 2018).

Sherwood, J. (2013). Colonisation – It's bad for your health: The context of Aboriginal health. *Contemporary Nurse, 46*(1), 28–40.

Smyth, C. (2013). Alcohol and violence – exploring the relationship. *Drugs and Alcohol Today, 13*(4), 258–266.

Snowball, L., & Weatherburn, D. (2007). Does racial bias in sentencing contribute to Indigenous over-representation in prison? *The Australian and New Zealand Journal of Criminology, 40*(3), 272–290.

Spivakovsky, C. (2012). *Racialized Correctional Governance: The Mutual Constructions of Race and Criminal Justice.* Farnham: Ashgate.

Spivakovsky, C., & Seear, K. (2017). Making the abject: Problem-solving courts, addiction, mental illness and impairment. *Continuum: Journal of Media and Cultural Studies, 31*(3), 458–469.

Storr, C. (2013). The High Court to soon decide on treatment of Aboriginality in sentencing decisions: *Bugmy v The Queen. Opinions on High,* 28 August. Available at: https://blogs.unimelb.edu.au/opinionsonhigh/2013/08/28/storr-bugmy/ (accessed 28 February 2019).

Storr, C. (2009). The Aurukun rape case, Indigenous sentencing and the normalisation of disadvantage. *Australian Indigenous Law Review, 13*(1), 107–113.

Tuhiwai-Smith, L. (2012). *Decolonizing Methodologies: Research and Indigenous Peoples* (2nd edn). Dunedin: Otago University Press.

Valverde, M. (2015). *Chronotopes of Law: Jurisdiction, Scale and Governance.* Milton Park: Routledge.

Walvisch, J. (2015). *Sentencing offenders with mental health problems: A principled approach.* Unpublished PhD thesis. Monash University, Clayton.

Watson, I. (2008). *The 'recognition' of cultural background in Indigenous sentencing.* Sentencing Conference Canberra, National Judicial College of Australia/ANU College of Law (pp. 1–17). Available at: https://ssrn.com/abstract=2476794 (accessed 28 February 2019).

Watson, I. (2007). Aboriginal women's laws and lives: How might we keep growing the law? *Australian Feminist Law Journal, 26*(1), 95–107.

Weatherburn, D. (2006). *Disadvantage, drugs and gaol: Re-thinking Indigenous over-representation in Prison.* Proceedings from the Conference of the Australasian Society on Alcohol and other Drugs, Cairns, 5–8 November.

West, R. (2001). Theories of addiction. *Addiction, 96,* 3–13.

White, H. R. & Gorman, D. M. (2000). *Dynamics of the Drug-Crime Relationship.* Washington: US Department of Justice. Available at: www.ojp.usdoj.gov/nij/criminal_justice2000/vol1_2000.html (accessed 28 February 2019).

## Cases

*Bugmy v The Queen* (2013) 249 CLR 571.

*Markarian v The Queen* (2005) 228 CLR 357.

*Munda v Western Australia* [2013] HCA 38.

*Neal v R* (1982) 149 CLR 305.

*R v Fernando* (1992) 76 A Crim R 58.

*R. v Gladue* [1999] 1 S.C.R. 688.

*R v Ipeelee* [2012] 1 SCR 433.

*R v Newman; R v Simpson* [2004] NSWCCA 102.

## Legislation

*Crimes Act* (1900) (New South Wales).

*Northern Territory National Emergency Response Act* (2007) (Commonwealth).

*Racial Discrimination Act* (1975) (Commonwealth).

*Sentencing Act* (1995) (Western Australia).

*Sentencing Act* (1991) (Victoria).

# 5    *Ethical practices*

## On rules, values and ethics as a 'matter of concern'

## Introduction

In previous chapters I examined how legal practices enact addiction, and considered some of the implications of this work. These included the potential to stigmatise and marginalise people who inject drugs and those labelled as 'addicts', and the implications for gender, race and governance of populations. In particular, I argued that these problems can occur through *practices of lawyering*. But what do lawyers think about all of this? Do they express similar concerns? Do they see these issues as something that lawyers should think about when they advocate for clients? What views, if any, do decision makers hold on these questions? This chapter examines these issues through an examination of lawyers' and decision makers' reflections on the ethics of legal addiction-attribution (following Sedgwick, 1993). Legal ethics tends to be dominated by two apparent modes of practice. For some, being an 'ethical' lawyer requires mere adherence to the technical rules that govern lawyers' conduct ('rules-based lawyering'), whereas for others, legal ethics is guided by something more subjective ('values-based lawyering'). A strict delineation between 'rules-based' and 'values-based' lawyering is problematic, however, in part because the rules which govern lawyers' professional behaviour are not value-free. In this, I see an analogy with the work of Bruno Latour (2004), particularly his challenge to the fact/value dichotomy in Western thought. Latour's idea is that 'facts' are intrinsically political. Against the tendency in critical social science to 'debunk' or deconstruct facts, Latour calls for a move towards 'matters of concern', a practice marked by a desire to 'protect and care'. Taking my cue from this work, I then explore how lawyers and decision makers reflect on the work that they do. Lawyers express apprehension about the central emphasis placed on addiction in their work, and question whether different approaches might be possible. They also express discomfort with the way they feel they must portray (or 'perform') addicted subjectivities and consumptive practices, the tendency to conceal the complexities of these processes from their clients and the failure to explore possibilities for doing things otherwise. In this sense, lawyers conceptualise their ethical obligations as being about more than compliance with their technical, ethical obligations (i.e. a narrow, rules-based reading of ethics), favouring a broader approach which incorporates *ethico-ontological* concerns, including concerns about the making of addicted realities, subjects and objects.

Lawyers are engaged in an ontological mode of inquiry that explores the role of law *in the making of worlds*. These are more weighty reservations about what legal practice *does* with alcohol and other drugs. In this chapter I also explore decision makers' reflections on these issues, and the perspectives of both groups on whether and how things might be otherwise. Here, lawyers emphasise the need for specific and subtle shifts in how they go about their work, as well as how they see their role. This includes the value of lawyering with clients as allies, the need to avoid assumptions and stereotypes, to explore what clients want and need, to care about the wider repercussions of their practices and to be open to new possibilities and priorities. In speculating about what changes are necessary or possible, decision makers take a different approach, drawing analogies with feminist and race-based lawyering, and urging lawyers to take heed of law's inherent fragility and capacity for change. This analysis sets the scene for the conclusion to this book.

## Background

Lawyers in all jurisdictions of Australia are governed by professional conduct rules. For solicitors, these rules include the *Legal Profession Uniform Law Australian Solicitors' Conduct Rules* (2015) ('the solicitors' rules') and for barristers, the *Legal Profession Uniform Conduct (Barristers) Rules* (2015). The solicitors' rules stipulate, for instance, that lawyers:

- Owe a paramount duty to the court and to the administration of justice (rule 3.1);
- Must act in the best interests of their client (rule 4.1.1);
- Be fair, honest and courteous in all dealings (rule 4.1.2);
- Must not act as the 'mere mouthpiece' of their client (rule 17.1);
- Must not deceive or knowingly or recklessly mislead the court (rule 19.1);
- Must not knowingly make a false statement to an opponent in relation to the case (rule 22.1); and
- Must not in any action or communication associated with representing a client: make any statement which grossly exceeds the legitimate assertion of the rights or entitlements of the solicitor's client, and which misleads or intimidates the other person […] [or] use tactics that go beyond legitimate advocacy and which are primarily designed to embarrass or frustrate another person (rule 34.1).

The rules also set out a series of ethical duties that lawyers owe to their clients, and these include duties to:

- Act in the best interests of their client (rule 4.1.1);
- Act with competence and diligence (rule 4.1.3);
- Act with loyalty, including by avoiding conflicts of interest (rules 10–12);
- Respect confidentiality (rule 9.1); and
- Follow their clients' lawful, proper and competent instructions (rule 8.1).

Similar rules and laws governing lawyer's conduct exist in other parts of the world. These include: in New Zealand, *Lawyers and Conveyancers Act* (2006) (NZ) and *Lawyers and Conveyancers Act (Lawyers: Conduct and Client Care) Rules* (2008) (NZ); and, in the United Kingdom, the *Legal Services Act* (2007) (UK); Solicitors Regulation Authority, *Practice Framework Rules* (on 6 December 2018); and Bar Standards Board, *Bar Standards Board Handbook* (on 21 January 2019). In Canada, each province has a separate professional legal regulator and suite of legislation and rules. In Ontario, for example, lawyers are governed by the *Law Society Act*, RSO 1990, c L-8; Law Society of Ontario, *Complete Rules of Professional Conduct* (at 26 April 2018). In the United States, lawyers are also regulated state-by-state, but all states other than California base their format largely on the *American Bar Association Model Rules of Professional Conduct* (2016). These various rules have been described as 'the law of lawyering' (Parker & Evans, 2014: 6). Like other areas of law, these rules have been scrutinised and interpreted by courts and tribunals, and form part of the overarching landscape that shapes legal practice. Importantly, however, grey areas remain. Lawyers must frequently decide whether a specific decision they are contemplating, or action they might take, is within the rules. Also, rules sometimes conflict with each other. Crucially, many questions that might cross the minds of lawyers, or be relevant in some way to their work, are not dealt with explicitly in the rules. There is no rule, for instance, that unequivocally prohibits the use of racial or gendered stereotypes by lawyers. As such, although it might be technically within the rules to do so, some might consider it to be morally wrong. There is also no rule that says that lawyers need to consider the wider implications of their work, including the potential ripple effects of pursuing a particular legal strategy, for how we come to think about subjects or subject categories (based on race, sex or class). Indeed, thinking about these broader effects of legal practice may be at odds with the lawyers' paramount duty to the court and their associated duty to their client.

The question of how lawyers should approach their roles has been dealt with extensively in the legal ethics literature. The key question is: 'By what standard should lawyers ultimately be guided when answering the question of how they should act: the law only, or the law and something else?' (Farrow, 2012: 164). In some legal ethics literature, a strict demarcation between two modes of lawyering is drawn.[1] These are referred to as 'rules-based' and 'value-based' approaches, respectively. The 'rules-based' approach is often considered to be the 'standard conception' of lawyering (Luban, 1988). It is characterised by partisanship, non-accountability and neutrality (see Wendel, 2010). Closely associated with zealous advocacy, this style of lawyering involves seeking to advance the client's interests at all costs, with the maximum zeal allowed by the rules, and 'regardless of what the lawyer herself thinks of the client's ends' (Dolovich, 2002: 1629). This 'gladiatorial champion' approach can be of great benefit to disempowered or vulnerable clients who must fight a more powerful opponent (Batagol, 2008), including criminal defendants who are facing loss of reputation or livelihood, liberty or life. Zealous advocates sometimes take their cue from legalism, claiming that lawyers only need to consider the technical rules when going about their work. This way of thinking has itself traditionally dominated legal practice and education, as Parker and Evans (2014: 6–7) explain:

> Much teaching and practical discussion of lawyers' 'ethics' in the legal profession is dominated by legalism. Legalism treats legal ethics as a branch of law – 'professional responsibility' or 'professional conduct' law. The professional conduct approach may cater to the need for certainty, predictability and enforceability in a context where people often consider ethics to be subjective and relative. By definition it abandons ethical judgement for rules.

In contrast, values-based lawyering is said to involve a consideration not only of what is technically permissible under the rules but of what is 'good', right or just (see Luban, 1983). Values-based lawyering, in other words, involves a more explicit engagement with putatively 'subjective', 'moral' and 'political' considerations in the practice of law. It may also turn upon an account of 'being' as a foundation for ethical action (e.g. Webb, 2002). Those advocating for values-based lawyering have offered advice on what this might entail. Most famously, David Luban (1983) called for people to be 'good' lawyers, noting – with recourse to Aristotelian principles – that a 'good lawyer' is a moral one. Similarly, Trevor Farrow (2012: 164) argues that 'the lawyering role must take into account some vision of the good (in addition to the right)'. He goes on to define this approach as one where lawyers might:

> take into account something more than law (contemplated by the right), which [...] amounts to something akin to a sense of morality that is animated by visions (albeit potentially contested visions) of justice.
>
> (Farrow, 2012: 164)

Farrow views moral deliberations as an inescapable element of legal practice. For example, a lawyer might need to advise a company director on their legal obligation to act in the 'best interests' of the corporation. As Farrow points out, even though existing case law might offer some insights into what 'best interests' mean, the lawyer may be dealing with a new or novel scenario. The company director may be considering a course of action that is technically within the rules but which is arguably immoral, or which is capable of having wide-ranging environmental or societal effects. Farrow argues that 'in all but the clearest of cases (involving the clearest of laws), morality is not incidental, but is rather central, to the lawyering role' (Farrow, 2012: 171). Sharon Dolovich offers another example of what values-based lawyering might entail, suggesting that lawyers should consciously choose to lawyer 'with integrity' (2002). This includes being true to one's commitments, having the capacity to reflect critically on one's values and principles, and nurturing an openness to change (see also Evans, 2014). Some writers have offered examples of what this might practically look like in different areas of law. Writing about corporate lawyering and corporate social responsibility, for instance, Bryan Horrigan (2015) argues that:

> The public interests that underlie the place of the legal profession in society mean that lawyers are not just guns for hire in the marketplace. The same is true of judges who seek to avoid personal responsibility for enforcing the values enshrined in particular laws that unjustifiably advantage rich people over poor people, by chanting the mantra that, whatever their personal sense of justice, they have no choice other than to enforce 'the law'. However, this stance treats the law as if it is always a fixed monolith, with judges' role as public officials being detached completely from any form of responsibility.

Horrigan might have some sympathy with Deborah Rhode (2000: 17), who argues that lawyers must take 'personal moral responsibility for the consequences of their professional acts'. Former Family Court justice Nahum Mushin (2018) has also sought to trouble the narrow conception of lawyers' ethical obligations, within the context of children's rights. Under Australian family law, the *Family Law Act* (1975) (Cth) holds that the best interests of the child are paramount. Mushin argues that this provision has implications for the way in which the ethical obligations of lawyers are to be interpreted. He argues that the lawyers' paramount duty to the court must be read in conjunction with the paramount purpose of the child's best interests, meaning that child welfare and safety should be at the centre of the way that lawyers approach their work. In other words, the unequivocal statutory emphasis on child well-being, welfare and safety is just as important, according to Mushin, as the technical legal rules that guide lawyers' conduct. Unlike Horrigan, Mushin's argument remains grounded to some extent in 'the law', even as it draws upon moral conceptions and considerations of the broader effects of lawyers' work.

Importantly, the tendency to reify legal practices as either 'rules-based' or 'values-based' is not without problems. First, this ignores the fact rules are shaped by values and reflect particular ethical and moral priorities. Second, when we analyse the motivations of lawyers who are typically understood to adopt a zealous, 'rules-based' orientation, it becomes clear that a set of values often continue to underpin their practice. Abbe Smith is a well-known American criminal lawyer, scholar and proponent of rules-based, zealous advocacy. Smith argues that a lawyer should do everything that is legally within the rules and necessary to represent their client. She nevertheless admits to experiencing some tension between her commitment to zealous advocacy and her identity as a feminist. In sexual assault cases, for example, Smith regularly cross-examines alleged victims, including women and young girls. In this work, she often tries to undermine the alleged victim's memory, perception and evidence, or attempts to discredit her. Smith (2016: 291) writes:

> The fact that I represent the poor is central to why and how I do this work and still sleep at night. I think of myself as a lawyer engaged in indigent criminal defense and, more generally, a poverty lawyer. This may be the moral heart of the matter for me. I was drawn to this work and remain drawn

because I believe there is a moral obligation to defend the poor. That we continue to fail miserably at fulfilling this obligation further spurs me on.

Smith (2016: 293) goes on to say:

> That the cards are 'stacked' is a familiar motivator in indigent criminal defense; we literally take on the *government*. This David versus Goliath feeling is amplified in a rape or child sex case because of the range of witnesses at the government's disposal, the intense investment of the prosecution (especially once the case goes to trial), the charged courtroom atmosphere, and the high stakes for the client.

My reading of both these passages suggests that even though Smith sees herself as a zealous advocate, whose practice is shaped by what the rules permit, other values and conceptions come into play (on these issues, see also Smith & Freedman, 2013; Smith, 2006). There is thus value in moving beyond accounts of legal ethics as shaped by either rules or values alone, or debates about which 'approach' is most suitable. I argue that different frameworks might be useful, both for assessing the work that lawyers do and for examining the way that they conceptualise this work. In this chapter, therefore, I propose a conceptual shift. For guidance in this respect and in this chapter I turn once again to the work of Bruno Latour.

## Matters of concern

In 2004, Latour published a famous article on the role of critique in the social sciences. Written in the wake of the attack on the World Trade Center on 9/11, and the growing challenge posed by climate change, Latour identified a curious 'coincidence' of sorts. There is a similarity between some forms of critique of scientific facts (including those Latour himself pioneered) and conspiracy theories designed to dismiss attacks such as that on 9/11, or global catastrophes, including climate change. Lamenting these developments, Latour sought to clarify his earlier work, describing it as an attempt not to dismiss the value of facts but rather to '*emancipate* the public from prematurely naturalized objectified facts' (2004: 227; original emphasis). Continuing, he explained that: 'the question was never to get away from facts but closer to them, not fighting empiricism but on the contrary, renewing empiricism' (2004: 231). Elsewhere Suzanne Fraser and I noted that Latour wants 'to salvage realism, but to remake it in doing so' (2011: 8). Central to this process of salvaging and remaking realism is Latour's claim that Western thought and practice is dominated by a demarcation between 'facts' and 'values'. This strict separation of 'facts' and 'values' cannot stand, however, since it overlooks the processes by which facts are produced:

> The category of fact attributes the properties of givenness and finality to the claims and ideas subsumed under its auspices, as though they suffered through no trials of strength along the way, as though they were simply

uncovered, or 'discovered,' without arduous innovation, without the formative influence of theory and speculation, of physical manipulation and field-
work, of inscriptions and their transportation and combination.

(McGee, 2014: 21)

Seeking to move beyond this simplistic account of 'facts', Latour called for a shift
from a preoccupation with 'matters of fact' in the social sciences to an interest in
what he called 'matters of concern'. He defines the difference between 'matters
of fact' and 'matters of concern' in this way:

Matters of fact are only very partial and, I would argue, very polemical, very
political, renderings of matters of concern.

(2004: 232)

In other words, as Suzanne Fraser has explained, Latour intends to provoke a
shift in 'our understanding of phenomena so that they are seen as intrinsically
political, built from continuous "dealing and dispute", and not only as unprob-
lematically objective, material and concrete' (2011: 95). In reorienting ourselves
to matters of concern, Latour further argues that we should aim not to 'debunk'
facts, but, following Donna Haraway, to 'protect and care' (Latour, 2004: 232).

I see two parallels between Latour's project and the argument I have been developing in this book so far. First, as the previous chapters have revealed, legal
'facts' about both alcohol and other drugs and addiction are (intrinsically) political
phenomena, constituted in practice, shaped by theory, speculation, effort and other
conditions. I also see an analogy of sorts between the rules-based/values-based
distinction that permeates debates about legal ethics and the fact/value dichotomy
that Latour wishes to challenge. In accounts of legal ethics, rules are sometimes
thought to be akin to 'facts', less nebulous, imprecise and 'subjective' than values,
and thus a more 'reliable' source of action. Of course, Latour's analysis disrupts di-
visions such as these and encourages us to pursue other ways of approaching issues.
So where does this leave us? If the constitution of realities, including facts, is always
already political, but we are not focussing on debunking facts, what might our focus
look like? Suzanne Fraser (2016: 12) takes up these ideas and calls for a remaking of
alcohol and other drugs through policy in 'more flexible, non-essentialising ways'
(see also Fraser & Seear, 2011). The focus is not, in other words, on producing alternative and 'less contested' matters of fact (Fraser, 2016: 8). In what follows, I take
up these ideas and explore them via lawyers' and decision makers' accounts of the
making of addiction in law. A common feature of these accounts is a profound res-
ervation about what legal practice *does* with alcohol and other drugs, and a concern
for the realities that the law makes possible. It is to those reflections that I now turn.

## Ethical ontologies and the 'necessary evil' of addiction

One of the first interviews I conducted for this project was with a Canadian
lawyer, Simone. As I explained in Chapter 2, Simone raised concerns about the

process of constituting drug use as addiction in order to ensure basic health care rights and harm reduction services for people who use drugs, as in, for instance, the aforementioned case of *Insite (Canada (Attorney General) v PHS Community Services Society* [2011] 3 SCR 134). We will recall that Simone described this form of advocacy as 'a sort of a "necessary evil", if you will, that there is a need to have some framing, that there needs to be discussion of addiction in cases involving drugs'. Simone was one of the first lawyers to express reservations of this kind to me, but would not be the last. Over the course of this study most lawyers raised similar misgivings about the work they did. The dual notions entailed in her comment – that these approaches were both 'necessary' and 'evil' – require some unpacking. For Australian lawyer Anne Marie, cases involving alcohol and other drugs raised difficult ethical questions. She noted that as a lawyer, you are always 'trying to get [clients] a better result', or 'the best result in the circumstance', and that lawyers are trained to see 'that as your legal obligation'. Despite this, she notes, 'you might have philosophical views outside of that', which makes for 'an interesting one to grapple with personally' (Anne Marie, Australia). In this sense, Anne Marie appears to be articulating a tension between 'rules-based' and 'values-based' lawyering: one of the classic legal ethics dilemmas I noted earlier. But what does it mean, precisely, to be grappling 'personally' with the work being done? What exactly were lawyers concerned about?

A frequent area of concern was the potential for legal practices to enact people who use drugs as addicts, and addicts as sick, non-agentive or irrational. As Barry, another Canadian lawyer, explained, the problem is not just with the language of addiction and key concepts (such as irrationality) that underpin it, but with the tendency to collapse drug use with addiction in ways that obscure the value of drugs in people's lives:

> BARRY: What's lacking [in law] is the holistic approach you know and the just the terminology, you know the designation of an illness, an addiction. That's pathologising. It gets in the way.
>
> KATE: What does it get in the way of, do you think, Barry?
>
> BARRY: It gets in the way of the person. They become identified as the label, you know, so their humanity gets lost. And the assumption in all of those designations is that something is wrong. In my perspective, these are actually indications something is right. Like these [drugs] are how people deal with their lives, there is a value in what they are doing and to eliminate it without replacing it with something, is I think like it's too moralistic. [Drug use] serves a purpose, right?

These practices may also have implications for how people come to understand themselves. As Australian lawyer Fern explained:

> So in a plea in mitigation you're, it's often unfortunately, I guess, [you are] presenting your client in the – not the most helpless light possible – but you're playing up the challenges they're facing and all the things going

wrong in their life, and how terrible it is for them and if they've got a disability, going on about their disability and so on. It's very – it's not a great model, and it's not great for clients.

(Fern, Australia)

For Australian lawyer Vaughan, enacting clients as 'addicts' was more harmful than helpful. He viewed it as more counterproductive than lawyers might assume, because it suggested that clients had an incurable problem that could not be solved. It was unhelpful,

> partly because the concept of addiction, as it's understood – and no doubt [I am] imperfectly understanding it – but as it's understood, gives that impression of it's a problem that can't be solved, it's intractable, it's addicted. 'He's been addicted so he'll always be addicted. He's addicted now, always will be'.
>
> (Vaughan, Australia)

The strategic imperative to perform drug use as addiction and addiction as a disease in legal contexts was also troublesome 'because of the stigma [...] that's associated with addiction' (Simone, Canada). These concerns extended to the use of similar terms such as 'alcoholic'. Australian lawyer Olivia accepted that 'alcoholism' might be a legitimate designation, and that she might even be dealing with clients who were alcoholics, or who considered themselves as alcoholics. Despite this, the use of the terminology concerned her, for what it implied about the person:

> I think when you call someone an alcoholic, you encompass a whole lot of meaning in that, which may be well beyond [the] things that really describe that particular person [...] With that term comes a lot of pejorative ideas about what someone might be like.
>
> (Olivia, Australia)

In these examples, lawyers are expressing concerns that are not (merely) about what legal conduct rules permit or require. They are also not grappling with how their professional legal role intersects with their personal value system, nor whether there is a clash between what the role demands and what their own values imply (although value considerations are present, to be sure). These are concerns, I suggest, of a more *ontological nature*. When Barry says that legal practice 'gets in the way' of the person, he is articulating a concern about the way that law undermines client autonomy and integrity, instantiates them as 'sick', directly challenges their perceptions of themselves and their practices, and performs them in ways he considers to be dehumanising. These concerns are also about interpellation (discussed in Chapter 2) and the instantiation of problematic stereotypes (of the kind discussed in Chapter 4). In other words, lawyers' accounts express doubts about the way subjects become abjects through law; this is an account of ethics which accords with Karen Barad's notion that 'the becoming of the world is a deeply ethical matter' (2007: 185).

Apart from the possible effects on individual clients, legal strategies pertaining to addiction can have more far-reaching consequences. Because law and policy are mutually co-constitutive (Seear & Fraser 2014a, 2014b), legal enactments of addiction may shape policy responses to drug use. As Erica pointed out:

> You know, you remove choice from a group of people that become victims and then the way that we design policy around them is arguably dysfunctional because of that.
>
> (Erica, Canada)

She went on to say that policy approaches to drugs can be 'harmful' as a result, particularly where they are informed by legal findings of 'fact' that constitute drug use as sickness and addicts as non-agentive. Caitlin, a judge, feared that focussing on 'addiction' as the root cause of problems was ethically fraught, not because of how the client might feel, but for what it implied about solutions. She noted that it 'may even exaggerate the extent to which at least some people [think they] can do something about it'. Caitlin's concerns echo those of Vaughan, quoted earlier, and overlap with those I outlined in Chapters 3 and 4 in that they trace concerns about what happens once we ascribe agency to alcohol and other drugs, and obscure the complex drivers of phenomena, such as violence. Celeste, another decision maker, also raised concerns about the way addiction was dealt with in the law. Like Caitlin, Celeste was uncomfortable with the tendency for broader systemic concerns to be elided when law enacted alcohol and other drug 'addiction' as central and causal. She explained:

> I totally get that your focus is on addiction and that's what you are looking into. But it also sort of doesn't make sense in isolation, because it is part of a much broader attitude to criminal conduct generally, and that is that there is zero compassion in that system, or very little room for that, and very little room for understanding why people commit offences. The treatment of addiction is really just systematic of a much bigger problem, which is that our system doesn't need to or seek to inquire into the factors that lead to people committing offences and once they are part of the system they generally never get out of that [...] I think the system is not equipped for any kind of nuance. It just has rigid rules you apply across the board. You're not really looking at the complexities of a case and coming up with a genuine solution. You are just ticking some boxes, basically. Especially when it comes to those [addiction] programs.
>
> (Celeste, Canada)

This was an ethical issue, too, for Celeste, who stated that:

> It's basically the people who are repeatedly the victims of that system can be none other than the victims of that system. They're fucked, from every angle.

This left Celeste feeling despondent about the system within which she operated. Systems enact people as damaged and disordered, centre 'addiction' and avoid broader societal factors that she felt likely to play an important role in the production of social problems.

## A necessary evil, but by what measure?

Several lawyers identified a key ethical tension in their work. On the one hand, many felt that it was often unethical to enact clients as addicts, for the reasons described above. On the other hand, it might also have been unethical to not make such arguments where they were available. Dana, a Canadian lawyer, stated that she didn't like labelling people as 'addicts', or as experiencing a 'disability', because she found those labels unhelpful and potentially offensive. However, 'accepting a label in one instance is going to open up doors that it wouldn't otherwise'. This was particularly so in Dana's area of practice (employment), which permitted workplace 'accommodations' to be made to people experiencing disabilities, including addiction. Lawyers ultimately perceive a 'huge tension' (Simone, Canada) between the strategic benefits of framing drug use as addiction through the disease model, and the paradoxical implications for those individuals affected:

> I think a lot of people who use drugs [...] really reject that idea of addiction and I think often times they draw analogies like I mentioned before, like people for who – addiction is so stigmatised – or the use of, people who are highly functioning and using drugs, all kinds of drugs and we just stigmatise people who use illicit drugs or drugs that have been criminalised [...] There's certainly a tension. And even if they understand why it might be useful as a legal tool to frame it in that way, I don't know if it hurts the overall movement to have people [who] use drugs recognised as [addicts ...] I don't really know the answer or how to resolve it.
>
> (Simone, Canada)

Although she does not draw any firm conclusions, Simone here touches upon two broader possible 'effects' of legal strategies on addiction. The first is that public understandings of all people who use drugs might be shaped by the narratives that lawyers produce, with all forms of illicit drug use constituted as sickness. Such an approach invariably forecloses alternative accounts of drug use as pleasurable, non-problematic and non-pathological. This has parallels with concerns raised by Barry in the previous section but can be distinguished in one important way. Here, Simone's fear is that legal strategies may operate to exclude alternative accounts of people who use drugs as anything other than irrational, non-agentive subjects, and that this will hurt 'the overall movement'. Simone's concerns appear to be for harm reduction and/or progressive drug law reform advocacy strategies more broadly. What can be done in the name of 'people who use drugs' if a view of such use as rigidly and intrinsically pathological becomes fixed in the legal/public imagination? How might the 'movement' advocate for decriminalisation, legalisation or other reforms if the practice at the heart of such advocacy (drug consumption) cannot now be seen as anything other than a form of sickness? A second concern raised by Simone is that only some people and some forms of drug use will be constituted as pathological through legal processes. This might occur because, for example, only certain kinds of substances feature in legal contexts, or because only certain people will be required to account for their use in legal settings. For instance, homeless people openly using illicit drugs in Downtown Eastside Vancouver are far more likely to be subjected to intensive policing and to be criminally sanctioned than wealthy Vancouverites who are able to consume drugs in the privacy of their own homes. In other words, even though 'addiction' can surface in legal proceedings through several means, the processes of subjectification described here are likely to disproportionately affect homeless, Indigenous and poorer people (among others). If 'addiction' is enacted as always already pathological, in other words, its pathology is most likely to be forged through intersecting forms of disadvantage and marginalisation, but in ways that obscure those same processes. 'Addiction' would come to be fixed to particular communities (if indeed it is not already), thus making it even more difficult to unmoor it from problems such as homelessness and poverty into the future. For Simone, these are profoundly ethical problems.

Although legal processes are not solely to blame for these issues, lawyering can entrench understandings of drug use that ultimately restrict the capacity of publics and governments to think differently about drugs, and the capacity for social change:

> [These ideas about addiction and agency] they come from all over the place, they come from lawyers, they come from people who are involved in NGO work, they come from the people themselves who are describing what they do. In the sense that they come from lawyers in the courts sometimes they are helpful and sometimes they are helpful and hurtful. Like, if you look at the *Insite* decision for example. You know the idea that addiction is an illness and causes compulsion is central, like that decision would not have suc-ceeded without that concept and the result is that there is a harm reduction facility available to people that saves hundreds of lives a year. So without that concept that wouldn't exist. But then you have a notion that only people who are compelled enough should be able to have harm reduction and that's not necessarily helpful. So that you're kind of, you know, there is always a sense of like trying to make sure you're not undermining something that you're really trying to enforce. Like are you undermining the dignity of people who are really suffering? To say that they, you know, that they really can't do anything else?
>
> (Erica, Canada)

Here, Erica touches upon the 'necessary' nature of the 'evil' earlier articulated by Simone. Addiction, that is, has been leveraged successfully to promote health and save lives. It is sometimes deployed in order to circumvent or overcome pu-nitive or problematic policies or laws that would otherwise complicate the lives of people who use drugs. Erica seemed to be grappling with a problem that was not simply about the specifics of lawyers' practices, but the systems they confront and work within.

The apparent advantages of advocating through the framework of addiction were emphasised repeatedly by Canadian lawyers. The situation was generally less clear in Australia, however. In Australia, there is no major high-profile case equivalent to *Insite*, and certainly nothing with the apparently major impact that case has had in Canada. This is an important distinction: a reminder that addiction's putative strategic 'value' is variable and contingent, that it depends on its perceived strategic worth as a device and that its salience will differ between jurisdictions. This has implications for how lawyers conceptualise the ethics and effects of their strategies, and what is at stake in the work that they do. It also extends to their perceptions about the ethics and politics of interpellating addicted identities. Most Australian lawyers I interviewed had given little thought to these issues. The situation was generally different in Canada, where lawyers appeared to be more conscious of these issues for reasons that are difficult to pin down. One exception was Australian lawyer Fern, quoted earlier. She believed that existing approaches to the construction of addiction were probably 'not great' for clients. In her experience, however,

> most clients seem to be okay with [how they are portrayed by lawyers]. And I think it's probably a really sad indictment on our justice systems and all the other systems that interfere in people's lives. That they're just so used to being talked about as though they're not there and talked about like they're useless individuals with no control over their own lives.
>
> (Fern, Australia)

Apart from a few examples, Australian lawyers otherwise often simply told clients what they needed to do and sought their instructions to proceed (an issue I touched upon in Chapter 2). Norman believed that some clients may experience 'dependence' or 'addiction' but still took issue with the ethical approaches some lawyers took, including the way they went about talking to their clients and their failure to ask clients what they wanted. Sometimes, lawyers did not bother to respectfully engage their clients in discussions about the strategies they were thinking about taking because 'they just don't present as somebody who's sufficiently capable, and so we step in'. He went on:

> NORMAN: And then the other thing – and this is just because of the way I think of things [...] is to respect client autonomy. I think the real risk with people with drug dependency, and a lot of vulnerable and disadvantaged people who present as clients, is for lawyers to simply go into legal overdrive and to take over and run the show, and not listen, and make decisions. And I don't think people with drug dependencies have forfeited their autonomy. I know I said before in practice, I always had a suspicion [those clients] were lying. But that's not a reason not to listen and talk and ask and respect their autonomy.

KATE: And so when you said 'go into legal overdrive', is that mainly about not accepting client's instructions, or thinking that you know better than the client?

NORMAN: It's not *not accepting* instructions because, in a way, lawyers always contrive to get instructions. It's just the instructions are the instructions that they've contrived to get. So I sit down with you and I say, 'Okay. So I've read the factsheet. And what I can see is this. And what you need to do is that. And you probably have to do this. What do you think?' And they just sit there and sort of nod. Well, I've just run the whole show. And I'll come out and I'll say, 'Well, I'm acting on their instructions'. And I haven't at all. But that's not an unfair characterisation of a lot of lawyer-client interactions. So that's lawyer overdrive. That's just taking control. We're very good at problem solving, so we see everything as a problem, and we offer our solution. And we're not very good at letting the person we deal with be a party to that solution.

Lawyers acting in the way Norman describes would appear to have a particular conception of legal ethics and the lawyer's role. Lawyers are to act competently and diligently, as the rules require, on the basis of the client's instructions, and in furtherance of the client's 'best interests'. Broader considerations, including the effects of instantiating stereotypes, producing and reproducing stigma, or interpellating people in certain ways, are less relevant. But what are the clients' 'best interests'? Who gets to decide this? And might 'best interests' extend to broader considerations involving the constitution of subjects, objects and phenomena? If the current approach is 'necessary', necessary by what measure? Norman's response provides some hints about these issues; who determines them; precisely how ethical dilemmas in legal practice arise; how ontological questions are elided; and, thus, how lawyers might begin to approach their practice differently. The ways in which lawyers interpret their role and the scope of their ethical duties are clearly important. So too is how they come to understand 'problems', 'solutions' and the crucial question of what is 'best' for clients. Recognising these challenges, some lawyers and decision makers were already trying to do things differently.

## Allies and alternatives

Several lawyers had ideas about how they might do things differently. Most commonly, lawyers emphasised the value of engaging with their clients in different ways. According to Australian lawyer Norman:

My immediate thought is – I think it's probably first a question for – explicitly for or guided by the client. I mean there are clients who will characterise their situation as being one of 'dependence' or 'disability'. And I think that's probably where you have to start.

(Norman, Australia)

Some lawyers described having a 'very long conversation' (Amy, Canada) with clients about how they understood themselves and wished to be portrayed through legal processes. Some lawyers invited their clients into the process of devising a legal strategy. As Amy explained:

> I think the way to navigate that tension [between the possible advantages and disadvantages of legal strategies] is to make sure the client decides and I don't, because it's not my life and I'm not there to speak for someone and make decisions for them. I'm there to make a space for them to be able to speak and then communicate that in the language of the court.
>
> (Amy, Canada)

The importance of non-judgemental practices was also emphasised. Olivia suggested that lawyers should be try 'not to be judgmental, and not to deal with that person in a way where that becomes the only thing that you're dealing with, and where that becomes the centre of everything about that person, because it's not everything about that person'. Betty took the view that this was 'exactly what the job is. In addition to making whatever clever legal arguments and things like that, but the *client is the centre of the whole thing*'. In these accounts, I see lawyers as motivated by a desire, not necessarily to build 'new' and 'different' facts (although this might happen), nor to 'debunk' existing facts, but to 'protect and care' for that which legal practices enact.

Given the large variety of terms (drug use, abuse, addiction, dependency) available to lawyers and the variation in key concepts underpinning it, discussions about what language to use, when they happened, were complicated and often drawn-out, as Erica, a Canadian lawyer, explained:

> So you know there is a lot of work done around how to use language, how to ask for legal solutions and how to kind of describe our clients and in particular, how to make sure that they are described in the ways that they want to be seen. So it's kind of wrestling with that spectrum of choice issue.
>
> (Erica, Canada)

In wrestling with this spectrum of choice, lawyers sometimes changed their original legal strategy, or were challenged on their own assumptions about the 'necessary evil' of addiction. Canadian lawyer Simone was acting for a man where 'strategically it would be more – it would probably be a stronger case [...] if we characterised him as having an addiction'. This was not a framework with which the client identified, however. She respected his opinion and had to reflect on her own practice, including whether it was essential to characterise him as addicted, chaotic, sick or irrational in order to secure the outcome he was looking for. The particular case concerned the availability of harm reduction services. As she reflected on her original assumptions, in collaboration with the client, Simone realised that it may be less important to position her client in the way she had assumed was necessary. Drawing on analogies from unrelated areas, she instead constructed an argument about people's right to be supported and safe, without judgement, rather than an argument about rights predicated on pathology:

> I remember [thinking about] the seat belts example [and that] it does not matter if the people will speed or not [...] we still provide seatbelts in cars. So [...] it shouldn't be relevant to the question of whether we have needle syringe programs [and other services].
>
> (Simone, Canada)

Simone later encouraged other lawyers to reflect on their practice, by always asking: 'How does [the client] feel about being identified in that way?' She also urged lawyers to look for alternative modes of framing drug use where addiction was not the preferred option. As in Fraser's (2016) work, noted earlier, Simone is here motivated to find more flexible and less essentialising ways of depicting alcohol and other drug use.

To this end, working collaboratively with clients was seen as particularly important. Theresa's workplace had expressly adopted this as a key feature of their practice. Canadian lawyer Theresa explained that:

> The model that the [service] has expressly adopted is lawyering as ally, and so what does that require of us? [...] A big part of that is an idea of trying to think of working *with* a client, and so that each of you bring different kinds of expertise and different knowledge. And, that a really important piece of that is also not to be judgmental, and also to be curious, and that there's often so much that we don't know. And to try to kind of shift away from really dichotomous thinking.
>
> (Theresa, Canada)

When doing advocacy work that did not necessarily involve representing a single client, such as law reform submissions, Simone said it was the 'centre' of her organisation's strategy to consult with user organisations. She noted that we 'take our guidance and leadership from [them]', ensuring that what they advocate for 'reflects what they would want to see in legislation'. These approaches to lawyering are consistent with a philosophy that many drug user organisations promote, encapsulated in the phrase 'Nothing about us, without us'. According to the Canadian HIV/AIDS Legal Network (2005: 4):

> As an ethical principle, all people should have the right to be involved in decisions affecting their lives.

Numerous user organisations have produced manifestos on both the importance of more inclusive practice and what a more inclusive practice might entail (e.g. Jürgens, 2008). On the question of what a more inclusive practice involves, Eliot

Albers, Executive Director of the International Network of People Who Use Drugs (INPUD), says that:

> Meaningful participation of the drug using community is not asking us to 'endorse' a document that we have never previously seen, had no role in developing, and not been consulted on. It is not a tick box exercise, a strap line, or an indicator, it is rather a fundamental principle and a value that should lie at the heart of all of your work whether you work in a multilateral agency, in service delivery *or in advocacy around drug law reform, harm reduction or human rights.*
>
> (Albers, n.d.; emphasis added)

There is a particularly strong history of collaborative advocacy of this kind in the Downtown Eastside area of Vancouver (see Boyd et al., 2017; Boyd, MacPherson, & Osborn, 2009). This way of practising law – as an ally, where the client's interests are centred, and where the possibility of different priorities is privileged – is also broadly consistent with one of Christine Parker's (2004) four modes of lawyering. Parker calls this the 'ethics of care' approach. It is an approach in which lawyers:

> are likely to spend more time listening to and discussing the broader concerns of clients and the way that legal issues are likely to impact on other aspects of their lives and relationships. At the very least, the ethics of care encourages lawyers and clients to consider the non-legal and non-financial consequences (eg, relational, psychological and to reputation) of different legal options.
>
> (Parker, 2004: 70)

Although many of the lawyers I interviewed for this research approached their practice in ways that were consistent with the ethics of care model, some others were less conscious of or concerned about what Parker called the 'wider consequences' of particular legal approaches to addiction. Those lawyers viewed their role more narrowly, consistent with zealous advocacy. While I acknowledge the utility of different approaches in different settings, some approaches to lawyering might, I suggest, be less appropriate or desirable with disadvantaged or stigmatised groups. It is also less appropriate in the context of drug user organisation calls for 'nothing about us without us', and their appeal for advocates to more explicitly and meaningfully engage with people who use drugs in decisions that affect their lives. In other words, once again, to protect and care about the intrinsically political nature of the worlds lawyers create. Where lawyers work with people who use drugs and those labelled as 'addicts', there appears to be considerable potential for that work to enact, reinforce and entrench stigma, or to produce, in Parker's terms, other 'consequences' for clients. Lawyers are rarely encouraged to consider these ontological dimensions of their work, or to think of them as ethical concerns (let alone ethical obligations). The reflections of lawyers in this chapter suggest that they do hold such concerns about their work even if they do not use the language of ontology, interpellation or subjectification. I argue that they are properly ethical concerns, however, and that there is a need to give more thought to these dimensions of lawyering. For this reason, there is value in encouraging lawyers who work with people who use drugs to reflect upon their work through what I call an explicitly *ethico-ontological* frame. I argue that this model is most appropriate to work involving stigmatised clients because it 'emphasises dialogue about ethics' (Parker, 2004: 70). Although the eventual legal strategy might end up being the same, this shift in philosophy and approach enables lawyers and clients to openly explore and examine the implications of various possible courses of action (while also acknowledging, importantly, that different courses of action are in fact available). In the process, lawyers may learn of assumptions and stereotypes that inform their work, including assumptions about the 'nature' and 'effects' of drugs and addiction; assumptions about what their clients hope to achieve in a legal proceeding; and assumptions about what constitutes a 'good' result in the minds of people who use drugs. Together, lawyers and clients may also discover alternative ways of talking about drug use and addiction that are less stigmatising and more generous. Importantly, decision makers also had views on the need for change. I now turn to those.

## The possibility of change

As I noted in Chapter 2, decision makers often afford themselves less agency in the enactment of legal truths than we might assume them to have. They also sometimes expressed concern about dominant approaches to lawyering, a theme I have returned to and expanded upon in this chapter. Several decision makers had a view about what kind of change was possible, as well as how, precisely, it might be achieved. Expressing ethical concerns about the treatment of 'addiction' in law, they drew both inspiration from and analogies with historic feminist practices as a source of change. One judge I interviewed took the view that lawyers were too conservative in their arguments. As this judge, Caitlin, explained:

> I also think that lawyers are pretty conservative in what they rely on. I mean I often said to people [...] I did it after a while though it was something I had to learn, but I'd often say, 'Well what about x?' Something that hadn't been [argued]. And quite often they'd say, 'No, no, no' [...] So I think lawyers are fairly conservative with what they'll go with generally speaking [...] So, you've got to have someone with either a crusading spirit or a very, very good, sympathetic case. I suppose a bit like what happened with family violence.
>
> (Caitlin)

This reference – to reforms in the family violence space – raised an interesting possibility: that feminist thinking and feminist activism, which was integral to reforms Caitlin described, could be utilised to do legal practice differently. Several other judges spontaneously emphasised the importance of feminist politics for challenging legal orthodoxies. Bethany, for example, explained it this way:

> It was very clear in my court back in the [earlier] days, not at the end of my time, but perhaps at about my middle of my time, when the court was really flirting in a, I think, a very proper and legitimate way with feminist thinking, and whether feminist thinking should be utilised to challenge some of the judicial ways, not just the way the court operated, although we did think about that, but legal principles and their application as well. And we just couldn't get counsel, even female counsel, to put arguments that were truly informed by feminist thinking, I think partly because the early women who were successful in the legal profession were relatively conservative the more they probably had been there, and also because they were a bit frightened about how it might be received, because there would have been courts, and there would have been judges, where they would have got a pretty unwelcoming response to those sort of arguments. But it meant that my court, that was really wanting to develop some jurisprudence around the changing roles of women and appropriate ways to be reflecting on women in the community just wasn't getting any opportunity or any real help to do it.
>
> (Bethany)

Another judge, David, drew upon feminist thinking as a way of thinking through how drug law might be reformed. His emphasis was on the role that judicial education might play in encouraging judges to think differently, but he also thought it was important for encouraging lawyers to think more critically about drugs in their work. He explained that he'd come to this realisation following a South Australian case in the early 1990s where a judge had famously found that a man could not be found guilty of raping his wife and that some degree of coercion was acceptable in marriage (*R v David Norman Johns* (1992), unreported, Supreme Court of South Australia). He explained to me that:

DAVID: It was a marital rape case with the 'rougher than usual handling' –
KATE: I know the case you mean.
DAVID: Famous case. But [the then Australian Prime Minister] decided we all needed some further judicial education, which I was very pleased he did because I was with a group of judges, [and] we went [overseas]. There was a judicial education [overseas]. It had two really outstanding women who were academics who helped [...] run these training courses, and we were particularly impressed with this, and we actually brought them out here, for seminars for judges here. But I think we really got a different approach to gender issues doing that. And I think that's what judges should – you could apply that to addiction if you'd like to – anywhere.

Finally, Bethany (a judge), called to mind a similar example of change, inspired not by feminist challenges to orthodox thinking, but challenges to racial stereotyping and the legacy of colonisation. Referring to the landmark decision *Mabo and Others v Queensland (No. 2)* [1992] HCA 23 (*Mabo*) noted briefly in the first chapter, Bethany explained:

> The [lawyers] that know every decision that was ever decided on a point, and look to find the case that's closest to one that says, 'Well, that's the outcome', without thinking through why it was the outcome in the earlier case, are not particularly helpful. And you've also got to have a sense, a little bit, about whether attitudes have been changing. I mean, the classic example that you'll be alert to, of course, is Ron Castan [a barrister], with native title [in the *Mabo* decision]. Every decision on the books was contrary to what the argument [he] wanted to put. There was a little bit of sympathy floating around in a few cases, but there was nothing that he could really point to. But not only could he analyse in principle, and chose a very clever case in which to do it, because it was so radically different from mainland Australia where the other cases had been decided, but the times were changing. It was a time when something could probably run in the superior courts of Australia, but wouldn't have run 15 years earlier. So, a really good lawyer can do that and it's why good lawyers don't spend all of their lives locked up in their chambers. They're not getting a sense about what's happening in the world, what people are thinking, how are attitudes shifting, what are the values that are beginning to inform the community's thinking about things.
>
> (Bethany)

Crucially, the decision in *Mabo* necessitated an exploration of Indigenous life and culture in pre-colonial Australia. A major, earlier case, *Milirrpum v Nabalco Pty Ltd* (1971) 17 FLR 141, had found that Indigenous peoples did not enjoy land rights, partly because the land was 'desert and uncultivated' upon the arrival of the British, and because the law would immediately come into force in any territory 'in which live uncivilized inhabitants in a primitive state of society'.[2] The judge in *Milirrpum* came to this conclusion even while finding that the Yolngu people who brought the claim had a thriving system of customs and laws at the time of the invasion (for a more detailed discussion, see Lavery, 2017). In *Mabo*, the High Court drew a different conclusion, finding that native title rights did exist in Australia. Crucial to this outcome was a reckoning with the original basis of the invasion, and a shift in the legal conceptualisation of Indigenous peoples. As Justice Brennan explained in *Mabo*, the:

> supposedly barbarian nature of indigenous [sic] people provided the common law of England with the justification for denying them their traditional rights and interests in land.
>
> (para. 38, Brennan J)

The court went on to say:

> The theory that the indigenous [sic] inhabitants of a 'settled' colony had no proprietary interest in the land thus depended on a discriminatory denigration of indigenous [sic] inhabitants, their social organization and customs. As the basis of the theory is false in fact and unacceptable in our society, there is a choice of legal principle to be made in the present case [...] it is imperative in today's world that the common law should neither be nor be seen to be frozen in an age of racial discrimination.
>
> (paras 39, 41, Brennan J)

In drawing an analogy between cases involving gender and race and 'addiction', decision makers reiterate something important about the ontology of addiction. At least some decision makers, that is, see addiction as a discriminatory, problematic object; more than a matter of 'fact', addiction is matter of concern, made in practice and capable of being made anew. In other words, they acknowledge the fragility and impermanence of subjects and objects in law, opening the door for a different kind of advocacy.

## Conclusion

This chapter explored the reflections of both lawyers and decision makers on the ethics of legal practices pertaining to alcohol and other drugs. As I noted at the outset of this chapter, thinking about legal ethics tends to be dominated by two apparent modes. For some, being an 'ethical' lawyer requires mere adherence to the technical rules that govern lawyers' conduct ('rules-based lawyering'), whereas for others, legal ethics is guided by what Trevor Farrow (2012: 164; emphasis added) calls 'the law *and something else*' ('values-based lawyering'). I then argued that a strict delineation between 'rules-based' and 'values-based' lawyering was problematic, in part because the notion that rules are value-free is unsustainable. In this, I saw an analogy with the work of Bruno Latour (2004), particularly his challenge to the fact/value dichotomy in Western thought. Latour's idea, simply put, is that 'facts' are the result of a process, and thus intrinsically political objects. Against the tendency in critical social science to 'debunk' or deconstruct facts, Latour calls for a move towards 'matters of concern', a practice marked by a desire to 'protect and care', following Donna Haraway. Taking my cue from this work, I then explored how lawyers and decision makers reflected on the work that they do. I argued that those working in law often expressed concerns about the work they did – concerns of an avowedly 'ethical' nature – and yet of a nature that exceeds the kinds of dilemmas often described in legal ethics literature. Lawyers reflecting on their practices are engaged in a mode of inquiry that explores not only how one's professional role aligns with/reflects/reconstitutes one's value system, and the responsibility of self to others, but the role of law *in the making of worlds*. Lawyers recognise the ontological weight of practices for subjects and objects; acknowledging the entanglement of legal practices with addicted realities, they articulate these as ethical problems with no simple answers. We might conclude, on the one hand, that these reflections are about 'values-based lawyering'. This is true to the extent that lawyers' concerns reflect things that they value and prioritise (such as reducing stigma). But this is also too narrow a reading. Lawyers worry about the becoming of the world through law. This is an *ethico-ontological* account of legal practice. An ethico-ontological account of lawyering highlights law's capacity to:

- Instantiate problematic stereotypes of alcohol and other drug use;
- Produce and reproduce stigma;
- Influence public understandings of 'problems' such as violence, poverty and homelessness;
- Centre alcohol and other drugs as the root cause of otherwise complex social problems, therefore obscuring or foreclosing other ways of understanding problems;
- Shape policy and other legal responses to phenomena such as violence, poverty and homelessness;
- Interpellate subjects as addicts, in ways that may be both helpful and harmful; and
- Directly shape materiality, including by directing resources to be applied to the 'problems' it makes possible, and foreclosing other possibilities.

Of course, lawyers also emphasised the capacity of legal practices to assist people, particularly by supporting them to gain access to much-needed services, including services the state may be otherwise unwilling to provide.

Recognising that realities, subjects and objects are inaugurated and stabilised through material-discursive practices, lawyers and decision makers also considered how things might be done otherwise. Lawyers emphasised the need for specific and subtle shifts in practice, beginning with the lawyer-client relationship. They underscored the value of lawyering with clients as allies (in ways that are consistent with the ethos of 'nothing about us, without us'), the need to avoid assumptions and stereotypes, the importance of exploring what clients want and need, and the value of caring about the wider repercussions of their practices and being open to the possibility that their perceptions of a client's 'best interests' may differ from the perceptions that clients hold (and thus, what clients want). In speculating about what changes are necessary or possible, decision makers took a different approach, drawing inspiration from and analogies with feminist and race-based lawyering. Importantly, they saw addiction as a discriminatory, problematic object, one that is made in practice and that can therefore be made anew. In other words, they acknowledged the fragility and impermanence of subjects and objects in law, opening the door for a different kind of advocacy. It seems to me that such advocacy must be both more flexible and less essentialising (following Fraser, 2016) than it has in the past. It is an advocacy that resists the stabilising tendencies of addiction and decentres it. This requires clients, lawyers (and decision makers) to unmoor alcohol and other drugs from the astonishing range of social problems they continue to be attached to and made to account for, including family violence, homelessness, sexual assault and poverty. It is a style of advocacy that also cares differently about what is produced, underpinned by a legal ethics that acknowledges legal 'truths' as always already the product of practices (rather than being stable, predictable phenomena pre-existing those practices). Most of all, it requires lawyers and decision makers to become open to new possibilities, including the notion that there are other ways of advocating for people who use drugs; ways that do not repeat the mistakes of the past, especially through rigidity of thought and repetition of method. On this final point, I want to return to Justice Brennan's observations in *Mabo*. Law involves choices; we can choose to be frozen in an age of addicted essentialism and stigmatisation, or we might make new choices and, in the process, forge new beginnings.

## Notes

1 This is not to be confused with Christine Parker's (2004) four modes of lawyering. She calls these the adversarial (or zealous) advocate, responsible lawyer, moral activist and ethics of care approaches (while noting there may be overlap between them).
2 *Milirrpum v Nabalco Pty Ltd* (1971) 17 FLR 141, 201.

## References

Albers, E. (n.d.). *Nothing about us without us*. Retrieved from: https://nuaa.org.au/about-nuaa/drug-user-organisation/nothing-about-us-without-us-2/.

American Bar Association. (2016). *Model rules of professional conduct*. Retrieved from: www.americanbar.org/groups/professional_responsibility/publications/model_rules_of_professional_conduct/model_rules_of_professional_conduct_table_of_contents/ (accessed 29 January 2019).

Barad, K. (2007). *Meeting the Universe Halfway: Quantum Physics and the Entanglement of Matter and Meaning*. Durham: Duke University Press.

Batagol, B. (2008). Fomenters of strife, gladiatorial champions or something else entirely? Lawyers and family dispute resolution. *Queensland University of Technology Law and Justice Journal, 8*(1), 24–45.

Boyd, S., MacPherson, D., & Osborn, B. (2009). *Raise Shit!: Social Action Saving Lives*. Halifax: Fernwood Publishing.

Boyd, S., Murray, D., SNAP, & MacDonald, D. (2017). Telling our stories: Heroin-assisted treatment and SNAP activism in the Downtown Eastside of Vancouver. *Harm Reduction Journal, 14*, 27, 1–14.

Canadian HIV/AIDS Legal Network. (2005). *'Nothing about Us without Us': Greater, Meaningful Involvement of People Who Use Illegal Drugs: A Public Health, Ethical and Human Rights Imperative*. Toronto: Canadian HIV/AIDS Legal Network.

Dolovich, S. (2002). Ethical lawyering and the possibility of integrity. *Fordham Law Review, 70*, 1629–1688.

Evans, A. (2014). *The Good Lawyer*. Port Melbourne: Cambridge University Press.

Farrow, T. (2012). The good, the right and the lawyer. *Legal Ethics, 15*(1), 163–174.

Fraser, S. (2016). Articulating addiction in alcohol and other drug policy: A multiverse of habits. *International Journal of Drug Policy, 31*, 6–14.

Fraser, S. (2011). Beyond the 'potsherd': The role of injecting drug use-related stigma in shaping hepatitis C. In S. Fraser & D. Moore (eds.), *The Drug Effect: Health Crime and Society* (pp. 91–105). Melbourne: Cambridge University Press.

Fraser, S., & Seear, K. (2011). *Making Disease, Making Citizens: The Politics of Hepatitis C.* Aldershot: Ashgate.

Horrigan, B. (2015). *The War against Poverty Is not Optional for Lawyers.* International Bar Association Online. Retrieved from: www.ibanet.org/Article/Detail.aspx?ArticleUid=f9ce20d3-15f9-417e-a9d8-59198ea304b2 (accessed 1 February 2019).

Jürgens, R. (2008). *'Nothing about Us without Us' – Greater, Meaningful Involvement of People Who Use Illegal Drugs: A Public Health, Ethical, and Human Rights Imperative, International Edition.* Toronto: Canadian HIV/AIDS Legal Network, International HIV/AIDS Alliance, Open Society Institute.

Latour, B. (2004). Why has critique run out of steam? From matters of fact to matters of concern. *Critical Inquiry, 30,* 225–248.

Lavery, D. (2017). 'Not purely of law' – The doctrine of backward peoples in Milirrpum. *James Cook University Law Review, 23,* 53–77.

Luban, D. (1988). *Lawyers and Justice: An Ethical Study.* Princeton: Princeton University Press.

Luban, D. (1983). *The Good Lawyer: Lawyers' Roles and Lawyers' Ethics.* Totowa: Rowman and Allanheld.

McGee, K. (2014). *Bruno Latour: The Normativity of Networks.* Oxfordshire: Routledge.

Mushin, N. (2018). Ethics in family law – Beyond legal principles and into value judgments. *Singapore Academy of Law Journal, 30,* 427–454.

Parker, C. (2004). A critical morality for lawyers: Four approaches to lawyers' ethics. *Monash University Law Review, 30*(1), 49–74.

Parker, C., & Evans, A. (2014). *Inside Lawyers' Ethics* (2nd edn). Port Melbourne: Cambridge University Press.

Rhode, D. (2000). *In the Interests of Justice: Reforming the Legal Profession.* Oxford: Oxford University Press.

Sedgwick, E. (1993). Epidemics of the will. In E. Sedgwick (ed.), *Tendencies* (pp. 130–142). Durham: Duke University Press.

Seear, K., & Fraser, S. (2014a). Beyond criminal law: The multiple constitution of addiction in Australian legislation. *Addiction Research and Theory, 22*(5), 438–450.

Seear, K., & Fraser, S. (2014b). The addict as victim: Producing the 'problem' of addiction in Australian victims of crime compensation laws. *International Journal of Drug Policy, 25*(5), 826–835.

Smith, A. (2016). Representing rapists: The cruelty of cross examination and other challenges for a feminist criminal defense lawyer. *American Criminal Law Review, 53,* 255–309.

Smith, A. (2006). Defending the unpopular down under. *Melbourne University Law Review, 30*(2), 495–553.

Smith, A., & Freedman, M. (eds.). (2013). *How Can You Represent Those People?* New York: Palgrave Macmillan.

Webb, J. (2002). Being a lawyer/being a human being. *Legal Ethics, 5*(1), 130–151.

Wendel, W. B. (2010). *Lawyers and Fidelity to Law.* Princeton: Princeton University Press.

### Cases

*Canada (Attorney General) v PHS Community Services Society* [2011] 3 SCR 134 (30 September 2011).

*Mabo and Others v Queensland (No. 2)* [1992] HCA 23 (3 June 1992).
*Milirrpum v Nabalco Pty Ltd* (1971) 17 FLR 141.
*R v David Norman Johns* (1992), Unreported, Supreme Court of South Australia.

## Legislation and Rules

*American Bar Association Model Rules of Professional Conduct* (2016).
*Bar Standards Board Handbook* (UK).
*Complete Rules of Professional Conduct* (Ontario).
*Family Law Act* (1975) (Cth).
*Law Society Act*, RSO 1990, c L-8 (Ontario).
*Lawyers and Conveyancers Act* (2006) (NZ).
*Lawyers and Conveyancers Act (Lawyers: Conduct and Client Care) Rules* (2008) (NZ).
*Legal Profession Uniform Conduct (Barristers) Rules* (2015).
*Legal Profession Uniform Law Australian Solicitors' Conduct Rules* (2015).
*Legal Services Act* (2007) (UK).
*Practice Framework Rules* (UK).

# Conclusion
## Making just habits. A blueprint for onto-advocacy

### Just habits?

Major changes in approach to drugs and the people who consume them sometimes feel elusive, in large part because of the persistence of punitive drug laws. Apart from a few well-known examples, such as reforms to laws in Portugal and Canada, most countries continue to criminalise drug consumption and/or persist with the 'war on drugs'. Advocates who are inspired by those countries that have reformed their laws often highlight the importance of the *political* process in bringing about changes in the lives of people who use drugs. Emphasising legislation and the political process has costs, however, potentially distracting attention from the multiple ways legal content is made and sustained, including through *practices of lawyering*. This book has been in part an exercise in disrupting assumptions about how and why present approaches to drugs and 'addiction' hold. It sought to shine a light on the significance of processes and practices in and of law and how these, too, stabilise alcohol and other drug realities. Focussing on five sets of practices (in legislation, advocacy, negotiations, sentencing and ethics) I argued that practices of these kinds play a vital and hitherto underappreciated role in constituting 'legal truths' about substances and those who consume them, materialising and stabilising links between use and 'addiction', 'addiction' and gendered violence, race and poverty. I have argued that these practices matter for various reasons, including because they are a means by which familiar addiction concepts such as irrationality are instantiated, and because they entrench ways of being 'properly' human. They also allow for the interpellation of 'addicted' subjects. Crucially, much of this work is hidden from view; it unfolds in lower courts and tribunals and in negotiations with others, including opposing lawyers and government departments. And perhaps most importantly, in that this book has traced only a handful of practices, leaving numerous practices, areas of law and processes of legal addiction-attribution (following Sedgwick, 1993) untouched, there is still much to be learned.

One of the most important implications of the analysis I have undertaken in this book is its highlighting of legal truths as 'fragile and constantly renegotiated' (McGee, 2015: 82). Law, in other words – and somewhat paradoxically – has a 'fragile force' (McGee, 2012: 1). Bruno Latour makes a similar point, noting that law's 'span is just as striking as its emptiness' (2015: 343). None of this is to suggest that punitive policies and legal frameworks are unimportant. Emptiness does not here equate to law being immaterial. Drug laws *matter*, and have substantial, sometimes lifelong, effects on the lives of people who use substances. But the function of these laws is scaffolded and complemented by a dazzling array of stabilising practices in the form of legal strategies, processes of anticipation, articulation, connection, expression, hailing, hesitation, veridiction, binding and un-binding, linking and de-linking, forged through associations and assemblages, sustained as habits. All of this reminds us of law's '*superficiality*' (Latour, 2009: 264; emphasis added). Put another way:

> The ethnographic 'tracing' that orientates Latour's approach finds its best expression in a proliferation of metaphors: of laces, webs, chains and nets. What these capture for the ethnographer is at one and the same time the fragility and strength of the fabric of law; the vocabulary is that of 'delicacy' and 'filaments', but also the 'persistence' and 'insistence' of the law's reticulum [...] the image of the net is precisely appropriate to that 'net-work' that is the law.
> (Matthews & Veitch, 2016: 355)

If we take seriously law's delicacy and instability, along with the fortifying accomplishments of practices, then practices become a pathway for remaking law, and the subjects and objects shaped by it. Throughout this book, I have gestured towards how we might begin such a task, whether by revisiting the way lawyers conceptualise their ethical duties or what it means to produce 'good' outcomes, whether it is through forging new and different connections or reflecting on our habits. What I have not done until now is articulated an overarching vision for how this might be accomplished. In the second chapter of this book, I hinted at an organising principle for this work. Questioning whether part of what the law does with addiction is just a product of habit, I asked *whether our habits were just*. This was a quite deliberate choice of words, given the special relevance and meaning of 'habit' to the alcohol and other drugs field. I also took inspiration from the work of Fraser, Moore and Keane (2014), especially their call for a recasting of habits as the very foundation of realities. Transposing these ideas to law, I question whether the realities that legal practices make are just.

It might seem curious, in a book about law, to have said so little up until now about justice. This is not an accident, but it connects to questions at the heart of certain STS critiques (some of which I flagged in the introductory chapter). There, I explained that Latour's concern with the supposed 'superficiality' of law had led some to question his interest in legal content. Does the Latourian project really care not what the law ultimately says or does? Does it not matter whether the law endorses slavery, condones genocide or perpetuates bigotry, oppression, suffering or violence? Is ideology irrelevant? Addressing these concerns directly, Kyle McGee notes that:

> Nothing prevents a successor from reifying, reducing, and otherwise translating a particular legal trajectory – by, for example, seizing on to a 'rule' or a *ratio decidendi* that may be drawn from it and discarding the remainder – for the successor's own purposes in some new course of action, including a moral or political one in which this instance of legality could become a

principle of constitutional politics or of moral action, held up as a standard, or denounced, critiqued, derided [...] In this respect, the account sketched here arguably renders the relations of law to justice, the good, and so forth *more* transparent than those traditions of legal thought that loudly proclaim their affinity for this problem.

(2018: 180; original emphasis)

In other words, although STS approaches to law may be concerned to identify, trace and expose what legal practices involve, along with how, precisely, they secure law's passage, this need not be the end of things. In fact, it may be just the beginning. Such work might inspire political actions taken in pursuit of more 'just' outcomes (however defined). I would also suggest that a decision to do nothing in response to a realisation of law's intrinsically political nature is itself a political choice (see also Latour, 2004). In other words, it is not possible to be politically or ethically 'neutral' in the face of such a project. The only question we are left with is: where to from here?

## Onto-advocacy: towards a blueprint for remaking 'addiction'

At the outset of this book, I noted that alcohol and other drug scholarship has undergone a kind of 'ontological turn' in recent years. Much of this has been inspired by STS work on complexities, social science methods and research. As I explained in the introductory chapter, realist claims to ontological singularity, stability and coherence have been critiqued by STS scholars, including Annemarie Mol (2002, 1999) and John Law (2004). In his book *After Method*, John Law (2004) suggests that these insights necessitate a new approach to research (see also Mol & Law, 2002). To recap: conventional social science methods are predicated upon realist assumptions, including the notion that there is a world that exists, 'out there', for social scientists to 'capture'. Traditional research methods also assume that reality is singular, stable and coherent, capable of being independently observed and documented by the researcher. Avoiding the multiplicity of realities, most conventional research methods are not sufficiently sensitive to the 'mess, confusion and relative disorder' (2004: 2) of the world. Indeed, mess, confusion, uncertainty and disorder are typically understood as challenges to be overcome by researchers, who see their task as producing order out of chaos. Viewed this way, researchers are in fact actively participating in the constitution of realities. The first step, according to Law, is to identify these stabilising tendencies and temptations. As he explains:

> If realities are enacted then many of the methodological certainties of the social and natural sciences are undone and we need debate about what follows.
>
> (Law, 2004: 154)

Law is less clear about what comes 'after method'. Despite this, he offers a few ideas as a starting point. For example, he urges researchers to look carefully at how 'anomalies' or other forms of 'mess' and 'complexity' are handled, 'resolved' or otherwise attended to (see also Law, 2002). Elsewhere he has encouraged researchers to move from studying 'nouns' to 'verbs' and from 'things' to 'processes' (Law, 1994). The recognition that researchers materialise the worlds they purport to merely describe has other consequences for research methods, too. They might cause us to rethink the kinds of research questions we ask, the objects and subjects we choose to study, the particular methods we use and the way we go about coding and writing up data. On this latter point, Law (2002: 6; original emphasis) reminds us that 'telling stories about the world also helps to *perform* that world'.

Recently, Suzanne Fraser has sought to extend these ideas further through a theoretical innovation she calls *onto-politically oriented research* (forthcoming; also 2017). An 'onto-politically oriented' approach to research recognises that reality is emergent and that all research projects are intrinsically performative. She argues that research methods:

> are as intimately involved in the making of everyday material realities as they are in reflecting them. As such, researchers have the obligation not only to track the realities being made by their research, but to approach the design and conduct of the research with this action in mind.
>
> (Fraser, Forthcoming)

In other words, Fraser's innovation goes beyond the idea that all research intervenes in and functions to constitute the realities it investigates, and instead focusses on how to design and conduct research *in light of this power*. She encourages researchers to 'consider the realities we wish to "research into being" and formulate our aims, questions, data sets and analyses accordingly, unconstrained by untenable aspirations to neutrality' (Forthcoming). On this latter point, Fraser notes that this 'is not interrupting the proper representation of objective reality but instead is the critical leveraging of an otherwise unacknowledged constitutive process' (Forthcoming). The aim is to 'embrace' rather than 'manage' research's performative functions. Fraser illustrated this through examples from her own research, including research which sought to document the lives of people understood to be experiencing 'addiction', or whose habits might be considered 'addictions' (a project which culminated in the website: www. livesofsubstance.org). Fraser identifies several key features of onto-politically oriented research. These include acknowledging the methodological performativity of naming (e.g. in the 'subjects' and 'objects' of research) and the ontological politics of data collection, which includes the recognition that terms used during recruitment (e.g. of those formally diagnosed as 'addicts') produce particular populations and data sets and that data sets, in turn, constitute realities. And so I ask: do lawyers have similar opportunities, or obligations? What might it mean to embrace law's constitutive dimensions? Is there a place for onto-politically oriented advocacy?

In law, this is a less controversial idea than it might seem. After all, law is intrinsically performative. Laws command and make possible, move to action and make worlds, often through 'mere' enunciation. The classic example advanced in this respect is the death penalty: with a 'mere' utterance, a judge can 'command' a person to be 'put to death'. Law isn't simply supposed to reflect realities, but to make them; *it is proof that law is working when we can say for certain that it constitutes them.* Other examples abound. Writing about drugs and the law, for instance, Kane Race (2011) points out that the explicit aim of many drug laws is to 'send a message' about drugs. Drug laws thus often intend, quite deliberately, to perform drugs as dangerous, risky and unhealthy, 'at the same time as they may also assert that the harmful "properties" of drugs pre-exist legislative and regulatory measures to manage their supply and consumption' (Seear, 2015: 69–70). And of course, one of the great claims made about law and lawyering is its capacity to provoke transformations and change worlds. In this potentiality for change lies the apparent *grandeur* of law: it is part of its great allure, especially for the socially minded. Indeed, law is less burdened with the pretense of neutrality than even research, since so much of what goes on in law is explicitly partisan and geared towards change (of whatever variety), as opposed to 'mere' description. That said, there is sometimes a tendency in law, as in conventional social science research, to remain steadfastly faithful to the claim that it produces truths (so-called 'legal truths'). But even here, the addition of the adjective is telling, for the truths law produces are legal, and thus they are always already truths *of a certain kind.* With this in mind, therefore, I want to consolidate and organise the insights from across this book, including, crucially, lawyers' *ethico-ontological* account of legal practice in Chapter 5. Lawyers recognise the constitutive power of their practices. Might they consider more deliberately and explicitly leveraging law's ontological fragility? Might we encourage them to rethink lawyering in light of the power they hold to constitute objects, subjects and outcomes?

To this end, drawing upon and combining ideas from the 'ontological turn' in alcohol and other drug studies, critical approaches to legal ethics and Suzanne Fraser's (Forthcoming) call to embrace rather than manage research's constitutive force, I here introduce the concept of *onto-advocacy*. Onto-advocacy is underpinned by five core principles. It:

1  Takes as its foundational premise the notion that legal practices do not simply describe or address pre-existing realities but actively participate in constituting them;
2  Takes seriously the notion that what becomes in the world through legal practices is a profoundly political and ethical problem. These becomings are not limited to final legal outcomes, judgements, verdicts or resolutions, but encompass realities generated, exacerbated and stabilised, along the way;
3  Urges lawyers to give consideration to such becomings, and to the constitutive power of legal practices;
4  Encourages modes of lawyering (and judging) that harness law's constitutive power, and that protect and care for the legal 'truths' that result;
5  Is work done in meaningful and explicit collaboration with drug user organisations and peers wherever possible, guided by the principle of 'nothing about us without us'. This work unfolds in partnership through recognition

that drug user organisations have a special stake in legal outcomes, since the implications of the realities lawyers bring into being impact on them most of all, and because realities have echoes and effects, heard and felt, far and wide.

As should be obvious by now, onto-advocacy must by necessity be emergent, multiple and adaptive to circumstance, and should not be prescriptive. As a tentative gesture forward I offer only a 'blueprint' for onto-advocacy: an early design or plan for the *kinds* of features of such a practice. I recognise that these possibilities are only that, and that they might be constrained by technical requirements and rules (a theme I will shortly return to). I offer them up here in the knowledge that they are only suggestions, in the hope that readers will debate, build on and adapt them.

Lawyers engaged in onto-advocacy might:

- Be more attentive to the power and performativity of the language they use;
- Draw on those insights to explore novel ways of constituting alcohol and other drug use including through a move away from the stabilising tendencies of the category of 'addiction' (and related terms);
- Seek out opportunities to mobilise or generate new alcohol and other drug use and/or 'addiction' concepts, including concepts that problematise or disrupt binary logic and persistent addiction tropes of the kind I described in the introductory chapter;
- Cultivate new techniques for questioning clients and taking instructions (following the discussion on lawyers' 'contriving' to gain instructions in Chapter 5), in recognition of the fact that the questions lawyers ask and the instructions they seek are performative of realities. In other words, the questions lawyers ask shape the answers they receive; in turn, this shapes what lawyers are able to say and the legal realities they are able to bring into being;
- Purposely leverage insights regarding the array of stabilising practices described earlier (legal strategies, processes of anticipation, articulation, connection, expression, hailing, hesitation, veridiction, binding and un-binding, linking and de-linking, forged through associations and assemblages, sustained as habits), so as to disrupt them by fashioning new links, connections, associations and habits;
- Decentre alcohol and other drugs by rethinking the pivotal role so frequently assigned to alcohol and other drugs and/or 'addiction' in law, including affordances of agency, causality and responsibility for various phenomena;
- Be more explicit with clients about both the fragility of law and the power of practices, inviting them to play a role in co-producing the realities they wish to bring into being.

Importantly, onto-advocacy presents challenges for traditional approaches to legal ethics and the regulation of the profession, as well as for legal education. Law schools are not in the habit, for instance, of teaching law students to think about their roles in the ways I have described here. Law students and lawyers are not routinely taught to critically reflect on the ontics of lawyering. This raises the question of whether legal education should include an enhanced dialogue with law students and lawyers about the implications and effects of this work. I believe that it should. Students and lawyers should be taught that what they do with the power they hold is an ethical and ontological matter, and that these things *matter* (both morally and materially). This requires legal educators and lawyers to move beyond thinking of legal ethics as a choice between two binary options – rules-based or values-based lawyering – and towards a broader conceptualisation of legal obligations.

Of course, a unique challenge for the onto-advocacy approach is that lawyers operate under technical and institutional constraints, including professional conduct rules (as I discussed in Chapter 5). Lawyers may well argue that they *need not consider*, and certainly *cannot be compelled to consider*, the broader implications of their work, given that such considerations may be at odds with their obligations to individual clients. In other words, a strategy used in an individual family violence negotiation (of the kind described in Chapter 3) might instantiate 'gendered' stereotypes regarding men's violence against women and/or women's responsibility for the violence perpetrated against them, on the one hand, but result in a positive outcome for the accused perpetrator, on the other. In this way, onto-advocacy as a mode of lawyering poses a direct challenge to the 'standard conception' (Luban, 1988) of lawyering, since it calls lawyers to attend to wider consequences beyond those for the individual client they represent. Is it possible to have concern for the ripple effects of their work, such as what it means to constitute women as having agency in the violence perpetrated against them, without breaching the duties they owe to their client? Perhaps it is not. But the answer to such questions also turns on a particular understanding of how we want lawyers to be obliged, and to whom. Lawyers, we will recall, owe a paramount duty to the court and to the administration of justice (see Chapter 5). But what forms of justice do we wish to help bring into being? If it were possible, is it worth restructuring lawyers' ethical duties so that these wider consequences were brought into focus somehow? And if this appears like too overtly political a question for lawyers to consider, let us keep in mind that the work lawyers do is *always already political and thus always already ontological*. It is about what choices we make for them.

The kind of advocacy I envisage here requires lawyers to reflect not only what is done in the moment, nor in the performance of specific tasks (a phone call to an opponent, a letter to an insurer, a negotiation with a government department, or a conversation with a client), nor in terms of 'outcomes' or even of 'justice', straightforwardly conceptualised (on which, see for instance, Fricker, 2007). Instead it asks lawyers to think carefully about how such practices connect to the production of worlds and whether these are the kinds of worlds worth occupying. I accept that people will reach different views on these issues, reflecting a long-standing debate about what it means to be a 'good lawyer' (see also Evans, 2014; Parker & Evans, 2014). Whatever conclusion one reaches, lawyers cannot escape the profoundly *ethico-ontological* dimensions of the work they do. And so

I urge a different approach for all the reasons I have already given, as well as two final ones I want to offer here. First, we live in an era where the very work of lawyering faces an unprecedented series of existential challenges. It is an age marked by the rise of artificial intelligence and robot lawyers, 'fake news' and a declining trust in experts, institutions and professions (e.g. Susskind & Susskind, 2015; Susskind, 2013; Macfarlane, 2008). Separately and collectively, these phenomena pose a challenge to the future of the profession. Several scholars have grappled with what these issues mean for the role of lawyers in the twenty-first century and whether it requires lawyers to work in ways they have never done before. On this, Melissa Mortazavi (2018) argues that the true value of lawyers is not in legal knowledge or technical know-how but in the interpersonal, social and relational aspects of their work. Robots, for instance, are no substitute for the emotional and identity work lawyers can do (at least not yet). Mortazavi argues that renewed value and confidence in law is possible, if only we conceptualise lawyers' work in those ways. I see parallels with my own project here, especially in drawing attention to the value and effects of lawyering beyond the 'technical'. There is value in lawyering that fosters dignity and respect for the historically disenfranchised, work that challenges entrenched and unjust realities including realities pertaining to gender, poverty and race, and that takes seriously its constitutive power. Of course, my argument for onto-advocacy is not supposed to be about renewing confidence in law or lawyers. I see these as worthwhile 'collateral realities' of the project (Law, 2011) subsidiary to my main goal, and to the communities this work is for. Second, and as I argued in Chapter 5, it bears repeating that even though lawyering practices are always already constitutive, the realities lawyers constitute have particular, acute and distinctly troubling implications for disadvantaged, stigmatised and marginalised groups. Historically, the realities lawyers chose to bring into being for people of colour, women and other populations (including people who use alcohol and other drugs) exacerbated and entrenched disadvantage, pain and suffering. We have an obligation to think through *with care* what we do to, for and with these populations going forward. How can our work be justified, when we think of it in this way? In other words, one need not care about renewing the purpose of and faith in the legal profession to accept the central premise of onto-advocacy. There are other, more compelling reasons for lawyers to re-evaluate their purpose, recognising, as they might, that harnessing law's power *together*, we can make for better, more just, more generous worlds.

# References

Evans, A. (2014). *The Good Lawyer*. Port Melbourne: Cambridge University Press.

Fraser, S. (Forthcoming). *Doing ontopolitically-oriented research: Synthesising concepts from the ontological turn for alcohol and other drug research and other social sciences.*

Fraser, S. (2017). *Doing ontopolitically oriented research: Investigating and enacting lives of substance.* Contemporary Drug Problems Conference, Helsinki, Finland.

Fraser, S., Moore, D., & Keane, H. (2014). *Habits: Remaking Addiction*. London: Palgrave Macmillan.

Fricker, M. (2007). *Epistemic Injustice: Power and the Ethics of Knowing*. Oxford: Oxford University Press.

Latour, B. (2015). The strange entanglement of jurimorphs. In K. McGee (ed.), *Latour and the Passage of Law* (pp. 331–353). Edinburgh: Edinburgh University Press.

Latour, B. (2004). Why has critique run out of steam? From matters of fact to matters of concern. *Critical Inquiry, 30*, 225–248.

Law, J. (2011). Collateral realities. In F. Rubio & P. Baert (eds.), *The Politics of Knowledge* (pp. 156–178). London: Routledge.

Law, J. (2004). *After Method: Mess in Social Science Research*. London and New York: Routledge.

Law, J. (2002). *Aircraft Stories: Decentering the Object in Technoscience*. Durham: Duke University.

Law, J. (1994). *Organizing Modernity: Social Ordering and Social Theory*. Oxford: Blackwell Publishers.

Luban, D. (1988). *Lawyers and Justice: An Ethical Study*. Princeton: Princeton University Press.

Macfarlane, J. (2008). *The New Lawyer: How Settlement Is Transforming the Practice of Law*. Vancouver: UBC Press.

Matthews, D., & Veitch, S. (2016). The limits of critique and the forces of law. *Law Critique, 27*, 349–361.

McGee, K. (2018). Hybrid legalities: On obligation and law's immanent materiology. In D. Matthews & S. Veitch (eds.), *Law, Obligation, Community* (pp. 163–182). Abingdon: Routledge.

McGee, K. (2015). On devices and logics of legal sense: Toward socio-technical legal analysis. In K. McGee (ed.), *Latour and the Passage of Law* (pp. 61–92). Edinburgh: Edinburgh University Press.

McGee, K. (2012). The fragile force of law: Mediation, stratification, and law's material life. *Law, Culture and the Humanities, 11*(3), 467–490.

Mol, A. (2002). *The Body Multiple: Ontology in Medical Practice*. Durham: Duke University Press.

Mol, A. (1999). Ontological politics. A word and some questions. In J. Law & J. Hassard (eds.), *Actor Network Theory and After* (pp. 74–89). Oxford: Blackwell Publishers.

Mol, A., & Law, J. (2002). Complexities: An introduction. In J. Law & A. Mol (eds.), *Complexities: Social Studies of Knowledge Practices* (pp. 1–22). Durham: Duke University Press.

Mortazavi, M. (2018). *Lawyers as intermediaries*. International Legal Ethics Conference 8: Legal Ethics in the Asian Century, The University of Melbourne, Australia, 7 December.

Parker, C., & Evans, A. (2014). *Inside Lawyers' Ethics* (2nd edn). Port Melbourne: Cambridge University Press.

Race, K. (2011). Drug effects, performativity and the law. *International Journal of Drug Policy, 22*, 410–412.

Sedgwick, E. (1993). Epidemics of the will. In E. Sedgwick (ed.), *Tendencies* (pp. 130–142). Durham: Duke University Press.

Seear, K. (2015). Making addiction, making gender: A feminist performativity analysis of Kakavas v Crown Melbourne Limited. *The Australian Feminist Law Journal, 41*(1), 65–85.

Susskind, R. (2013). *Tomorrow's Lawyers*. Oxford: Oxford University Press.

Susskind. R., & Susskind. D. (2015). *The Future of the Professions: How Technology Will Transform the Work of Human Experts*. Oxford: Oxford University Press.

# Index

Note: Page numbers followed by "n" denote endnotes.

ableism 12
'Aboriginal community': assembling
127–9; geotemporal dimensions of 128;
mutual force of addiction, race and place
129–32; wider effects of the Munda
decision 132–4
Aboriginal women 133; sexual assault
by white men against 123; 'special
vulnerabilities' faced by 133; violence
against 123
*addicere* 3
addiction: and addicts 2; American
drunkenness 6; concepts across cultures
and time 5–7; concepts of 3–5; as
a disability 12; as a disease 93–5;
emergence of 1; and 'enslavement' 3;
episodic drinking as 103; judging 81–4;
in the law 9–12; mutual force of race,
place and 129–32; nature and meaning
of 2; 'necessary evil' of 149–53;
nomenclature of 1; onto-advocacy and
170–5; and ontological politics 13–16;
overview 1–3; proactively asserted 10;
reactively asserted 10–11; theories of
7–9; *see also* dependence
addiction-related stigma 5
addicts 1, 159; and addiction 2; coercive
practices and 5; conceptualising 4–5;
paternalistic policies and 5; and stigma 5
advocacy practices: alcohol and drug
use 66–72; anticipation in law 62–6;
hesitation in law 62–6; interpellating
'addicted' subjects 75–80; making of law
62–6; overview 61–2
*After Method* (Law) 170
Albers, Eliot 158–9

alcohol: 'addicted' to 6; and drugs 5; and
law 66–72; reclassified as drug 6; *see also*
drugs
'alcohol and other drugs' (AOD) 6
'alcohol-fuelled violence' 115, 132–3
Alcoholics and Drug-Dependent Persons
Act 38; detention and treatment
order 39; objectives 38
Alcoholics Anonymous 9, 104
alcoholism 6, 100, 113, 129, 132–3; *see
also* addicts
allies and alternatives 156–60
alternative dispute resolution (ADR)
89–90
Althusser, Louis 66
American Bar Association Model Rules of
Professional Conduct 145
American drunkenness 6
American Psychiatric Association 2
anaemia 13
Andrews, Daniel 39
anticipation: and drug use 67–71; judging
81–4; in law 62–6
Anti-Discrimination Act (1977) 10
Arendt, Hannah 34, 41–2, 54
artificial intelligence 175
assemblage thinking 114, 116–19; Duff
on 118; reimagining sentencing through
134–6; study of alcohol and other drugs
and 116–17
assembling: 'Aboriginal community'
127–9; alcohol effects 125–7
*attenuated will* 49
Australia: addiction in 9–10; Anti-
Discrimination Act 10; dependence in
9–10; Drug and Alcohol Treatment

Act 10; drug test welfare recipients 39–40; Infringements Act 10; invasion and colonisation of 120; legal system 35; paternalistic policies in 133; policymakers' views on addiction 77; proposed bills 38–41; rights protection in 35–7; *stare decisis* 18; three-tiered system of government 35

Australian Bureau of Statistics 116

Australian Capital Territory (ACT) 35

Australian Constitution 35

Australian Council of Social Service 52

Australian High Court 114, 119, 120

Australian Institute of Health and Welfare 114

Australian Labor Party 45

'autonomous' selfhood 47

Bacchi, Carol 65

Barad, Karen 151

Bar Standards Board 145

*Bar Standards Board Handbook* 145

Berridge, Virginia 55

Bill of Rights (United States) 35

'binary logic' 4

binge drinking 103, 131

*The Body Multiple* (Mol) 13

Boughey, J. 37

'brain disease model' 8–9

*British American Tobacco Australia Services Limited v Cowell (as representing the estate of Rolah Ann McCabe, deceased)* (2002) VSCA 1) 11

Brook, H. 8

*Bugmy v The Queen* (2013) 249 CLR 571 120, 123–4

Bunn, Rebecca 12

Butler, Judith 61, 66

Campbell, Nancy 8

Canada: drug use and illnesses 72–3; lawyers positioning clients as addicts 73–4; legal addiction-attribution 73; policymakers' views on addiction 77

*Canada (Attorney General) v PHS Community Services Society* (2011) 3 SCR 134 11, 69, 72, 78, 93

Canadian *Charter of Rights and Freedoms* 1982 93

Canadian HIV/AIDS Legal Network 158

Canadian Supreme Court 93

Charter of Human Rights and Responsibilities Act 35

Charter of Rights and Freedoms (Canada) 35

child protection, veridicting 100–7

Children and Young Persons (Care and Protection) Act 101

colonialism 121

Commonwealth Constitution 35

Commonwealth of Australia Constitution Act 35

*Commonwealth v Julie A. Eldred* (2018) SJC 12279 11–12

Complete Rules of Professional Conduct 145

'compulsive' drug use 4, 8

*Contemporary Drug Problems* 15

Controlled Drugs and Substances Act 93

constructionism 13, 118

Convention on the Elimination of all forms of Racial Discrimination 41

Convention on the Rights of Persons with Disabilities 41

Convention on the Rights of the Child (CRC) 41, 50; Article 3 50–1

criminal law: sentencing Indigenous offenders in 120–4; sentencing offenders in 119–20

culture: Aboriginal 122, 134–6; and addiction 5–7; and American colonial period 5

Davis, Megan 35

Davies, J. B. 4–5

Deleuze, Gilles 65, 117

dependence 10, 96; *see also* addiction

Derrida, Jacques 4

detention and treatment order 39

*Diagnostic and Statistical Manual of Mental Disorders* 2

'dialogue model' 33

disability, addiction as 12, 72, 78

'The discovery of addiction' 5

disease, addiction as 93–5

Dolovich, Sharon 146

domestic violence 101, 106

Douzinas, Costas 34, 41–2; on human rights 42–3

Drug and Alcohol Treatment Act (2010) 10

drug courts 2, 12, 73

drug-related harms 15

drug-related stigma 24

drugs: and alcohol 5; defined 3; as 'inherently criminogenic' 7; *see also* alcohol

drug test welfare recipients 39–40; and
income management 40; Social Services
Legislation Amendment (Drug Testing
Trial) Bill 40; Social Services Legislation
Amendment (Welfare Reform) Bill
39–40
drug use: and criminal law 70; and family
law 68, 70; illicit 6, 70, 84, 93, 99,
114, 117, 153; and illnesses 72–3;
and jurisdictions 69–70; and lawyers'
anticipation 67–71; 'perceptions' of 80;
'realities' of 80
DSM-5 2
Duff, Cameron 117–18, 138

Edney, Richard 121–2
Education Act 1990 101
Edwards, Griffith 55
Eldred, Julie 11–12
'enslavement,' and addiction 3
'epidemic of addiction-attribution' 1
episodic drinking 103
Erni, John 34, 42, 53; on sexual health 43
*'the essence of law'* 16–1
ethical ontologies and 'necessary evil' of
addiction 149–53
ethical practices: allies and alternatives
156–60; background 144–8; ethical
ontologies and 'necessary evil' of
addiction 149–53; matters of concern
148–9; necessary evil, but by what
measure? 153–6; overview 143–4;
possibility of change 160–3
'Euro-American common-sense realism'
*see* realism
Evans, A. 146

'fake news' 175
family law: addiction and 9; alcohol and
other drug issues 67, 70
Family Law Act 147
family violence: defined 95; jurisdiction
96; veridicting 95–100
Family Violence Protection Act 95
Farrow, Trevor 146, 163
Federal Court of Australia 89
feminist activism 160
feminists, and performativity theory 16
feminist thinking 160–1
Fitzgerald, J. 5
Fomiatti, R. 66
Fraser, Suzanne 3, 7, 10, 15, 16, 22, 65–6,
77, 117, 126, 137, 148–9, 171

gambling addiction 21
Gans, Jeremy 37
Garriott, William 7
gender: dimension 79, 88, 99, 105;
implications 24, 122; reflections
on 107–8; stereotypes 83; violence
107, 168
'gladiatorial champion' approach 145
Goffman, E. 5
Grosz, Elizabeth 4
Gutwirth, Serge 61–6, 68, 84–5; 'formal
sources' of law 63; law as 'mode of
habit' 62; law's two modes 62; on
lawyers' role in making the law 64–5

habits 15, 49, 85–6, 168–70
*Habits: Remaking Addiction* (Fraser,
Moore and Keane) 15
Haraway, Donna 149
hesitation: defined 64; in law 62–6
High Court of Australia 123–4
'hijacked brain' 8–9
Hopkins, Anthony 120–1
Horrigan, Bryan 147
Huberman A. M. 23
human rights 41–6; defined 41; Douzinas
on 43; scrutiny, process of 46–51;
subject of 51–4
Human Rights (Parliamentary Scrutiny)
Act 36, 41
Human Rights Act (United Kingdom) 35
Human Rights Bill 2018 35
human rights protection: in Australia
35–7; in Canada 35; in United Kingdom
35; in United States 35

illicit drug use 6, 70, 71, 84, 93, 99, 114,
117, 153
Infringements Act (2006) 10
*An Inquiry Into Modes of Existence
(AIME)* (Latour) 17, 90
inhabit 47, 128, 162, 163
*Insite (Canada (Attorney General) v PHS
Community Services Society* [2011] 3
SCR 134) 98, 108, 150
International Covenant on Civil and
Political Rights 41
International Covenant on Economic, Social
and Cultural Rights (ISECR) 37, 41
International Network of People Who Use
Drugs (INPUD) 159
interpellation 66; 'addicted' subjects
75–80; Althusser on 66

Joh, Elizabeth 12
judicial decision making 64
jurimorph 34; defined 44; Latour on 45;
    McGee on 44–5
just habits 86, 168–70

Karasaki, Mutsumi 104
Keane, Helen 3, 7, 15, 22, 75, 85,
    117–18, 128
Klugman M. 5

'lace' 18, 169
Latour, Bruno 16–20, 22, 88, 90, 108,
    129, 148; '*the essence of law*' 16–17; *An
    Inquiry into Modes of Existence* 17; on
    jurimorph 45; on studying importance
    of law 17
law: and addiction 9–12; and alcohol
    66–72; Bruno Latour on importance
    of 17; and drug use 66–72; 'formal
    sources' of 63; 'materiological' account
    of 20; as 'mode of habit' 62; science and
    technology studies (STS) 16–18; STS
    approach to 18–22
Law, John 3, 13, 14, 22, 170
'Law1' 62–3
'Law2' 62–3
Law Society Act, RSO 1990, c L-8 145
Law Society of Ontario 145
lawyers: on addiction 23; and addiction
    facts 21–2; constituting alcohol and
    other drugs 72–5; engaged in onto-
    advocacy 173–4; 'ethical' 163; ethical
    duties that lawyers owe to their clients
    144; and formal 'diagnosis' of addiction
    80–1; interpellating 'addicted' subjects
    75–80; positioning clients as addicts 73;
    practice of negotiation 24; robot 175;
    role in making the law 64–5; rules and
    laws governing lawyer's conduct 145
Lawyers and Conveyancers Act (2006)
    (NZ) 145
Lawyers and Conveyancers Act (Lawyers:
    Conduct and Client Care) Rules (2008)
    (NZ) 145
legal addiction-attribution 1, 73, 88,
    143, 168
legal content: critiques of 19; generation
    of 45; McGee on 33, 43
legal education 173, 174
legal ethics 143, 145, 148–50, 156,
    163, 172–4
*Legal Profession Uniform Conduct
    (Barristers) Rules* 144

*Legal Profession Uniform Law Australian
    Solicitors' Conduct Rules* 144
Legal Services Act (UK) 145
legal strategy 22, 61, 66, 67, 69, 71,
    72, 77, 79, 81, 145, 152, 153, 157,
    160, 169
legal system, Australia 35
'legal systems abuse' 102
legal veridiction 22, 90–3, 98, 103, 107
legislative process 23; background 34–8;
    introduction 33–4
Leshner, Alan 8
Levine, Harry 5–6
Lezaun, J. 15
Liberal National Coalition 45–6
Luban, David 146
Lynch, Michael 21

*Mabo and Others v Queensland (No. 2)*
    (1992) HCA 23 35, 162
McCabe, Rolah 11
*McCabe v British American Tobacco
    Australia Services Limited* (2002) VSC
    73 11
McDonald, K. 5
McGee, Kyle 17, 19–20, 22, 33–4, 169;
    on jurimorph 44–5; on legal content 43;
    and 'reasonableness' 44
MacLean, S. 115, 129
*The Making of Law* (Latour) 17, 64, 91–2
'managerial judging' 90
Marie, Anne 71, 150
*Markarian v The Queen* (2005) 228 CLR
    357 119, 134
Marrati, Paola 65
Martin, Wayne 89
'materiological' account of law 20
'matters of concern' 143, 148–9, 163
medical model, and addiction 7
Miles, M. 23
*Milirrpum v Nabalco Pty Ltd* (1971) 17
    FLR 141 162
'mode of habit' 62, 85
modernity 7, 41–2
Mol, Annemarie 3, 13–14, 22, 170
Moore, David 3, 7, 15, 16, 22, 65–6, 115,
    117–18, 129, 137
moral model, and addiction 7
Mortazavi, Melissa 175
*Munda v Western Australia* [2013] HCA
    38 114, 124–5; wider effects of 132–4
Mushin, Nahum 147
mutual force of addiction, race and place
    129–32

*Neal v R* (1982) 149 CLR 305 120
necessary evil 73; of addiction, ethical
 ontologies and 149–53; but by what
 measure? 153–6
negotiation practices 24; background
 89–90; further reflections on gender
 107–8; legal veridiction 90–3; overview
 88–9; stabilising legal 'fact' of addiction
 as a disease 93–5; veridicting child
 protection 100–7; veridicting family
 violence 95–100
neoliberalism 12
New South Wales Supreme Court 121
'night time economy' 115–16, 118, 129
Northern Territory National Emergency
 Response Act ('the Intervention') 134

*obiter dicta* 18
objective 'reasonableness' 44
obligations 21, 41, 47, 54, 75, 137, 143,
 147, 159, 171, 174
Ombudsman 71, 89
'ontics' *see* 'ontological politics'
onto-advocacy: five core principles of 172–
 3; lawyers engaged in 173–4; towards
 blueprint for remaking 'addiction'
 170–5
ontological multiplicity 13, 22
ontological politics: and addiction 13–16;
 defined 14–15
onto-politically oriented research 171

'parental responsibility contract' 102
parliamentary rights scrutiny 36, 37
Parker, Christine 146, 159, 165n1
Parliamentary Joint Committee on Human
 Rights 36
Parnet, Claire 117
'pathological gambling' 21
performativity theory: described 16; and
 disciplines 16; and feminists 16
policy making 65
possibility of change 160–3
Practice Framework Rules 145
prescription drugs 71; *see also* drugs
proposed legislation: on alcohol 23; on
 drug issues 23
*Providence Health Care Society v Canada
 (Attorney General)* [2014] BCSC 936 72

Race, Kane 172
Racial Discrimination Act (1975) 134
'racialised peoples' 116
*ratio decidendi* 18

realism 13, 148
'reasonableness': legal tests of 44; objective
 44; of rights limitations 47
*Reassembling the Social* (Latour) 118
Recommendation 77; of the Family
 Violence Royal Commission 110
'recovering addict' 66
reimagining sentencing through
 assemblage thinking 134–6
Reinarman, Craig 6
repetitive drug use 8
Rhode, Deborah 147
rights assessment 47
rights limitation 47–8
'risky drinking' 114
Ritter, Alison 49
robot lawyers 175
robots 175
Room, Robin 6
Rose, Nikolas 47, 49
Royal Commission into Family
 Violence 110
'rules-based lawyering' 143, 145, 147,
 149–50, 163, 174
*R v David Norman Johns* (1992) 161
*R v Fernando* (1992) 76 A Crim R 58 120
*R. v Gladue* [1999] 1 S.C.R. 688 120
*R v Ipeelee* [2012] 1 SCR 433 120
*R v Newman* 122
*R v Simpson* [2004] NSWCCA 102 122

SARC (the Scrutiny of Acts and
 Regulations Committee) 36
science and technology studies (STS):
 approach to law 18–22; Bruno Latour
 16–18; and law 16–18
Second World War 42
Section 54 of Victims of Crime Assistance
 Act 67–8
Sedgwick, Eve 1, 4, 6, 53
Senate Community Affairs Legislation
 Committee 39
sentencing practices: assemblage thinking
 116–19; assembling 'Aboriginal
 community' 127–9; assembling alcohol
 effects 125–7; background 114–16;
 Indigenous offenders in the criminal
 law 120–4; *Munda v Western Australia*
 [2013] HCA 38 124–5; mutual
 force of addiction, race and place
 129–32; offenders in the criminal law
 119–20; overview 113–14; reimagining
 sentencing through assemblage thinking
 134–6; sentencing Indigenous offenders

in criminal law 120–4; sentencing offenders in criminal law 119–20; wider effects of Munda decision 132–4
'severe substance dependence' 34, 38
Severe Substance Dependence Treatment Bill 34, 38, 47, 53
sexual health 43
sexual violence 99, 107, 115; 'slowing down, peering in' 1, 20
Smith, Abbe 147–8
social constructionism 118
social deprivation 130–1
social oppression 131, 138–9
Social Services Legislation Amendment (Drug Testing Trial) Bill (2018) 34, 40, 53; compatiblity with rights and freedoms 41; objectives 40
Social Services Legislation Amendment (Welfare Reform) Bill (2017) 39–40
Solicitors Regulation Authority 145
Spivakovsky, Claire 116
*stare decisis* 18–19, 63
State of Victoria *see* Victoria
stigma: addiction-related 5; and addicts 5; drug-related 24; lifetime effects of 5
Storr, Caithleen 122
Stringer, R. 8
Supreme Court of Canada 11, 72, 93
Supreme Court of Western Australia 89, 125

'terra nullius' 34–5
time and addiction 5–7
Tuhiwai-Smith, Linda 134
Tupper, Kenneth 3

unconscious emotional needs 104
United Nations 35

Universal Declaration of Human Rights (UDHR) 35
US National Institute on Drug Abuse (NIDA) 8

values-based lawyering 143, 146–7, 149–50, 163–4, 174
Valverde, Mariana 6
'veridiction' 17; child protection 100–7; family violence 95–100; legal process of 88–3, 100, 108–110
Victims of Crime Assistance Act (1996) (Victoria)) 67
Victoria 10, 35, 65, 67, 95
Victorian Charter 39
Victorian Equal Opportunity and Human Rights Commission 37
Victorian laws 110
Victorian *Sentencing Act* 119
violence: alcohol-fuelled 115, 132–3; domestic 101; family 95–100; sexual 99, 107, 115
Volkow, Nora 8

Watson, Irene 122–3
Weatherburn, Don 116
Western Australian *Sentencing Act* 119
Western colonisation 116
West, R. 7
Woolgar, Steve 7, 15
World Health Organization (WHO) 6, 43
World Trade Center attack 148

Young, Michael Brett 37

Ziegler, S. 6

For Product Safety Concerns and Information please contact our EU
representative  GPSR@taylorandfrancis.com
Taylor & Francis Verlag GmbH, Kaufingerstraße 24, 80331 München, Germany

www.ingramcontent.com/pod-product-compliance
Lightning Source LLC
Chambersburg PA
CBHW070427270326
41926CB00014B/2972